D1117661

DEMOCRACY AND THE CULTURE OF SKEPTICISM

DEMOCRACY AND THE CULTURE OF SKEPTICISM

POLITICAL TRUST IN ARGENTINA AND MEXICO

MATTHEW R. CLEARY AND SUSAN C. STOKES

VOLUME XI IN THE RUSSELL SAGE FOUNDATION SERIES ON TRUST

Russell Sage Foundation • New York

The Russell Sage Foundation

The Russell Sage Foundation, one of the oldest of America's general purpose foundations, was established in 1907 by Mrs. Margaret Olivia Sage for "the improvement of social and living conditions in the United States." The Foundation seeks to fulfill this mandate by fostering the development and dissemination of knowledge about the country's political, social, and economic problems. While the Foundation endeavors to assure the accuracy and objectivity of each book it publishes, the conclusions and interpretations in Russell Sage Foundation publications are those of the authors and not of the Foundation, its Trustees, or its staff. Publication by Russell Sage, therefore, does not imply Foundation endorsement.

BOARD OF TRUSTEES
Thomas D. Cook, Chair

Alan S. Blinder	John A. Ferejohn	Alan B. Krueger
Kenneth D. Brody	Larry V. Hedges	Cora B. Marrett
Christine K. Cassel	Jennifer L. Hochschild	Eric Wanner
Robert E. Denham	Kathleen Hall Jamieson	Mary C. Waters
Christopher Edley Jr.	Melvin J. Konner	

Library of Congress Cataloging-in-Publication Data
Cleary, Matthew R.
    Democracy and the Culture of Skepticism : political trust in Argentina and Mexico / Matthew Cleary and Susan Stokes.
        p. cm. — (Russell Sage Foundation series on trust ; v. 11)
    ISBN 0-87154-166-1
        1. Democratization—Argentina.   2. Democratization—Mexico.   3. Trust—Argentina.
    4. Trust—Mexico.   5. Political culture—Argentina.   6. Political culture—Mexico.
    7. Public opinion—Argentina.   8. Public opinion—Mexico.   I. Stokes, Susan Carol.
    II. Title.   III. Series.

JL2081.C53   2006
320.972′09′49—dc22   2005048996

Copyright © 2006 by Russell Sage Foundation. All rights reserved. Printed in the United States of America. No part of this publication may be reproduced, stored in a retrieval system, or transmitted in any form or by any means, electronic, mechanical, photocopying, recording, or otherwise, without the prior written permission of the publisher.

Reproduction by the United States Government in whole or in part is permitted for any purpose.

The paper used in this publication meets the minimum requirements of American National Standard for Information Sciences—Permanence of Paper for Printed Library Materials. ANSI Z39.48–1992.

Text design by Suzanne Nichols.

RUSSELL SAGE FOUNDATION
112 East 64th Street, New York, New York 10021
10 9 8 7 6 5 4 3 2 1

The Russell Sage Foundation
Series on Trust

THE RUSSELL Sage Foundation Series on Trust examines the conceptual structure and the empirical basis of claims concerning the role of trust and trustworthiness in establishing and maintaining cooperative behavior in a wide variety of social, economic, and political contexts. The focus is on concepts, methods, and findings that will enrich social science and inform public policy.

The books in the series raise questions about how trust can be distinguished from other means of promoting cooperation and explore those analytic and empirical issues that advance our comprehension of the roles and limits of trust in social, political, and economic life. Because trust is at the core of understandings of social order from varied disciplinary perspectives, the series offers the best work of scholars from diverse backgrounds and, through the edited volumes, encourages engagement across disciplines and orientations. The goal of the series is to improve the current state of trust research by providing a clear theoretical account of the causal role of trust within given institutional, organizational, and interpersonal situations, developing sound measures of trust to test theoretical claims within relevant settings, and establishing some common ground among concerned scholars and policymakers.

Karen S. Cook
Russell Hardin
Margaret Levi

SERIES EDITORS

Previous Volumes in the Series

Contents

About the Authors

Matthew R. Cleary is assistant professor of political science in the Maxwell School of Citizenship and Public Affairs at Syracuse University.

Susan C. Stokes is John S. Saden Professor of Political Science at Yale University.

Preface

THIS BOOK is about the place of trust in democracy. In recent years, democratic theorists have elevated trust—among citizens, and of citizens toward elected governments—to the status of necessary component of a smooth-functioning democracy. When public opinion polls turn up large numbers of citizens who declare that they do not trust their government, such findings become a cause for much hand-wringing by academics, the press, and commentators.[1] Equally common among political theorists and some empirical researchers is the contention that civic activism and an intense organizational life are the hallmarks of a healthy democracy. When citizens do not join organizations, or attend meetings, or bowl in leagues, we are told to expect that government will function badly.

Our own research into trust and associational life in two new Latin American democracies, as well as a closer scrutiny of the logic underlying the civic culture theory of democracy, has led us to reject both ideas. The research and reasoning contained in the chapters that follow lead us to the conclusion that the political culture most supportive of democracy is not a political culture of trust, but a political culture of skepticism. And we make the case that, as democracies mature, people in them may turn away from certain forms of civic activism in favor of more private activities. Our picture of the mature democratic community should not necessarily be of people spending a lot of time meeting with their neighbors and directly monitoring government action. Instead it may be a picture of people occupying themselves with private pursuits. They may interest themselves in political and community affairs, they may be regular voters, and they may welcome and even provide financial support for interest organizations that monitor government actions. But they are not themselves necessarily active participants in civic associations. Nor do they trust government, except in the sense that they believe it will pursue their interests when institutional arrangements make it in the government's interests to act in this way.[2] The older picture may be more normatively appealing to some, but the latter one is more descriptively accurate.

Acknowledgments

WE COULD not have carried out this study without the encouragement and financial support of the Russell Sage Foundation's Program on Trust. We are grateful to Eric Wanner and to Karen Cook, Margaret Levi, and Russell Hardin for their leadership in this important area of social science inquiry. We received stimulating and helpful comments from many people who attended presentations of our work at the Russell Sage Foundation, meetings of the Latin American Studies Association, the University of Notre Dame's Kellogg Institute, Yale, Michigan, and the University of California at San Diego. We are especially grateful to Michael Coppedge, Paul DiMaggio, Edward Gibson, Alan Houston, Joy Langston, Margaret Levi (again), Scott Mainwaring, and Mariela Szwarcberg, all of whom made comments that forced us to rethink our work. We also thank Caroline Beer for sharing her data on Mexican state legislatures, David Samuels for sharing data on malapportionment in Argentina, Valeria Brusco, Marcelo Nazareno, and Mario Riorda for helping us develop and implement the surveys in Argentina, and Francisco Abundis and Rene Bautista for their assistance with the Mexican surveys. We are grateful to Helen Glenn Court for excellent editing of the manuscript. Our warmest thanks, of course, go to our families: Heather Cleary and Adam and Jacob, Steve Pincus and Sam and David.

PART I

POLITICAL CULTURE IN DEMOCRATIC THEORY

Chapter 1

The Place of Trust in the Political Culture of Democracy

THE CONCEPT of trust has been rediscovered of late by students and theorists of democracy. They have revived the idea that civic participation generates trust, and that trust among citizens is crucial for democracy to function well. But an equally long, if currently less fashionable, tradition views democracy (or representative government) as functioning best if citizens retain a sense of the fallibility of their leaders and hence the importance of constraining institutions. Distrust is good for democracy. And this latter tradition places rather more weight on the delegation of political involvement from the citizenry to its elected representatives than on civic participation. On the first view, the political culture of democracy is a culture of activism and trust; on the other, it is one of delegation and skepticism.

In the discussion that follows we examine critically the civic culture theory of democracy. Before turning to empirical tests of the theory's causal propositions, in this chapter we raise several theoretical objections to it. We then turn briefly to traditions in democratic theory that suggest that well-functioning democracy requires skeptical citizens, rather than trusting ones. We also outline a trajectory of change from poor and class-divided democracies, which feature clientelism and a culture of personal trust in politicians, to wealthier and more equal democracies, which feature accountability and a political culture of skepticism toward politicians and conditional trust in political institutions.

Trust, Social Capital, and the Civic Culture

Citizens trust one another more if they are actively engaged in civic associations, and democracy works better if citizens trust one another. So contends a growing number of theorists of democracy. According

3

to this neo-Tocquevillian line of thought, not only is it good for democracy that citizens trust each other, but this trust should be of the strongest possible sort. Rather than discrete quid pro quos (you scratch my back, I'll scratch yours), interpersonal trust should take the form of a generalized expectation of mutual aid (you scratch my back today, I'll help you with some yet to be determined task at some future date).

Forty years ago, Gabriel Almond and Sidney Verba's *The Civic Culture* (1963) explored the idea that a nation's civic life shaped the quality of democratic governance. They wrote that democracy is sustained by a certain political culture—a set of attitudes and beliefs regarding the self, politics, and government. The civic culture was one with "high frequencies of political activity, of exposure to political communications, of political discussion, of concern with political affairs" (1963, 31). Their explorations of beliefs and activities of citizens in five countries (Britain, the United States, Germany, Italy, and Mexico) revealed mixtures of parochial culture (in which citizens have little knowledge of political process or policy and little sense of self as an active participant), subject culture (in which they have more knowledge of system), and participant culture (in which they are knowledgeable and participate actively; 1963, 16–24). But, in general, Almond and Verba discovered a trend from subject to participant to an emerging civic culture as their study shifted from more autocratic to more democratic systems.

Recent incarnations of the civic culture tradition are intimately linked to the concept of social capital. Social capital, according to Robert Putnam, "refers to . . . social networks and the norms of reciprocity and trustworthiness that arise from them" (2000, 19). Similarly, Pamela Paxton writes that social capital requires two dimensions: "objective associations among individuals, and . . . associations of a particular type—reciprocal, trusting, and involving positive emotion" (2002, 256). In places rich in social capital, people form many civic associations, participate frequently in these associations, and develop bonds of trust. The central claim of social capital theorists is that social capital makes democracy more likely to arise and better able to function well. In the tradition of Tocqueville, Mark Warren writes that a "multifaceted" associational life "provides a dense social infrastructure enabling pluralistic societies to attain a vibrant creativity and diversity within a context of multiple but governable conflicts" (2001, 3).[1]

Why, according to these theorists, does social capital enhance democracy? One reason is that civic associations are schools of democracy, teaching participants how to pursue collective goals (Warren 2001; see also Sandel 1996). According to Joshua Cohen and Joel Rogers (1995), democracy grounded in a rich associational life nurtures "civic consciousness," by which they mean decision making in which the deliberators consider the general good, rather than narrow self-interest.

Another claim of social capital theorists is that a trusting citizenry makes democracy work better by encouraging cooperation with government in the provision of services. In his landmark book *Bowling Alone*, Robert Putnam writes,

> Light-touch government works more efficiently in the presence of social capital. Police close more cases when citizens monitor neighborhood comings and goings. Child welfare departments do a better job of "family preservation" when neighbors and relatives provide social support to troubled parents. Public schools teach better when parents volunteer in classrooms and ensure that kids do their homework. When community involvement is lacking, burdens on government employees—bureaucrats, social workers, teachers, and so forth—are that much greater and success that much more elusive. (2000, 346)

Another slightly different account of why social capital and interpersonal trust produce better-functioning democracy is that interpersonally trusting communities free the government from the need to enforce compliance and therefore allow it to spend time and resources on other activities. Carles Boix and Daniel Posner write: "By giving citizens more optimistic expectations about the behavior of their fellow citizens, social capital can relieve the government from the burden of enforcing compliance and free up resources that can be applied towards increasing the efficiency or expanding the range of the services that it provides" (1998, 691).

A central tenet, then, in the civic culture theory of democracy is that an active civic life encourages interpersonal expectations of cooperation. It encourages the expectation that others will comply with public demands that are burdensome but critical to the functioning of democracy. It also leads to greater accountability among public officials. Putnam writes,

> If decision makers expect citizens to hold them politically accountable, they are more inclined to temper their worst impulses rather than face public protests. . . . Where people know one another, interact with one another each week at choir practice or sports matches, and trust one another to behave honorably, they have a model and a moral foundation upon which to base further cooperative enterprises. (2000, 346)

Similarly, in his 1993 account of why democracy works better in parts of northern Italy than in the south, Putnam explains that in the north the "civic community is marked by an active, public-spirited citizenry, by egalitarian political relations, by *a social fabric of trust and cooperation*," whereas other regions "are cursed with vertically structured politics, a social life of fragmentation and isolation, and *a culture of distrust*" (15, emphasis added).

Theoretical Criticisms of the Civic Culture

Whether civic engagement encourages interpersonal trust and whether interpersonal trust improves government performance are ultimately empirical questions. Later we present evidence from Argentina and Mexico that lends little support to the civic culture tradition. Before turning to this evidence, however, we suggest several theoretical objections to the idea that trust improves democracy.

Consider first the proposition that interpersonal trust facilitates the monitoring of government, that if people "trust one another to act honorably," decision makers will "expect citizens to hold them politically accountable" (Putnam 2000, 346). But, in fact, in all but the smallest polities, and all but the most local levels of government, most government monitoring in contemporary democracies is carried out not by individual citizens but by professional organizations, interest groups, and the press (see Arnold 1993). Most people rely on these institutions to monitor government, not on their personal acquaintances. If you are worried about air pollution, it's a small comfort that you have a close and trusting relationship with your neighbor—you have no expectation that your neighbor will monitor the government's environmental policies. More important is whether you trust the Nature Conservancy or the environmental reporting in your newspaper. Civic culture theorists may regret this development (see Putnam 2000, 343–44). But the fact that governments are monitored by professionals and institutions severs the link between trust in one's neighbors and the quality of democratic governance.

Second, social capital theory deems social networks of reciprocity very important to making democracy work. But reciprocity is not always good for democracy. Democracy in some ways works best if actors are unknown to one another (rather than known and deeply enmeshed in a fabric of organizations), and autonomous (rather than mutually dependent for favors). Consider campaign finance. When candidates receive donations from known benefactors, this knowledge may create pressure for quid pro quo legislative concessions. The benefits to democracy of donor anonymity inspire Bruce Ackerman and Ian Ayres (2002) to envision a donation booth, which recreates the anonymity of the voting booth, where donors anonymously write checks for candidates and parties.

If reciprocity between donor and legislator can vitiate democratic principles, so can reciprocity between voters and parties. Consider the dynamics of vote buying by the old machines of many U.S. cities and in developing democracies today, from Bulgaria to the Philippines to Benin to Mexico. Vote buying does not work if the party attempting to buy the vote cannot punish the voter for defecting and voting for someone else. Vote buying does work if the party has enough information about individuals' partisan predilections and likely vote that it can punish defection (Stokes 2005). It is precisely the rich fabric of social networks, associations, and interactions—celebrated by civic culture theorists—that reduces the potential vote seller's anonymity and provides the vote buyer with information indicating likely defections.[2]

To get a sense of the tension between the theory of democracy as resting on reciprocity, and the coercion that this reciprocity can sustain, consider first Putnam's depiction of a community rich in social fabric, and then the reflections of two residents interviewed in a town in Argentina.[3] First, Putnam:

> An effective norm of generalized reciprocity is bolstered by dense networks of social exchange. If two would-be collaborators are members of a tightly knit community, they are likely to encounter one another in the future—or to hear about one another through the grapevine. Thus they have reputations at stake that are almost surely worth more than gains from momentary treachery. In that sense, honesty is encouraged by dense social networks. (2000, 136)

Now the couple in Argentina:

Interviewer: When people come and give things out during the campaign, are they people whom you know?

Husband: Yes, they're people from here, they're neighbors. Here everyone knows each other. Small town, big hell. (Pueblo chico, infierno grande.)

Interviewer: Do they know how you voted?

Husband: For many years we've seen, people will say, "So-and-so voted for so-and-so." And he wins, and they come and say, "You voted for so-and-so." I don't know how they do it, but they know.

Wife: We were at the unidad básica [a neighborhood Peronist locale] and they say to me, "[Your cousin] voted for Eloy" [the given name of a Radical Party candidate]. And I asked my cousin, "did you vote for Eloy?" And she said "yes"! They knew that my cousin had voted for Eloy!

Husband: The person who didn't vote for them, they discriminate against him a little, he might go ask for a favor, and they say, "He voted for so-and-so."

Regarding civic participation, we will show that, in Argentina and Mexico, people in more democratic regions often retreat from civic participation to more private concerns. Civic activism may, indeed, be self-limiting. People in developing countries collectively press for infrastructure improvements, economic opportunities, and political rights. If these goals are achieved, civic engagement becomes less pressing. Of course, in the countries we studied, even in the relatively democratic regions the challenges of economic development and political representation are far from resolved. Yet, to the extent that existence becomes less precarious and community development advances, the pressing needs that drew people into the public sphere attenuate.

To summarize, social capital theorists claim that the culture of democracy is, or should be, a culture of civic activism, reciprocity, and trust. We have raised several theoretical objections to this view of democratic political culture. Citizens turn not to their neighbors but to specialized organizations to monitor politicians and governments, raising questions about any link between interpersonal trust and accountable government. Anonymity, and not intense social interaction, enhances some democratic goals, from campaign funding to voting. Social capital theory fails to provide persuasive arguments about why community organizational life is critical to the quality and consolidation of democracy, just as it fails to provide persuasive arguments about why interpersonal trust among citizens enhances democratic governance.

The Skeptical Tradition in Democratic Theory

The seeds of a more skeptical democratic theory lie in the civic culture tradition itself. For all its protestations that citizens need to trust one another for democracy to work—that they must take part in associations that are "reciprocal, trusting, and involving positive emotion"— note that a central reason they must trust one another is that they cannot automatically trust politicians. Even though Putnam finds reasons to despair in light of data suggesting declining trust of Americans in their government, the reason why (Italian) citizens had to trust one another is that only by doing so would they be willing to monitor their government. The belief that government acts in constituents' interests only as long as it is under constituents' watchful gaze is a weak form of trust, however, as we shall explain. And we have raised doubts about any connection between citizens who trust one another and the accountability of governments.

To the extent that it views interpersonal trust (among citizens) as necessary to overcoming the untrustworthiness of politicians, the civic culture tradition taps into a more skeptical political theory, one with roots in the eighteenth century. From Montesquieu and Hume, James Madison drew the idea that some elected officeholders would inevitably lack the qualities that would make them trustworthy. In the tenth *Federalist*, Madison explained that most men elected into the "chosen body" of his hoped-for federal republic would have "the wisdom [to] best discern the true interests of the country," as well as "patriotism" and "love of justice" (1787/1982, 47). Still, Madison continued, "Enlightened statesmen will not always be at the helm" (45), and "Men of factious tempers, of local prejudices, or of sinister designs, may by intrigue, by corruption or by other means, first obtain the suffrages, and then betray the interests of the people" (47). The beauty of repeated elections was that they lessened the importance of personal trustworthiness of politicians; even those who, left to their own devices, might act against the interests of constituents, would be constrained to be trustworthy. In the fifty-seventh *Federalist*, Madison sketched a notion that in the twenty-first century would be called accountability:

> Before the sentiments impressed on their minds by the mode of their elevation . . . can be effaced by the exercise of power, they will be compelled to anticipate the moment when their power is to cease, when their exercise of it is to be reviewed, and when they must descend to the level from which they were raised; there for ever to remain, unless a faithful discharge of their trust shall have established their title to a renewal of it. (294)

Today, the idea that politicians who face future elections may be held accountable is pervasive in academic and popular understandings of democracy. Perhaps overlooked is the skeptical turn of mind that accountability assumes. Were politicians to be inherently trustworthy—were they all, in Madison's language, wise, patriotic, and justice-loving—we would not need to rely on their baser desire to retain office to keep them in line.

Not all contemporary theorists have lost sight of the centrality of skepticism to democracy. Vivien Hart's *Distrust and Democracy* (1978) opens with an epigraph from Demosthenes: "There is one safeguard known generally to the wise, which is an advantage and security to all, but especially to democracies against despots. What is it? Distrust" (xi). And Hart insists, against the grain of other theorists and some interpreters of public opinion, that "distrust is democratic and thoughtful, not an anti-democratic outburst of emotion, and is potentially constructive, threatening only to vested political interests" (xii).

Just as Hart's distrust is thoughtful and constructive, the skepticism that, we believe, infuses the culture of democracy is an engaged skepticism. And it is an active skepticism. Citizens of the more democratic regions we studied were not driven by skepticism to cynicism or inaction. Indeed, they sought more information about politics, voted more regularly, and discussed political matters more readily than did their counterparts in less democratic regions. (But, as we shall see, they were less active in civic associations.) Too much skepticism about politics might lead to aloof detachment; but this was far from the posture of the citizens in the mature democratic regions we studied.

Some contemporary theorists lead us to expect that, as democracy develops, accountability increases, and therefore the trustworthiness of government also grows, displacing personal trust in politicians with institutional trust in government.

If it were never in politicians' interests to be constrained by institutions, then voters who believed in their accountability might simply be deluded. Yet trustworthiness may in fact be in politicians' interests. John Ferejohn (1999) posits that the more accountable (and hence trustworthy) politicians are, the more power voters are willing to grant them. Voters are willing to empower institutionally constrained politicians because voters know that, should the politicians abuse this power, they can be discovered and punished. By analogy, a building contractor who is constrained by an enforceable contract will be more successful in soliciting projects than one who works without contracts because his clients know that, should something go awry, they can turn to a court for help. Therefore, even though the contract in a sense constrains the contractor, it also empowers him. It is in the interest of both parties that an enforceable contract can be signed.

By the same logic, institutional constraints can work in the interest of both officeholders and constituents. For this reason, under some conditions they have a shared interest in building mechanisms of accountability and institutional trust. As evidence that growing institutional accountability and growing scope of government action go hand in hand, Ferejohn points to a general correspondence in time between the widening policy range of the U.S. government and congressional reforms that made government more accountable. These reforms included recorded teller votes, opening of the committee markup sessions, and changes in how campaigns are financed (139).

Drawing on Ferejohn's insight, we posit the following stylized scenario. A poor and class-divided society democratizes. Poverty and inequality tempt political parties to deploy a strategy of clientelism: the trading of votes and political support in return for small, private payoffs to voters. Clientelism functions only when both voters and political brokers are tightly enmeshed in personal networks, networks that allow the brokers to punish individual voters who defect from their implicit contract—to hold them "perversely accountable" for their votes (Stokes 2005). Clientelism is then, by necessity, a highly personalized form of politics. It also requires that voters take actions that cannot be fully monitored by the patron party, such as voting for their candidates in exchange for handouts. To improve compliance, parties cultivate relations of friendship and trust with their clienteles.

If the society travels a path toward economic development and—

eventually—a more equal distribution of income, clientelism becomes a less effective strategy for parties in search of votes.[4] Instead, it becomes attractive for parties and political leaders in this more developed and more egalitarian society to forge relations of accountability with voters, for the reasons we have just reviewed. Hence a belief in accountability or institutional trust—a belief that does not imply personal trust in politicians but, quite to the contrary, a certain skepticism about their motives and unchecked actions—displaces the personal trust of the earlier era.

There is nothing inevitable about this process. Economic development and social leveling are by no means bound to occur in poor democracies. But they may, and indeed sometimes do, occur. That countries, and regions within countries, do sometimes follow the path we have described means that we expect to find an elective affinity between low-quality democracy, clientelist strategies, and personal trust in politicians on one side, and high-quality democracy, programmatic or performance-oriented mobilization of voters, and institutional trust in government on the other. In later chapters, we discover just such patterns of political culture in Mexico and Argentina.

Does civic activism generate trust? Does trust improve the quality of democracy? Are politicians who operate in more active polities more trustworthy and accountable? Does development undercut personal trust in politicians and encourage trust in the institutions of government? One can answer all these questions with empirical data. In later chapters we translate many of these questions into causal hypotheses, and test them with data from two new democracies. We hope that this discussion leaves readers predisposed to doubt that trust, rather than skepticism, informs the political culture of democracy.

Conceptualizing Trust

The belief that a politician acts in one's interests because he or she is monitored and will be held accountable is, we have asserted, a weak—some might even say a strange—form of trust. Here we explain what we mean by concepts such as trustworthiness and distrust, weak and strong trust, trust in people and trust in institutions, and trust in one's fellow citizens versus trust in politicians.

First, trust. Trust involves a relationship between actors regarding an action. If A and B are actors and X is an action that is in A's interest, then if A believes that B will do X, A trusts B.[5] Trust then is someone's (A's) belief about the likely action (X) of someone else (B). Theorists of trust are quick to observe, and rightly so, a distinction between trust and trustworthiness. Trust is a belief (that is, A's belief that B will do X). Trustworthiness is a quality or predisposition (that is, B's predisposition to do X). And trust may therefore be ill-founded: A may trust B to do X even though B is in fact unlikely to do X and, hence, is untrustworthy.

Distrust can be stated as the contrapositive of trust: A distrusts B if A does not believe that B will do X. (X, again, is an action that A wishes B to undertake).

But we need to say more about the concept of trust. There are many circumstances in which A believes B will take an action X that is in A's interest, and yet the belief falls short of common language usages of trust. Our purpose here is not to parse definitions, but rather to show how common understandings of trust vary along a dimension (from weak to strong) that we find theoretically important.

Consider, first, an example of spontaneous coincidence of interests. Farmer B lives next door to an orchard owned by Farmer A. Farmer B, with an eye on her bottom line, installs beehives on her farm. The bees fly into Farmer A's orchard and help pollinate his trees. Farmer A experiences better harvests and increased profits. Farmer B's profits also improve. Looking forward to next year, Farmer A expects Farmer B to keep her hives. This scenario seems to conform to our preliminary definition of trust. Yet if Farmer A were to say that he "trusts" Farmer B to continue with her hives, we would find the expression awkward. The two actors happen to have converging interests, but the convergence is not the result of any institutional arrangement or mutual consideration. Thus, we exclude such situations of spontaneous coincidence of interests from our conception of trust (see Hardin 1998, 2002).

Consider next punishment for noncooperation. For instance, two opposing parties are negotiating after the fall of a long-standing dictatorship. Each can either stick with an agreement to hold elections, or it can instigate a coup. If both stick with the agreement for elections, the result is a democracy in which each party will win some future elections and lose some others. If one party defects and the other sticks with the agreement, the coup-maker gets all power for a delimited period. If both attempt coups, a civil war will erupt, which both parties consider a worse outcome than either becoming the new authoritarian rulers or entering into a democracy. Their preference order from first to last is: become new authoritarian, share power in a democracy, civil war, and become subject to opponent's authoritarianism. Knowing that they will face one another and similar decisions into the indefinite future, they institute a democracy that lasts for many years.

According to our generic definition, the two parties trust each other not to instigate coups. Yet the usage of the term trust strays from common usage. Here, A expects B to do X because both know that if B does not do X, A will sanction B, and the sanction makes carrying out X more attractive to B than not carrying it out.

The situation is a prisoner's dilemma. Cooperation produces payoffs (democracy) for both that are higher than the payoffs when they both defect (civil war) but not as high as when one defects and the opponent cooperates, in which case the defector gets all power (and the cooperator gets no power). In a one-shot game, the Nash equilibrium is civil war. But in the repeated game we assume the parties are playing, they can sustain the cooperative equilibrium of democracy. Both may cooperate as long as they anticipate being punished by the other if they defect, and both anticipate that the cost of future punishment—a period of civil war—outweighs the current gain from defection (see Axelrod 1984). Each party then trusts the other in the sense that each knows that his credible threat of punishment forces the other to sustain democracy. We consider this instance of trust sustained by direct punishment for noncooperation to be a form of weak trust.

Punishment for noncooperation can also be imposed by third parties. For instance, in the new democracy just described, voters know that politicians are under the ongoing scrutiny of the courts, and believe, therefore, that their elected officials will act honestly. Institutional accountability induces them to be responsive. In this case, A (voters) trusts B (elected officials) to do X (act honestly and efficiently) because they believe that, if B does not do X, institutional arrangements provide for third parties to punish B, and B prefers to do X than to endure the punishment. These are situations of trust sustained by third-party punishment for noncooperation. Trust sustained in this manner is a stronger form of trust than is trust by direct punishment: the former does not have the gun-to-the-head, coercive sense of the latter. Still, the reliance on punishment makes this a weaker sense of the term than those considered next.

Other examples can be marshaled that better get at what is commonly meant by trust. For instance, voters in a small community elect as mayor a neighbor who is known as honest and frugal, and expect him to be a good mayor. Or a leader proposes that his country go to war, claiming to have private information that justifies the action. Some citizens believe him and support the war. In this example, unlike in the previous two, A's trust in B does not rely on external sanctions, wielded either by A or by a third party. A's trust relies on some inherent quality of B. B's honesty, efficiency, or good judgment will induce him to do X. They are subtly different from the first example in that here, if B did not have the inherent quality on which A's trust rests, B might act against A's interests. If dishonest, the mayor would stand to gain by diverting funds to his personal account or shirking on the job. If lacking in judgment, the leader might initiate a war that is not really in his country's interest. As is frequently the case in common usage, trust sustained by the trustee's (perceived) inherent qualities connotes some willingness on the part of the trustee to sacrifice his own interests. B could hurt A and get away with it, but A trusts B and therefore expects him not to. This is the understanding of trust most consonant with common usage. We call this personal trust: in contrast to the previous examples in which trust was based on institutional incentives or fear of punishment, personal trust is based on the inherent qualities of the trustee. Personal trust is a strong form of trust.

To summarize, we exclude from our definition instances in which A's belief that B will do X rests on spontaneous (rather than engineered, reflexive, or future-oriented) coincidence of interest. We accept beliefs that rest on direct punishment of the trustee by the truster, or on third-party punishment for noncooperation. Both of these are, however, weak senses of trust. A trusts B to do X in a strong sense when his belief that B will do X is sustained by B's inherent qualities, qualities that induce B to do X even though he would gain from not doing X.[6]

A central claim of this book is that political accountability requires at most a weak form of trust, one that rests on second- or third-party enforcement. Belief in accountability implies institutional trust: the belief that institutional constraints induce officeholders to act in the interests of their constituents. But accountability implies distrust of officeholders: the belief that, without institutional constraints, they are prone to disregard the interests of constituents. Institutional trust is deeply in tension with personal trust in politicians, the latter the belief that their personal qualities leave them disposed to act in constituents' interests even when they would benefit from disregarding these interests. Personal distrust, accompanied (in the best of circumstances) by institutional (weak) trust, enhances the quality of representative government. Or, perhaps, institutional trust allows citizens the luxury of not needing to evaluate a politician's personal trustworthiness. Institutions increase the range over which trust is possible; when one has to rely only on personal trust, the likely result is less trust overall. Our perspective is therefore far from that of social capital theorists, for whom democracy rests on strong trust.

Methods and Plan

What sort of evidence might one find to test these theoretical propositions? The remainder of this book is an effort to test them against the experiences of two new democracies in Latin America: Argentina and Mexico. If the theory gives us any good guidance about how to think about trust and the political culture of democracy, we should find the following:

- In places where democracy is relatively consolidated and works relatively well, we should find institutional trust in government to be the more common form of trust. In places where it is unconsolidated or functions badly, to the extent that we find political trust it should be of a personal sort.

- In regions where democratic practices are marred by political clientelism and vote buying, we expect to find a political culture of personal trust in politicians, and relatively little awareness of the possibility of institutional trust or accountability. Indeed, clientelism may rely on a personalization of political relations and on personal trust in politicians and in party operatives.

- We should not find systematic differences in the quality of associational life, or the prevalence of social capital, in places where democracy works relatively well and in places where it works badly. And we should not be able to predict people's levels of institutional trust in government from their levels of personal trust in their neighbors.

Methods and Data

Our strategy in the book is comparative. We make comparisons at multiple levels and across multiple units. These include:

Comparisons Across Countries   Most of our cross-national comparisons are based on data we gathered in two countries that lie at the geographic extremes of Latin America: Mexico in the north and Argentina in the south. The two countries have different histories and different trajectories of democratization and they face different challenges in the consolidation of democracy. Their histories also contrast starkly. Mexico was a center of colonial life beginning in the sixteenth century; Argentina was a backwater until well into the nineteenth century. Mexico has a large indigenous and mestizo population; Argentina is largely a nation of European immigrants. Mexico's proximity to the United States deeply shaped its history; Argentina is geographically remote from the hemispheric hegemon. Mexico underwent a transformative social revolution; Argentina did not. The most recent processes of democratization had sharply different dynamics. In Mexico democratization happened when a party that had maintained hegemonic control for seven decades finally lost power in a peaceful presidential election. In Argentina democratization meant ousting a brutal military regime and reinitiating elections. In Mexico democratization took decades, in Argentina it took but a few months. Democratization in Mexico started with reforms undertaken by a ruling party that was embarrassed by the weakness of its electoral opponents, and bubbled up slowly from below, from municipalities and states to the presidency. Democratization in Argentina relied on a backdrop of economic failures by the regime but happened, in large part, because of a bungled military adventure. It took place simultaneously at all levels of government. What varied from region to region in Argentina was not democratization but the quality of subsequent democratic governance.

Despite these many differences, our general expectation is that we will find similarities between the two countries. Indeed, our primary purpose in studying the political culture of democracy in two countries rather than one is to suggest that our results are likely to hold for many new democracies in the developing world. The difficulties that citizens face in ascertaining the trustworthiness of governments and of politicians grow out of the very workings of democracy. Clientelism is a strategy of mobilization that makes sense in all democracies in which many voters are very poor, and it may generate personal trust wherever it is deployed.[7] The theory linking politicians' bids for more power and authority with greater self-imposed accountability, and hence greater institutional trust, is general.

We recognize, however, that our research strategy precludes us, in a strict sense, from using survey data to compare Argentina and Mexico. This is because the sample surveys on which much of our analysis rests were not national, but instead were drawn from particular regions in each country (see the appendix for more details). The reader will find that when we do make such two-country comparisons, we add the caveat that apparent differences (or, for that matter, similarities) would have to be confirmed with national samples.

Our original plan was to complement our Mexico-Argentina comparisons with large-N cross-national analysis, drawing from publicly available surveys. Yet, to our dismay, our conceptualization of trust as A's belief that B will do X rendered many survey questions on trust unhelpful to us.[8] Given these shortcomings, we have not made extensive use of these more broadly cross-national surveys.

Comparisons Across Regions   Comparisons across regions within each of the countries we study are at the heart of this book. We undertook two kinds of cross-regional analyses. One was cross-state or cross-provincial comparisons across the full range of subnational units. We gathered certain kinds of information from all thirty-one states in Mexico and all twenty-three provinces in Argentina.[9] These data allow us to make comparisons and draw inferences about, for example, the causes of variation in efficiency of elected state or provincial governments. The second set of comparisons consisted of cross-regional ones across a subset of regions. In both countries we gathered data from a subset of regions to characterize the quality of democracy in each. Ultimately we selected four regions (four states in Mexico, three provinces and one region within a province in Argentina) that represented a range from better to worse functioning regional democracy. The quality of democracy is then the explanatory variable, and we are able to compare the nature of trust, strategies of electoral mobilization, and endowments of social capital, as a function of the quality of regional democracies.

Some of the data we collected in these regions were qualitative. We interviewed political leaders and drew from secondary accounts of regional politics. Some of the data were ecological. We gathered information about the social structure and electoral dynamics of each of the selected regions. And some of the data were individual, drawn from our own sample surveys. But these individual data also allow us to make cross-regional comparisons, and these cross-regional comparisons represent the core of our analytical strategy. By recording in which of the four regions in each country individual respondents lived, we were able to use statistical analysis to study the effect of region and, behind it, the quality of democracy, on phenomena of theoretical interest. Hence, for example, we were able to estimate the effect that living in the province of Buenos Aires (rather than, say, Misiones) had on an Argentine's likelihood of trusting her neighbors, or the effect of living in Chihuahua (rather than, say, Puebla) had on a Mexican's perceptions that his neighbors were influenced by clientelism in deciding how to vote.

Comparisons Across Municipalities   The political dynamics that interest us theoretically often unfold at more local levels than the state or province. In Mexico, for example, opposition victories in important municipalities in the north gave a stimulus to national democratization. In Argentina, municipal governments could either encourage or stifle mechanisms of accountability. We use qualitative research (our own and others') into local politics to assess the quality of democracy across regions. And we use quantitative ecological data that we and others have gathered at the municipal level to compare, for example, the effect of municipal poverty rates on whether, and in what ways, individual residents trusted government.

Comparisons Across Individuals   Trust, as we have defined it, is a belief that individuals hold about other individuals' likely actions. In theories linking trust (personal, institutional, interpersonal) to the quality of democracy, trust is sometimes a cause and sometimes a consequence of democracy. Hence to study political cultures of trust and skepticism, we need to compare people who hold a variety of beliefs, and we need to compare people who are different in other ways—the wealthy versus the poor, the well educated versus the little educated, a resident of one region versus a resident of another—and observe the levels and types of trust that they evince. Data most relevant for these cross-individual comparisons come from our sample surveys.

Plan of the Book

The central objective of part II, chapters 2 and 3, is to rank a subset of regions within Mexico and Argentina, respectively, according to the quality of regional democracy. Part II draws on a wide range of sources: interviews with citizens and political leaders, qualitative municipal and regional studies in the secondary literature, and ecological databases with measures at state, provincial, and municipal levels. Part III, chapters 4 and 5, exploits this cross-regional variation in the quality of democracy to test causal hypotheses about the political culture of democracy. In chapter 4 we explore whether cross-regional differences in the quality of democracy have counterparts in regional differences in political culture, particularly in beliefs about accountability and the trustworthiness of politicians. In chapter 5 we test propositions concerning the effect of social capital, development, and inequality on the political culture of democracy. Last, in chapter 6 (part IV), we reexamine questions about the political culture of democracy in light of our theoretical and empirical findings. Having started by assessing theories that link democracy with trust, we end by suggesting that a healthy democratic culture is as much a culture of skepticism as it is of trust.

PART II

REGIONAL VARIATION IN THE QUALITY OF DEMOCRACY

Chapter 2

Regional Variation in the Quality of Democracy in Mexico

ERE, WE introduce the concept of subnational democracy and discuss several approaches to cross-state measurement. Borrowing from Linz and Stepan's (1996) definition of democratic consolidation, we analyze the nature of electoral competition in Mexico, and then turn our attention to regional and local political institutions, party behavior, and public opinion. The evidence attests to substantial variation in the pace of democratization and quality of democracy across the Mexican states.

Cross-State Variation in the Level of Democracy

Mexico has a three-tiered federal system, with thirty-one state governments and more than twenty-four hundred municipalities.[1] Many of the northern states, such as Baja California and Nuevo León, are relatively industrialized, wealthy, and educated. They also have higher divorce rates and lower infant mortality rates (INEGI 2000). By comparison, many states in the south, including Oaxaca, Puebla, and Guerrero, are rural, agricultural, and poor. Social problems in the south are exacerbated by violent conflicts across ethnic, economic, and ideological cleavages. Several southern states have large indigenous populations, and indigenous languages are widely spoken.[2] The north and south of the country also have deep cultural differences that extend to cuisine, music, and sports. Soccer is the most popular sport in most of the country (including the south), but northerners prefer baseball. Occasionally, southerners can be heard blaming the national soccer team's losses on the north's failure to produce top-quality players.

Politics differs across these regions as well. Some states have a vibrant political sphere, with competitive elections, pluralism in munici-

21

pal councils and state legislatures, and public and journalistic scrutiny of government affairs. These governments tend to be more transparent and efficient, and have a greater capacity to generate their own revenue (Courchene and Díaz Cayeros 2000). Other states have less competitive elections, widespread clientelism, and dominant governors whose power is not significantly checked by state legislatures or other local political groups.

Electoral Competition and Party Alternation

The most dramatic evidence of varying levels of democracy across the Mexican states can be found in the electoral arena. For fifty years after its founding, the Institutional Revolutionary Party (Partido Revolucionario Institucional, PRI) held hegemonic political power throughout the country. The first serious challenge to this electoral hegemony came in the early 1980s, when opposition politicians defeated PRI candidates, primarily in Chihuahua and Baja California, but also in scattered municipalities throughout the country, including in the southern states of Oaxaca and Chiapas. After the surprisingly competitive (and fraudulent) presidential election of 1988, true multiparty competition in municipal and state contests became more prevalent, especially in the northern half of the country. By the late 1990s, non-PRI parties had captured ten governorships and several hundred municipal administrations, including twenty-six of the thirty largest cities in the country (Lujambio 2000). But the spread of electoral competition and the alternation of parties in state and municipal offices were not uniform. In some states the shift to competitive elections was swift and dramatic. In others, the PRI continues to dominate even today, and local politics has only a small measure of competition or pluralism.

Scholars offer several explanations for increased electoral competition in Mexico. Hernández Valdez (2000) argues that state-level "subnational democracy" is a function of relative income equality, the effectiveness of electoral institutions, and ethnic homogeneity. Others find a link between democratic transformations and development, modernization, or integration with international trade (see, for example, Díaz Cayeros, Magaloni, and Weingast 2003; Rodríguez and Ward 1994; Valdiviezo Sandoval 1998). We offer our own reasons for this subnational variation in chapter 5. But what interests us here is that these studies share a conceptual understanding that the degree of democratization and the quality of democracy vary across the Mexican states. Most Mexicanists can intuitively agree that however democratic the country as a whole is at any moment, Baja California, for instance, is more democratic than Guerrero, and Chihuahua is more democratic than, say, Hidalgo.

We turn now to quantitative measures of state-level democracy that have been introduced in the literature on Mexico. We start with a simple claim: states that have truly competitive multiparty elections are more democratic than states without such competition.[3] Before 1983, the PRI's margin of victory in gubernatorial contests throughout the country—the gap between its vote total and that of the party finishing second—rarely fell below 60 percent. In the eleven gubernatorial contests held in 1980, for example, official returns show the PRI winning by an average margin of 80 percentage points, equivalent to a 90 percent to 10 percent outcome. The average margin for the seven elections held in 1981 was 76 percent. Slowly and unevenly, however, the level of competition increased, especially in the north. Opposition victories in some cases may have been masked by PRI-sponsored election fraud (for example, Chihuahua in 1986), but the first officially recognized opposition win in a statewide race was in Baja California's gubernatorial race in 1989. Opposition parties won several more governorships in the 1990s. Today, even in the states in which the PRI has never lost the governorship, elections are closely contested.[4]

Table 2.1 lists the first year in which a party other than the PRI won the governorship of each state (if one ever has), the number of party alternations in the governor's office from 1989 until the end of 2003, and the year in which the PRI first lost its majority in the state legislature (if it ever has). In some of the states where parties have alternated in office the opposition party has become dominant. For example, the National Action Party (Partido Acción Nacional, PAN) won the governorship of Baja California three times in a row, in 1989, 1995, and 2001. But in Chihuahua and Nuevo León, the PRI won back the governorship after a one-term opposition interlude. Because gubernatorial elections occur just once every six years, it will be some time before we know whether elections in these states will remain competitive. But note that of the six states that have held another election after an opposition (non-PRI) victory, four have returned the opposition to power a second time, and two have reverted to the PRI. All six have been relatively close contests, and in these states ex ante uncertainty about election outcomes has become the norm. In contrast, governor's races in many of the states near the bottom of the list in table 2.1 have never been closely contested. Still, even in states that are traditional strongholds of the PRI, the trend toward competition is undeniable. State legislative elections show a similar pattern. Opposition parties have broken the PRI's state legislative majority in most of the states where they have won governorships, often in the same election. States in which opposi-

Table 2.1   Party Alternation in the Mexican States, 1989 to 2003

State	Year of First Gubernatorial Alternation	Number of Gubernatorial Alternations	Year PRI First Lost Majority in State Legislature
Baja California	1989	1	1989
Guanajuato	1991	1	1997
Chihuahua	1992	2	1992
Jalisco	1995	1	1995
Nuevo León	1997	2	1997
Querétaro	1997	1	1997
Aguascalientes	1998	1	1995
Zacatecas	1998	1	1998
Baja California Sur	1999	1	1999
Tlaxcala	1999	1	2001
Nayarit	1999	1	1999
Chiapas	2000	1	never
Morelos	2000	1	1997
Michoacán	2001	1	2001[a]
Yucatán	2001	1	2001
San Luis Potosí	2003	1	2003[b]
México	none	0	1996
Sonora	none	0	1997
Guerrero	none	0	2002[c]
Tabasco	none	0	2003
Coahuila	none	0	never[d]
Colima	none	0	never[e]
Campeche	none	0	never
Durango	none	0	never
Hidalgo	none	0	never
Oaxaca	none	0	never
Puebla	none	0	never
Quintana Roo	none	0	never
Sinaloa	none	0	never
Tamaulipas	none	0	never
Veracruz	none	0	never

Sources: Banamex (2001); Lujambio (2000); Keesing's Record of World Events (various).
[a]The PRI held 50 percent of the seats in the 1989 to 1992 legislature, then regained a clear majority until 2001.
[b]The PRI lost a majority in 2003 but retains a plurality.
[c]The PRI lost a majority in 2002 but retains a plurality.
[d]The PRI held 50 percent of the seats in the 1997 to 1999 legislature, then regained a clear majority until 2002.
[e]The PRI held 50 percent of the seats in the 1997 to 2000 legislature, but maintained a clear majority after that.

tion parties have failed to break the PRI's legislative majority are generally also states that have not experienced alternation in the governor's office.

Yet we are concerned with more than the mere presence of electoral pluralism in the Mexican states. We are also interested in whether competition has produced party alternation and other significant changes in state and local governments. Our logic here builds on Huntington's (1991, 266–67) definition of democratic consolidation. Writing about national-level democracy, Huntington argues that consolidation requires two peaceful alternations of the party in power. The second alternation, he maintains, shows that the new incumbents are also willing to cede power, thus distinguishing cases in which the legitimacy of electoral competition has been accepted by all parties from those in which authoritarianism reemerges after only one competitive election. Because state governments controlled by former opposition parties in Mexico would not have the power to commit massive vote fraud or nullify unfavorable electoral outcomes without the collaboration of the federal government (controlled by the PRI until 2000), the second competitive election is less important for demonstrating democratization in Mexico.[5] Even a single alternation is significant evidence of a democratic shift.

In Mexico, there is only one major party whose willingness to submit to fair contests remains in question. Before 1989 it was clear that the PRI was not willing to cede gubernatorial power under any circumstances. Often the official election returns were so skewed that they were highly suggestive of fraud, in the counting if not in the voting. In the 1990s, with opposition power growing, the PRI had to adapt. State PRI organizations reacted to electoral competition in a variety of ways. In some states the PRI accepted the new reality and changed its strategy. In Chihuahua, for example, it reacted to its 1992 loss in the governor's race by acquiescing to some electoral reforms and changing its candidate-selection procedures. In other cases, the PRI pursued a more obstructionist strategy. Although indisputable evidence of election fraud is hard to come by, serious accusations were leveled against the PRI in several state elections, including Guanajuato in 1991, Michoacán in 1992, and Tabasco in 1994 (Eisenstadt 2004). Perhaps the best evidence comes from the Tabasco contest, in which the PRI's candidate, Roberto Madrazo, grossly exceeded campaign spending limits, employed typical "'get out the vote' promotions and petty ballot stuffing," rigged the vote-counting computer on election day, and dissuaded the state's election courts from hearing charges of fraud (Eisenstadt 2004, 111–12). In response to protests by the Party of the Democratic Revolution (Partido de la Revolución Democrática, PRD), President Zedillo's administration attempted to force Madrazo's resignation. Not only did

Zedillo fail, but in 2002 Madrazo was elected to the presidency of the national PRI.

Hence, whereas the PRI recognized opposition victories in Baja California and Chihuahua, it actively subverted such victories in Guanajuato, Michoacán, and Tabasco.[6] One might expect such subversive strategies to be less viable, and therefore less common, after the national transition to democracy in 2000. Yet in 2001 the PRI governor of Yucatán orchestrated fraudulent elections in that state. The state PRI attempted first to pack the state electoral commission with its own partisans, and then to prevent the federal electoral commission from using its oversight authority to correct the partisan abuse (Eisenstadt 2004, 245–49). Fraud may also have determined the outcome of the 2004 gubernatorial election in Oaxaca. José Murat, the governor from 1998 to 2004, is an infamous and colorful cacique who governed in an authoritarian manner (Gibson 2004). In the 2004 election, his handpicked successor officially won a close contest, but the election was marred by violence, both before and after the vote, and by charges of fraud. Violence and voter intimidation were widely reported by the press, and independent observers judged the elections to be unfair.[7]

Thus, in the relationship between electoral competition and democracy among Mexican states, the real question is whether the PRI is willing to relinquish power once it loses a state election. As Adam Przeworski argues, democracy becomes consolidated when elections become self-enforcing, meaning that "all the relevant political forces find it best to continue to submit their interests and values to the uncertain interplay of the [electoral] institutions," even when they lose (Przeworski 1991, 26). Of Mexico's thirty-one states, the opposition has won the governor's office and the PRI has stood aside in seventeen (in addition to the Federal District). Hence in these seventeen, the PRI has shown itself to be willing to subject its interests to the uncertainty of election outcomes, even if it had not been prepared to do so in the recent past. In the fourteen remaining states it is hard to say whether the state PRI is committed to democratic procedures.[8] In a few states, such as Oaxaca, Tabasco, and Yucatán, the PRI appears unwilling to cede power, even as recently as 2004. In others it may be willing to submit to electoral results, but has not been forced to do so because of its continued electoral dominance.[9]

Political Violence and Human Rights

The PRI's uneven record of submitting to fair elections and abiding by their results suggests a broader way of thinking about variation in the level of democracy across Mexico. When the PRI lost elections but refused to yield, the refusal was often followed by political violence. Eisenstadt (2004) chronicles many postelection conflicts, in which an opposition party believed the PRI had committed fraud and responded with protest and civil disobedience. Small-scale violence was common, especially when the PRD was involved. Eisenstadt estimates that as many as two hundred people were killed in these conflicts between 1989 and 2000 (2004, 140).

It is reasonable to argue that the outbreaks of postelection violence indicate a low level (or complete lack) of democracy in that state. Political violence can also happen outside of the electoral arena. The most famous example, in 1994, is armed rebellion in the southern state of Chiapas, which the Ejército Zapatista de Liberación Nacional (EZLN, or Zapatistas) initiated against the government. But opposition groups are far more often the targets of political violence than the perpetrators. To give just one example, in December 1997, forty-five indigenous people (mostly women and children) were murdered by paramilitary gunmen in the village of Acteal, Chiapas. The violence revolved around a land dispute, and the killers were working with the tacit approval of local PRI officials. Within weeks, dozens of villagers, including the mayor, were arrested in connection with the murders.[10]

These events show that some political actors are willing to subvert democratic institutions and resort to violence in pursuit of their political goals. Their actions reveal a lack of democratic consolidation. In Przeworski's language, adherence to democratic institutions has not become "self-enforcing" (1991). This more expansive understanding of democracy, which entails not just competition or alternation of parties in power but also adherence to democratic norms, suggests additional ways to measure the level of democracy across the Mexican states. Hernández Valdez (2000) constructs a state-level measure of democracy based largely on the amount of electoral competition in the state. But he supplements the electoral indicators with two measures of each state's human rights record: the number of human rights violations per capita, and the number of recommendations sent to each state by the Mexican Commission on Human Rights (Comisión Nacional de Derechos Humanos) from 1990 to 1996.[11]

He then uses principal components analysis to translate these measures into a single, composite indicator of local democracy. The first column in table 2.2 contains what Hernández Valdez calls the Comparative Index of Local Democracy (CILD). The principal components procedure generates a variable with a mean of zero and a standard deviation of one. States with positive CILD scores (including Baja California and Chihuahua) are more democratic than average, and states with negative CILD scores (including Michoacán and Puebla) are less democratic.

It is fair to ask whether the CILD scores are accurate reflections of

Table 2.2   Mexico: Indicators of State-Level Democracy and Legislative Independence

State	Comparative Index of Local Democracy (CILD)	Legislative Budget (Pesos per Capita)	Percent of Bills Proposed by State Legislators
Baja California Sur	1.33	10.77	13
Nuevo León	1.21		55
Querétaro	1.20		
Baja California	1.15	5.26	
Aguascalientes	1.01	5.85	
Zacatecas	0.89		
Guanajuato	0.81		38
Chihuahua	0.73	3.54	
Jalisco	0.59	1.62	47
Tlaxcala	0.58	6.30	12
Durango	0.48	6.33	
Colima	0.44	5.93	39
Yucatán	0.29	2.88	
Coahuila	0.24		
Sonora	0.19	4.47	50
Sinaloa	0.09	2.74	45
Nayarit	−0.04	5.10	13
Morelos	−0.09	6.09	55
Campeche	−0.10	10.07	
San Luis Potosí	−0.10	3.30	25
Quintana Roo	−0.10		5
Tamaulipas	−0.10		49
Hidalgo	−0.29	1.99	15
Michoacán	−0.40		15
Mexico	−0.41	3.08	
Tabasco	−0.69		
Veracruz	−0.99		
Puebla	−1.14		11
Guerrero	−1.51	0.71	6
Oaxaca	−1.87	2.85	
Chiapas	−3.27	3.18	

Sources: CILD indicator from Hernández Valdez (2000, 120, table 3); legislative data from Beer (2003); population data from INEGI (2000).
Notes: CILD: Comparative Index of Local Democracy (principal components index), 1989–1999.
Budget: 1996 legislative budget divided by 2000 population, except Jalisco and Chiapas use 1995 budget data.
Empty cells are missing data.

the exact level of democracy in each case, and whether the small differences between pairs of states carry substantive significance. For example, we could not be confident that Baja California (which scores a 1.15) is really less democratic than Nuevo León (which scores 1.21). But Hernández Valdez's procedure does give us an accurate reflection of overall trends. The states at the high end of the CILD scale are clearly more democratic than those at the low end, according to nearly any conception of democracy. Thus, accounting for each state's human rights record produces a ranking comparable to those based only on the level of electoral competition.

The Independence of State Legislatures

Hernández Valdez's scale, based on electoral competition and human rights records, correlates closely with the indicators developed in another cross-state comparative study of Mexican democracy. Caroline Beer (2003) analyzes the relationship between electoral competition and institutional changes in the Mexican states. She finds that competition has caused several changes, including increased autonomy of state legislatures, a greater reliance on open methods of candidate selection (such as primary elections, rather than party appointments, for gubernatorial candidates), and more fiscal autonomy vis-à-vis the federal government. To show these relationships empirically, Beer develops several original measures of state legislative activity. During the period of PRI hegemony, state legislatures were largely ineffective and subservient to governors. With the rise of democracy in many states, legislatures became more active. Beer shows that the most active legislatures generate more bills (rather than simply debating bills sent to them by the governor), have larger operational budgets, and have members who appear in the media and in public more often. Other Mexicanists agree that these are good indications of legislative independence and therefore of a robust state-level democracy (see Ward and Rodríguez 1999, chap. 4).

The last two columns of table 2.2 list two of Beer's measures. The first is the size, in pesos per capita, of the legislative budget—not the state's spending budget that the legislature approves, but rather the operational budget for the legislature itself. We expect more active legislatures to have larger budgets for members' expenses, and Beer argues that legislatures use the extra money to hire more (and better) staff, improve office resources, and in other ways enhance their legislative productivity. The last column is the percentage of bills brought to the floor of the state congress that were generated by the legislators themselves, rather than by the governor.[12] Beer interprets this measure as an indicator of legislative independence and initiative: legislatures

Figure 2.1   Mexico: Level of Democracy and the Size of Legislative Budgets, 1989 to 1999

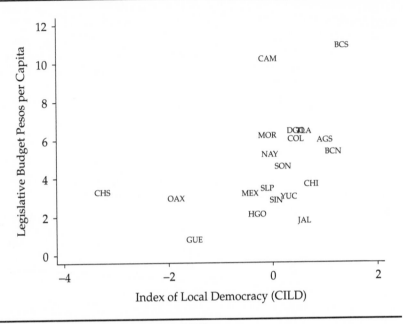

Sources: Hernández Valdez (2000); Beer (2003).
Notes: N = 20, correlation coefficient rho = .45.

that generate more law on their own are more independent (and more powerful) than legislatures that only debate bills presented by the governor.

Beer's two measures and Hernández Valdez's CILD scores are correlated, though only weakly so. Figures 2.1 and 2.2 present graphical representations of the same data that we list in table 2.2. In Figure 2.1, we can see that the states scoring lowest on the CILD index also tend to have small legislative budgets (the correlation coefficient is 0.45, p = 0.048). The three least democratic states in the graph are Chiapas, Oaxaca, and Guerrero; all three have legislative budgets that are well below average. The most democratic states have larger legislative budgets. Similarly, figure 2.2 shows that the least democratic states tend to have less independent legislatures, according to Beer's measure. Legislatures in states such as Guerrero and Puebla are among the least active, whereas those in Sonora, Jalisco, and Nuevo León are among the most active. The relationship, however, is only weakly significant (the correlation coefficient is 0.42, p = 0.096).

Beer's indicators are far from perfect for our purposes: they are mea-

Figure 2.2   Mexico: Level of Democracy and Legislative Bill Generation

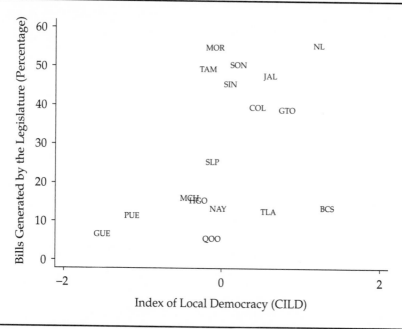

Sources: Hernández Valdez (2000); Beer (2003).
Notes: N = 17, correlation coefficient rho = .42.

sures taken with error, and at only one point in time. The measure of legislative bill generation draws from a survey of legislators, and hence reflects the legislators' own estimates of their productivity. Further-more, we have shown bivariate correlations that do not account for possible confounding factors, such as the wealth (and potential tax base) of each state. We therefore might be less confident in our assess-ment of state-level democracy if these two indicators were the only information available. Yet Beer's and Hernández Valdez's measures re-inforce one another and also match the qualitatively driven intuitions of most Mexicanists about which states in Mexico are the most and the least democratic.

Public Opinion About Democracy

One final dimension on which democracy is thought to vary is with regard to mass attitudes toward democratic forms of government. For example, in the context of consolidation, Juan Linz and Alfred Stepan write that a democratic regime is consolidated when a strong majority of public opinion holds the belief that democratic procedures and institutions are the most appropriate way to govern collective life in a society such as theirs and when the support for antisystem alternatives is quite small or more or less isolated from the pro-democratic forces. (1996, 6)

In this view, the quality of democracy varies with the degree to which most citizens view democratic institutions and practices as legitimate.

The legitimacy of democracy cannot be taken for granted in Mexico. Historically, Mexicans have demonstrated a weak ideological commitment to democratic institutions. Although Almond and Verba found Mexicans to be surprisingly proud of their political institutions, they combined this pride with the perception that their political system was inefficient and unfair (1963, 102). Mexicans responding to the Civic Culture survey in 1959 were five times as likely as respondents in the other four countries to say that they did not expect equal treatment from the government bureaucracy and the police.[13] They were also less likely than respondents in other countries to feel obligated to participate in politics (171), to believe that their political efforts would be successful (185), and to report having "attempted to influence the local government" (188).

Richard Fagen and William Touhy's 1966 survey in Jalapa, Veracruz, produced similar evidence of ambivalence towards democracy. Citizens of Jalapa were apathetic about politics, disbelieved in their ability to influence political outcomes, and recognized the undemocratic nature of the political system. Eighty-two percent of respondents agreed that "it is useless to vote in municipal elections because our leaders are pre-selected by the Party," and 85 percent agreed that "almost all the decisions in Jalapa are made by a very small group of local people" (1972, 110). Sixty-four percent agreed that "every politician is a crook" (112). Yet these bitter feelings about politics did not lead Jalapa residents to wish to democratize their political system. Fagen and Touhy write that

our analysis emphasizes the extent to which centralized and hierarchical forms of governance are accepted by the citizenry. Although the behavior of politicians is frequently seen as corrupt and self-serving, and the operation of certain institutions is often viewed quite negatively, the tradition of strong, centralized, authoritarian rule is seldom challenged. However much citizens may be stung by individual experiences with centralized and arbitrary authority, they do not react by demanding that participation be democratized or that decision-making be decentralized. (1972, 137)

If Mexicans surveyed forty years ago recognized that their government was corrupt, unresponsive, and undemocratic, but still accepted their political institutions, we should not be surprised to learn that many scholars, like Fagen and Touhy, identified weak public support for democracy as one of the major obstacles to democratization in Mexico.

Much has changed in Mexico since Fagen and Touhy's survey. But we should not assume that the public opinions they identified have disappeared. On the contrary, there is ample evidence that many Mexicans remain skeptical about democracy. The persistence of authoritarian enclaves in much of Mexico is partial evidence of continuing authoritarian tendencies (see, for example, Cornelius 1999; Fox 1994; and Lawson 2000).

Survey responses provide direct evidence of authoritarian attitudes and ambivalence about democracy among many segments of the Mexican public. Jorge Domínguez and James McCann (1996) reviewed a number of public opinion surveys, from the Civic Culture surveys collected in 1959 to pre-election surveys conducted in the 1990s. The review led them to conclude that Mexico's transition to democracy was "facilitated by"—though "not caused" by—a democratic shift in public values (1996, 6). Although they present persuasive evidence that political attitudes became increasingly democratic in Mexico in the 1980s, their evidence also reveals a striking persistence of antidemocratic attitudes. And, the regional pattern they uncover matches our characterization of cross-state differences in democracy.

Domínguez and McCann note that Mexicans were more likely to "talk freely about politics with anyone" in 1991 than in 1959 (1996, 36). But the increase is small (from 19 percent to 27 percent), and may merely reflect that 1991 was a federal election year, whereas 1959 was not. The percentage of respondents saying they "never talk about politics" remained virtually unchanged, at 21 percent in 1959 and 20 percent in 1991. Another question that has a long history in Mexican public opinion surveys asks respondents whether they agree that "a few strong leaders would do more for Mexico than all the laws and talk." Agreement indicates support for authoritarian or hierarchical political arrangements. In 1959, 67 percent of Mexicans agreed. In 1988 and 1991, agreement fell to 59 percent and 54 percent, respectively (Domínguez and McCann 1996, 41). The decline indicates that public support for authoritarian leaders has diminished over the past few decades. Even at 54 percent, however, the level of agreement is remarkably high.

Critically, respondents in the northern region were least likely to agree with this statement, and those in the central region were most likely to agree. In fact, the correlation between these responses and socioeconomic factors steadily declined over time, but region continues to be a powerful explanatory factor: "Regionalism rose in importance from 1959 to 1988, and by 1991 it was the only factor that helped to explain variance in authoritarian attitudes" (42). In sum, even if Mexi-

Figure 2.3   Map of Mexico

Source: Generated by the authors using ArcGIS 8.0.

can political culture has changed over the past forty years, many Mexicans are still ambivalent about their democracy and some have authoritarian leanings. There is also wide regional variation in what Linz and Stepan would call the attitudinal dimension of democracy.

Democracy in Four Mexican States

The measures introduced so far offer a consistent and intuitive way to think about variation in the level of democracy among the Mexican states. A closer look at four cases offers a more detailed understanding of how politics differs between the more democratic and less democratic states. A dozen states held elections in 2001. Among these, we carried out in-depth research and conducted surveys in two where democracy was relatively well established, and in two where politics was relatively undemocratic.[14] Here we describe the quality of democracy in each: Baja California, Chihuahua, Michoacán, and Puebla (see figure 2.3 for the location of these states).

Baja California Norte

Baja California Norte occupies the northern half of the Baja California peninsula, in the northwest corner of Mexico. Its northern border abuts

California and is only fifteen miles from San Diego. Geographically, Baja California is as far as one can get from Mexico City without leaving the country. Socioeconomically and politically, the distance is just as great. Before the twentieth century, the region was sparsely populated and relatively unimportant. The peninsula had no rail or highway connection to the rest of Mexico until the late 1940s. Baja California Norte did not gain statehood until 1952.[15] Since then, the region's economy and demography have been heavily influenced by its proximity to the United States.

Maquiladora industries, assembly factories that import parts and re-export finished products, gained importance in the 1960s, especially in the border city of Tijuana. At about this time, the state began a trajectory of rapid population growth, from just over half a million inhabitants in 1960 to more than two and a half million in 2000 (see Rodríguez and Ward 1994, 20; INEGI 2000). Today, maquiladoras remain important, but agriculture, fishing, business, and tourism are also dynamic sectors of the state's economy. The diverse economy, foreign investment, and relatively prosperous and urban middle class distinguish Baja California from most of the rest of Mexico. Even the more traditional sectors, such as agriculture, illustrate the region's distinctiveness. Whereas the agricultural sector in other parts of the country consists primarily of small plots producing for local or personal consumption, or of communally owned ejidos, agriculture in Baja California is centered in the Mexicali Valley and features commercial and export production using modern irrigation techniques (Rodríguez and Ward 1994, 17).

This distinctiveness extends to politics. As in all of Mexico, the PRI dominated Baja California from the 1930s, when the party was formed, until the 1980s. But even during the peak of the PRI's hegemony, Baja California was different. The PAN has been a serious competitor in the state since its strong showing in the 1959 gubernatorial election.[16] In the 1970s and 1980s, when the PRI was winning most other state elections with 85 to 100 percent of the vote, the PAN regularly garnered 30 percent or more in Baja California's contests. Espinoza Valle argues that the state had a two-party system as early as 1971, even though the PAN did not actually win an election before 1986 (1998, 3). That year, the PAN's candidate, Ernesto Ruffo, won the mayoral election in Ensenada.[17] Ruffo was a charismatic businessman with experience in the city's fishing industry. As would be true of successful opposition candidates in the years to come, Ruffo was a relative newcomer to the PAN, having joined the party only in 1984.

The political scene changed dramatically three years later, when Ruffo won the governor's race in 1989. This was the first opposition victory in a statewide election in modern Mexican history. Ruffo

Table 2.3   Mexico: Winning Party in Municipal Elections in Baja California, 1986 to 2004

	Ensenada	Mexicali	Tecate	Tijuana	Playas de Rosarito[a]
1986	PAN	PRI	PRI	PRI	—
1989	PAN	PRI	PRI	PAN	—
1992	PAN	PRI	PAN	PAN	—
1995	PRI	PAN	PRI	PAN	—
1998	PRI	PAN	PRI	PAN	PAN
2001	PAN	PAN	PRI	PAN	PAN
2004	PAN	PAN	PRI[b]	PRI	PAN

Sources: Banamex (2001); Keesing's Record of World Events (various).
[a]Playas de Rosarito was created in 1995 and held its first elections in 1998.
[b]In a coalition (PRI-PEBC-PT-PVEM).

needed to win not just the vote but also the count, and both victories require explanation. His winning of the vote is easier to explain: the PAN had a strong social base in the state, the previous PRI administrations had lackluster performances and were dogged by corruption charges, and Ruffo himself was a popular and charismatic politician. His winning the count is more difficult to explain. The PAN's widely publicized protests following the 1986 elections in Chihuahua and its willingness to cooperate with the PRI in the federal legislature (where the PRI, no longer a supermajority, sometimes needed the PAN's help) gave the party a good deal of negotiating power. Some scholars also highlight President Carlos Salinas's personal motives for recognizing the victory. In light of widespread doubts about the legitimacy of his own election in 1988, Salinas was under pressure to allow a democratic opening in the country. Salinas also seems to have thought that the pressure for opposition representation could be contained, and may have been attempting to limit opposition wins to PAN victories in the periphery (see Espinoza Valle 1998; Rodríguez and Ward 1994, 32–39; Guillén López 1993).

All elections in the state became much more competitive after 1989. The PAN won the governorship in the three consecutive elections of 1989, 1995, and 2001. Yet a closer look at recent elections shows that Baja California did not simply switch from PRI to PAN dominance. Elections in the state's five municipalities allowed the opposition to take power on several occasions, and at least once in each municipality (see table 2.3). Even in Tijuana, where the PAN won five consecutive mayoral elections from 1989 to 2001, contests were hard fought and had close finishes. The PAN won most of these elections by small margins, including a 48 to 46 percent margin in 1992. The PRI, even after having failed to win the municipality five times in a row, eventually did succeed, winning the 2004 race by just 1 percent over the PAN. Elections for the state legislature show a similar pattern of intense two-party competition.[18]

Ruffo's insistence on cleaning up the election rolls, implementing campaign finance reform, and creating a photo identification system for the 1992 election heightened multiparty competition (Guillén López 1995; Rodríguez and Ward 1994, 44). Reform of the state's electoral institutions is just one example of a broader pattern of institutional and social change in Baja California. Immediately after the 1989 election, the unicameral state congress became an important veto player in the state legislative process, because the PAN held only nine of nineteen seats. Thus "Ruffo's early years offered a historic first: a Mexican governor facing willful and often successful opposition from a divided state legislature" (Rodríguez and Ward 1994, 122). Ruffo also returned legal powers to the state judiciary and to the municipalities, powers that had traditionally—though unconstitutionally—been exercised by the governor (Rodríguez and Ward 1994, 122–23).

Along with these institutional changes came a social transformation that began long before 1989 and continues to the present day, with significant political implications. The rise of the maquiladora system, an increase in daily commuting to the United States for work, and the expansion of the state's economy into sectors that were lightly unionized, all served to weaken the grip of corporatist organizations in Baja California (Espinoza Valle 1998, 31–33). Baja California's relatively large middle class, and the ties that its business class developed with the United States, also limited the reach of the state's corporatist organizations (Rodríguez and Ward 1994, 33–34; Espinoza Valle 1998, 32). Additionally, urban popular organizations that the PRI had used to mobilize voters became less influential once their connection to the governor's office was severed in 1989 (Guillén López 1993, 30).

In an electoral sense, Baja California is clearly very democratic. Increasingly after 1989, state electoral institutions became independent, elections became cleaner and more transparent, and outcomes of all state and local elections are now ex ante uncertain (see Espinoza Valle 1998). But politics in Baja California also conforms to more expansive conceptions of democratic consolidation, such as Linz and Stepan's (1996). Baja California is a state in which all key actors have clearly accepted the legitimacy of democratic institutions.[19] Parties now compete in free and fair elections, and respect the results even when they lose. In contrast to the old days, when the governor's power was unchecked, legislative and judicial branches of state government have gained authority, as have municipal governments. Clientelism is relatively infrequent, and corporatism is not an effective means of voter mobilization or social control. By most accounts, state government is relatively efficient and transparent (see Espinoza Valle 1998; Rodríguez and Ward 1994).

After a brief period of disarray, the PRI recovered, showing a willingness to accept the new reality and adjust its political strategy. Just three years after the devastating loss of the governorship, the PRI changed its candidate selection method in Baja California. Before 1992, nominations had always been under the control of senior party officials, and sometimes even of the PRI's national council. But in 1992 the PRI switched to primary elections, in which any party member could vote. This change allowed the PRI to identify and nominate its most popular local candidates, who it hoped would be competitive in the increasingly free and fair electoral system (Guillén López 1993, 28).

In the state's four municipalities where the PRI retained or recovered control, it modernized its recruitment practices for city bureaucrats, and placed a greater emphasis on efficiency and good governance (Rodríguez and Ward 1994, chap. 3). The PRI got the message that continuing in office depended on how it performed in office. Democracy is far from perfect in Baja California. But the rise of electoral competition, the horizontal and vertical decentralization of political power, and the parties' willingness to operate within the new institutional framework indicate that Baja California is one of the most democratic states in Mexico.

Chihuahua

Like Baja California, Chihuahua is a relatively wealthy, industrialized state located in the north of Mexico, adjacent to the U.S. border. Also as in Baja California, competitive elections involving the PAN came early in the process of Mexico's democratization. The first major opposition victory came in 1983, when the PAN won the municipal elections in eight large municipalities, including the state's two largest cities, Chihuahua and Ciudad Juárez.[20] At a time when the PRI held all thirty-one state governorships, every one of the seats in the federal Senate, 75 percent of the seats in the Chamber of Deputies, and 98 percent of municipal governments across the country, victory in these municipal contests was a startling political opening.

The factors explaining the PAN's strong showing in these elections were similar to those at work in Baja California: Chihuahua and Juárez were wealthier, more urban, and less enmeshed in PRI corporatist networks than cities in other parts of the country. Like Tijuana, Ciudad Juárez also had burgeoning maquiladora industries. Support for the opposition came from a wide array of urban social classes and economic sectors, many of them tied to the new industrial economy. The PAN victory in 1983 also owed much to a reaction from the entrepreneurial classes in those two cities, who were angered by the antibusiness economic reforms, such as bank nationalizations, of the outgoing López Portillo administration, and by the debt-crisis-induced recession of 1982 (Chand 2001; Mizrahi 1995). The opposition in Chihuahua benefited from newly inaugurated President de la Madrid's "new policy regarding municipal elections: henceforth, municipal-level victories by opposition party candidates would be recognized, wherever they occurred" (Cornelius 1986, 124). As we shall see, the PRI's willingness to respect election outcomes once again proved to be the crucial element in the state's democratization.

The 1983 contests were midterm elections only, limited to mayoralties and to the powerless state legislature. But the strong showing by the PAN raised the possibility of further opposition gains in the 1985 election for the federal Chamber of Deputies and the 1986 gubernatorial election. The PAN administrations in Chihuahua City and in Juárez proved to be popular and effective, giving the PAN reason to expect further electoral successes. Yet such successes did not materialize. The PRI captured 54 percent of the vote in the 1985 congressional elections, and in 1986 it claimed not only the governorship, but also a majority in the state legislature and sixty-five of sixty-seven municipal elections (including the important cities of Juárez and Chihuahua).

Election fraud, and not voter displeasure with the PAN, was responsible for the PAN's setbacks in 1986. Chand writes, "the elections themselves were characterized by almost every conceivable kind of irregularity from ballot box stuffing to expulsion of opposition representatives from polling stations to intimidation by soldiers, among others" (Chand 2001, 37). Circumstantial evidence of fraud is most striking in the rural parts of the state, where it was harder for the opposition to monitor the polls. The number of voters on registration lists increased dramatically between 1983 and 1986, and in some rural areas turnout approached 100 percent, with more than 80 percent of the votes going to the PRI.[21] Wayne Cornelius places these elections in the context of a national pattern, in which less progressive elements in the PRI quickly closed down de la Madrid's political opening. In the aftermath of the relatively fair elections in July of 1983 (and writing in 1986), Cornelius notes that

> the government has not recognized a single important electoral victory by any opposition party. Traditional, heavy-handed electoral manipulations were used to deny victory to the opposition (mainly PAN candidates) in cities like Puebla and Mexicali in 1983 and several cities in the states of Coahuila and Mexico in 1984. (124–25)

So harsh was this reversal that the most significant opposition victory of the next several years was Ernesto Ruffo's 1986 mayoral win in Ensenada (Baja California).

As Ruffo was capitalizing on his newfound celebrity by winning the Baja California governorship in 1989, Chihuahua was on a different trajectory. The 1986 election was widely denounced as fraudulent, and the PAN opted for a strategy of postelection protest and civil disobedience. Several prominent PAN leaders went on a hunger strike, and one of them, Luis Alvarez, then led a protest march to the city of Querétaro. Protesters also blocked the bridges linking Ciudad Juárez to El Paso, Texas, "for days at a time," thus ensuring international press coverage of the protest movement (Chand 2001, 39). These events sparked a nationwide social movement that included sympathy protests in other states and expressions of solidarity from clergy, nonpartisan business and community groups, and even from left-wing political parties. The protests raised the costs of election fraud in subsequent years. As mentioned, some scholars attribute the PRI's conciliatory stance in the 1989 Baja California elections to the 1986 protests in Chihuahua. They did not alter the official election outcome, however, and the PRI's candidate, Fernando Baeza, served his full constitutional term.

The PRI's willingness to resort to fraud was not the only factor explaining the PAN's poor performance after 1983. The entrepreneurial class that had provided so much energy in the PAN election campaigns became by 1986 discouraged by the party's lack of success, and many felt a need to return to their businesses (Mizrahi 1994, 144–45). Others were persuaded to return to the PRI. A conspicuous example of a businessman who turned away from the PAN and reengaged with the PRI was Jaime Bermúdez, an entrepreneur and industrialist with a strong hand in the formation of the maquiladora industries in Ciudad Juárez. In 1983, he financed Francisco Barrio's PAN campaign for the mayoralty of that city. Yet in 1986 he was persuaded to run for that office himself, as a candidate for the PRI (Chand 2001, 113–14).

The PAN never consolidated the social and political mobilization that had accompanied its success in 1983. The business class itself was not fully integrated into the PAN, and though it made important financial and organizational contributions to campaigns, it was not otherwise active in the party. The same can be said of several important civic associations that the PAN administrations in the cities of Chihuahua and Juárez had promoted. These organizations had been successful in mobilizing electoral support in 1983 and 1986, but were tied more to the entrepreneurial class than to the party per se, and when the entrepreneurs demobilized after 1986, "many of these civic organizations ... disintegrated" (Mizrahi 1995, 88). Hence, as the PAN fell into disarray after 1986, the PRI solidified its support base and enhanced its profile for the 1989 election. The result was both surprising and difficult to reconcile with the view that a new democratic culture was emerging in Chihuahua. On July 2, 1989, the same day that the PAN captured the governorship in Baja California, the PRI in Chihuahua won all sixty-seven municipal elections and seventeen of eighteen state legislative districts.[22]

Yet in the immediate aftermath of the fraudulent 1986 elections and in the PRI's resounding midterm victories in 1989 lay the roots of democratization in Chihuahua. A shift in political strategies revealed itself in several ways. First, on taking the governor's office in 1986, Fernando Baeza adopted a conciliatory tone toward the PAN and the business class, with whom he met frequently. This deactivated the business class's fervent opposition to the PRI, though business leaders still supported the PAN in the 1992 governor's race. Their behavior signaled that, from the late 1980s on, it was an independent and pragmatic political force, ready to evaluate individual candidates and support the ones that seemed most promising for its interests (Mizrahi 1994, 143–45).

Democratization in Chihuahua after 1986 is also evident in several major changes in the electoral arena. In 1988 the Baeza administration adopted a new electoral code that increased the ability of all parties to monitor polling stations, witness the tabulation of votes, and pursue formal complaints about electoral misconduct or fraud (Chand 2001, 250–52). And, in fact, the 1989 election was indeed relatively free of fraud. We should not overstate the case, however. The PRI still enjoyed significant advantages, including access to government largesse and huge disparities in campaign spending (Mizrahi 1994, 138; Chand 2001, 42). Nevertheless, the increased transparency in elections after 1986 was an important step toward democracy, as would become evident in the 1992 elections. These institutional reforms were matched by internal changes within the PRI, which "decided to democratize the selection of its candidates for municipal and state legislative offices" (Chand 2001, 42).

If the evidence presented up to this point is merely suggestive, the 1992 election outcome is more revealing. In 1992, just one term (six years) after the fraudulent election of 1986, the PAN's candidate, Francisco Barrio, won the governorship. The PAN also captured a majority in the state legislature and won thirteen municipalities, including Ciudad Juárez and several other major cities. The PRI and PAN had jointly updated the voter registration lists, and the PAN was able to place monitors at almost every polling station, even in rural areas (Chand 2001, 43). Hence, as in 1989, the election was generally free of fraud. This was the PRI's most resounding defeat in a statewide election. It did not dispute the results or try to disrupt the transfer of power to the new PAN governor. This single election was enough for most scholars

Table 2.4   Mexico: Elections in Chihuahua, 1992 to 2004

| Year | Type of Election | Party | | | | Total |
		PAN	PRI	PRD	Others	
1992	Governor	**51.2%**	44.3%	1.4%	3.1%	100.0% (756,292)
1994	President	28.3	**60.4**	6.2	5.1	100.0 (1,089,006)
1994	Federal deputies	27.5	**58.0**	5.7	8.8	100.0 (1,114,877)
1995	State deputies	40.1	**47.5**	6.2	6.2	100.0 (822,919)
1997	Federal deputies	41.2	**42.1**	10.3	6.3	100.0 (889,826)
1998	State deputies	41.9	**47.4**	7.3	3.5	100.0 (979,954)
1998	Governor	42.2	**50.3**	5.5	2.0	100.0 (988,199)
2000	Federal deputies	**47.1**	41.2	7.4	4.3	100.0 (1,119,844)
2000	President	**48.7**	40.9	6.8	3.6	100.0 (1,128,099)
2001	State deputies	41.4	**46.0**	5.1	7.5	100.0 (867,647)
2003	Federal deputies	37.5	**47.4**	6.2	8.9	100.0 (757,095)
2004[a]	State deputies	44.0	**53.2**	—	2.8	100.0 (988,674)
2004[a]	Governor	41.4	**56.5**	—	2.1	100.0 (993,511)

Sources: Banamex (2001); *Instituto Estatal Electoral de Chihuahua,* data accessed at http://www.ieechihuahua.org.mx on April 1, 2005.
Notes: Winning party's vote proportion noted in boldface; total votes cast in parentheses.
[a]In 2004 state elections the six registered parties formed two coalitions, PAN-PRD-PC and PRI-PT-PVEM.

to conclude that Chihuahua was in the vanguard of democratic consolidation in Mexico.

Although we largely agree with this assessment, we disagree with the literature's exclusive focus on Barrio's win, which remains anomalous.[23] With the exception of the federal elections in 2000, the PAN never won another statewide election (see table 2.4). In the 1994 federal election the PRI won all of the state's federal congressional districts, and its presidential candidate (Ernesto Zedillo) won over 60 percent of the vote in Chihuahua. In 1995 the PRI regained the majority in the state legislature, and won every major municipality except Ciudad Juárez. In 1998 it won back the governorship. Although the PAN fared well in the 2000 election that brought Vicente Fox into the presidency, the PRI reasserted its dominance after that election, winning statewide races in 2001, 2003, and 2004. The electoral evidence on its own might therefore give the impression that the PAN could muster only an occasional win in what remained basically a PRI-dominant state.

But the political changes in Chihuahua before 2000 ran deeper than a single PAN term in the governor's office. Competitiveness also matters, and table 2.4 reveals a two-party tendency in most state elections. The PAN regularly garnered more than 40 percent of the vote, and parties have alternated in power in several municipalities and legislative districts. Elections in Chihuahua are a vibrant source of democratic legitimacy, even if the PRI is on an impressive winning streak.

The new political atmosphere in Chihuahua, which set in during the aftermath of the 1986 fraud, forced the PRI to change its tactics in ways that favored democratic consolidation. As in Baja California, the most important political change in Chihuahua was internal change within the PRI. In addition to its willingness to pass electoral reforms and clean up fraudulent voter registration rolls, the state party changed its own candidate selection mechanisms to adjust to the newly competitive electoral environment. In 1989 it democratized the nomination procedure for local contests. This change produced a cohort of candidates that had deeper local roots and higher public profiles than had been the norm in the past (Chand 2001, 246–47; Langston 2003). The new PRI cohort looked like PAN candidates. Many were from the business sector, and some had experience with business organizations such as the Mexican Employers' Confederation (Confederación Patronal de la República Mexicana, or COPARMEX).

The PRI failed to extend this reform to the gubernatorial nomination in 1992, but did in 1998. The consequences were significant. The dominant leader in the party after 1992 was Artemio Iglesias, a long-time party figure who was credited with unifying the party and improving its performance in elections. Under the old rules, Iglesias almost certainly would have received the party's nomination for governor, despite his lack of popularity outside the PRI. But Iglesias lost the party primary to Patricio Martínez, a more popular, charismatic, and pro-business politician who had been mayor of Chihuahua City. Martínez then won the general election, beating a PAN candidate who had not been selected though a primary election (see Langston 2003; Aziz Nassif 2000, 147–61). Thus the PRI's change in political strategy led directly to electoral success in 1998: rather than engaging in election fraud or questionable forms of voter mobilization, the PRI adjusted to the new democratic reality and became competitive in a free and open race.

We interpret Chihuahua's competitive elections and occasional opposition victories as indicating a high level of democracy in the state. Our assessment also takes into account changes in the strategies of political actors. The PRI's new approach to operating under conditions of electoral competition bodes well for the future of democracy in Chihuahua. After 1986, the PRI increasingly accepted the sanctity of election rules and the legitimacy of an active opposition. As we shall see, the PRI has occasionally responded to these kinds of conditions with fraud and even violence. But in Chihuahua, the response was to run better candidates. And the strategy worked.

Michoacán

Michoacán is a large state on the Pacific Ocean, due west of Mexico City. With approximately four million inhabitants the state is one of the largest in the Mexican federation, and it is relatively densely populated. It is also largely rural: 108 of its 113 municipalities have fewer than a hundred thousand residents, and the economy is dominated by agriculture. Michoacán is usually described as a traditional state, with high levels of religiosity and a hierarchical social structure.[24] Michoacán's politics are also distinct from states like Baja California and Chihuahua. Before 1988 the PRI thoroughly dominated politics in Michoacán, as it did in the country as a whole. But while signs of change became evident in 1983 in the northern states, there was no such political opening in Michoacán. The PRI dominated elections, winning about 99 percent of municipal contests and 100 percent of the plurality seats in the state legislature in 1980, 1983, and 1986. (The introduction of proportional representation in 1977 allowed the opposition to win a few seats in the state legislature.) The PRI won the gubernatorial election in 1980 with 93 percent of the vote and in 1986 with 85 percent. Politics also had a more traditional feel. In Michoacán, clientelism and caciquismo are common forms of political mobilization. This means that voters are closely linked to parties through personal ties to a local strongman, and are therefore more likely to provide stable (and less self-conscious) support for a given party over time.[25] Politics also tends to be more violent than in many other parts of the country.

The first time Michoacán witnessed a truly competitive multiparty election was in the 1988 presidential contest, when Cuauhtémoc Cárdenas, the state's former governor, ran for president under an opposition party banner. The ruling party's apparent manipulation of the election sparked further competition, the creation of a new political party with strong roots in Michoacán, and (eventually) an opposition victory in the 2001 gubernatorial election. In this strictly electoral sense, then, it might appear as though Michoacán has gone through the same process of political opening as did Baja California and Chihuahua, albeit a few years later. But the timing, causes, and defining characteristics of the shift to multiparty competition in Michoacán are starkly different from those in Baja California and Chihuahua, and the details paint a less positive picture of democracy in Michoacán.

The roots of Michoacán's political opening lie not within the state but in Mexico City, where in 1986 Governor Cárdenas, then a leader in the PRI, began meeting with like-minded reformers about strategies for initiating changes in the PRI and influencing its policy positions. The group would eventually form a faction within the party known as the Democratic Current (Corriente Democrática, CD). The CD pressed for a return to the PRI's populist and nationalist roots and criticized the neoliberal economic policies of the de la Madrid administration. It also proposed "internal democracy," or major changes in the way the party selected its leadership and candidates. The CD proposed ending the tradition of the dedazo (finger-pointing), by which the outgoing president personally selected the PRI's next presidential candidate and, therefore, the next president (see Bruhn 1996; Garrido 1993; Sánchez 1999, 43–53).

The CD had many sympathizers within the PRI. Yet the ideological and personal antagonisms between the CD faction and the PRI's national leadership quickly escalated, leading to a split in the party. The rupture was also fueled by personal ambition. Cárdenas aspired to be president, but it was clear that he would not secure the nomination from the party's ruling faction, which was dominated by neoliberal technocrats. In October 1987, a week after the PRI announced that Carlos Salinas would be its presidential candidate, Cárdenas announced his own candidacy by accepting the nomination of a small opposition party, the Partido Auténtico de la Revolución Mexicana (PARM). Cárdenas went on to form an electoral front that united several leftist parties in a coalition for the 1988 election. In 1989 most of these parties joined to form the PRD, which has been Mexico's major leftist party ever since (see Garrido 1993; Bruhn 1996).

Cárdenas was not the only senior member of the PRI involved with the CD; nor was he the only one to leave the party as a result of the rupture between the CD and the PRI. But among the members of the CD, he was the one who had the broadest political network and the strongest base of popular support (Bruhn 1996, 76). His network and base were strongest in Michoacán, where he had been governor and where his family had deep political roots. Cuauhtémoc Cárdenas is the son of Lázaro Cárdenas, the revered former president of Mexico (1934 to 1940). The elder Cárdenas, also from Michoacán, was a populist who instituted many early social reforms. Cuauhtémoc Cárdenas's unique position made him the most likely candidate to emerge from the CD movement, and also made it likely that Michoacán would provide his strongest base of support if he did run. Events bore out this proposition: although Cárdenas officially lost the election by a wide margin, his strongest result came in Michoacán, where he won 61 percent of the vote (compared to 24 percent for Salinas). No other opposition candidate could have deprived the PRI of so many votes in Michoacán, especially had Cárdenas remained in the ruling party. Thus the original political opening in the state resulted from an elite-level event, not from a locally inspired grass roots mobilization effort.

The elite nature of the political opening in Michoacán does not make it less real. We know that democratization in many countries is born of exactly the sort of division among elites that occurred in Mexico from 1986 to 1988 (see O'Donnell and Schmitter 1986). But in this case, the political opening led neither to a democratic pact in Michoacán nor to a stalemate among political forces that would have made full-scale democratization an attractive option. Rather, Cárdenas's split from the PRI precipitated a period of political conflict that was routinely rancorous, often fraudulent, and occasionally violent.

Michoacán held midterm state elections in 1989, just a year after the tumultuous presidential election.[26] By this time Cárdenas and his allies had formed the PRD, which ran candidates for the state congress and all 113 municipalities. If we look only at the election results, we see signs of healthy competition. The PRD won six state congressional districts (out of eighteen) and almost half of the municipal contests, including the capital city, Morelia. The PRI won most of the remaining offices, giving the sense that Michoacán had undergone a quick transformation to a two-party system.

But the 1989 elections were marred by fraud and violence. The split between Cárdenas and the PRI created personal antagonisms; the PRI was also more vulnerable to the PRD because the two parties had overlapping social bases of support. Kathleen Bruhn and Keith Yanner note that there was "an unusually deep antagonism" between the PRI and the PRD (1995, 120), and other observers note the personal hatred that many PRI members felt toward Cárdenas for having left the PRI. These animosities had an immediate impact on the state legislative election: "In exchange for Cárdenas's 'embarrassment' of Salinas by defecting from the PRI . . . Salinas punished Cárdenas and the PRD in the [July] 1989 Michoacán legislative elections, widely viewed as among the most fraudulent state elections ever" (Eisenstadt 2004, 206). The PRD cried foul, and their supporters blocked roads and occupied government buildings in several municipalities in protest.

With municipal elections just a few months away, Eisenstadt (2004) reports, the PRD attempted to compromise with the state leadership of the PRI, with some success. The PRI recognized PRD victories in fifty-two municipalities in December of 1989. But this concession did not prevent violent protests in other places. PRD supporters occupied municipal offices in thirty-three municipalities, citing PRI election fraud as their motivation. Violence erupted in several of these municipalities. Eisenstadt (2004, 206–7) estimates that nineteen people were killed, and many more injured, in at least nine municipalities. The dead included protesters, municipal police officers, and several PRD mayoral candidates. The state PRI, under pressure from Salinas, did not concede much ground to the PRD. The standoff continued until April 1990, when Salinas sent in several thousand troops, with tanks, to arrest the protesters.[27] Violent protests arose again in 1992, when the PRD disputed the official victory of the PRI's gubernatorial candidate, Eduardo Villaseñor, as well as the results in about twenty municipalities (Eisenstadt 2004, 208). PRD supporters protested at Villaseñor's inauguration, and physically blocked the entrances to the governor's palace to prevent him from going to work. Villaseñor resigned less than a month after his inauguration, and was replaced by another PRI politician. Similar cycles of allegations of election fraud, protest, and violence continued through the 1990s.

Violent protests erupted in Michoacán at exactly the time that the PRI was recognizing opposition victories in Baja California (1989) and Chihuahua (1992). The PRD's strategy of postelection protest followed the lead of the PAN in Chihuahua. But whereas the strategy had eventually yielded success in Chihuahua, it led to bloodshed in Michoacán. Eisenstadt attributes the difference to the PRI's hostility toward the PRD, and in particular to Salinas's hostility toward Cárdenas (2004, 109). But the particularly conflictual relationship between the two parties in Michoacán might also have resulted from the challenge that the PRD posed to the PRI's traditional bases of support in the state (the poor, peasants, and laborers). In either case, the PRI was clearly unwilling to abide by the results of elections in Michoacán, subjugating democratic institutions to its own desire to remain in power.

The PRD had undemocratic tendencies as well. Of course, democratic reform was one of the foundational ideological components of the CD, and the leftist groups that joined the PRD in 1989 could rightly claim to have been persecuted and excluded from the political process in Mexico for many decades. The PRD never advocated antisystem, antidemocratic, or violent political behavior.[28] But many PRD activists were skeptical about the possibility of an electoral route to power, and others were clearly interested in democracy only for instrumental reasons (Bruhn 1996, 169–71). Bruhn notes,

> The ex-CD leaders [from the PRD, such as Cárdenas] were even more vulnerable to accusations that their commitment to democracy lacked

conviction. Critics repeatedly questioned why—if they truly valued democracy—they had not done more to promote it while they had positions of power in the PRI. (171)

Recall that Cárdenas himself had won the governorship of Michoacán
in 1980 with 93 percent of the vote. His administration was not responsible for any serious democratic reforms in the state, which his successor won in 1986 with 85 percent of the vote.

The PRD's style of mobilization closely resembled that of the PRI—
not surprisingly, given that former PRI figures dominated the PRD.
Personal ties and local loyalties drove the policy and personnel decisions of the early PRD. Cárdenas was accused of bending the party to
his will, and other politicians relied on local networks of support they
had established long before the PRD was created (Bruhn 1996, 190–4;
Sánchez 1999; Semo 2003). The PRD also had a tendency to replicate
patronage networks common in the PRI: Bruhn reports that many in
the PRD advocated replacing PRI appointees with PRD supporters in
local administrative positions, and some "expected special treatment,
like' preferences in contracts, because of their party affiliation" (1996,
239). Bruhn is careful to point out that pro-patronage activists did not
always get their way, and it would be hard to show empirically that
the PRD was more prone to patronage than were other political parties.
Yet clearly the PRD adopted many of the PRI's mobilization tactics.
Therefore the shift to two-party competition in Michoacán was not accompanied by a shift in the way parties mobilized support or distributed favors.

The shift to two-party (and occasionally three-party) electoral contestation in Michoacán was a thin form of democratization. At least in the
more formal, electoral sense, it marked a shift toward a more democratic politics, punctuated by party alternation in 2001, when the PRD
finally succeeded in winning the governorship. But the key political
actors in Michoacán routinely demonstrated a lack of respect for democratic rules and a propensity toward violence. Part of the problem was
institutional. Michoacán lacked viable election courts and had no other
institutions with independent oversight of election processes. The
courts that did rule on election disputes were part of the state's PRI
administration, and were biased against the PRD (Eisenstadt 2004). Because PRD leaders (and other political forces) saw little chance that a
disputed election would be adjudicated fairly, protest strategies were
attractive. But the lack of respect for democratic procedures and norms
was also personal and ideological. The animosity between the two parties fed the conflict. We should not underestimate the power of personalistic politics in the state even today. Although the change of party in
the governor's office in 2001 certainly signified a democratic advance

in Michoacán, it is notable that the winning candidate was Lázaro Cárdenas Batel, son of the former governor and grandson of the former president.

Puebla

The state of Puebla is one of the most traditional areas of Mexico. Its capital city (also called Puebla), located between Mexico City and the port city of Veracruz, has been a center for industry and commerce since colonial times. Countless colonial churches dot the landscape, reflecting the area's conservative Catholic legacy. The city was the site of many battles, including the Battle of Puebla on May 5, 1862 (which is commemorated in the Cinco de Mayo holiday). Today, the city is at the center of a sprawling metropolitan area with a diverse economy and a major industrial sector. Rural areas and small towns dominate the remainder of the state. About 30 percent of the state's population lives in and around the city of Puebla. Most of the remainder live in rural areas. More than 200 of the state's 217 municipalities have fewer than fifty thousand residents, and these comprise more than 50 percent of the state's population.

The state of Puebla is a reliable PRI stronghold. The party has never lost the governorship, and remains dominant in most other contests. Until the 1990s, elections in Puebla were distinctly uncompetitive. Macías Palma (1998) describes a typical example, the nomination in 1968 of Rafael Moreno Valle for the state governorship. Several senior figures in the PRI were known to be seeking the nomination, yet public discussion was practically nonexistent. Party leaders, affiliated labor unions, and other popular sector groups may have had their preferred candidates. But public endorsements before the nomination, which might put the endorser in the awkward position of having publicly backed the wrong candidate, were rare. Once the party announced Moreno Valle as its nominee, these same political groups quickly purchased ad space in Puebla's newspaper of record, El Sol de Puebla, expressing approval of the party's choice and vowing unity in support of Moreno Valle. The election itself was little more than a formality: with the main opposition parties (the PAN and the PPS, Partido Popular Socialista) failing to field candidates for the governorship, Moreno Valle won with an overwhelming percentage of the vote. The PRI also won all sixteen seats in the state legislature and 216 of 217 mayorships; the sole loss (to the PAN) was "surely pre-arranged (concerta-concesionado) 'to make the election democratic'" (Macías Palma 1998, 12).

This sort of election profile did not distinguish Puebla in the 1960s and 1970s from any other state in Mexico. But by the 1980s and 1990s, when several states witnessed dramatic transformations in the way elections were carried out, politics in Puebla changed little. One scholar summarizes the state of competition thus:

> In the recent history of the state there has not been competition for the governor's office. The candidate of the official party has always won with a large majority of votes. Senate elections have always been the same. In contrast elections for federal deputies are competitive in the metropolitan area of the state capital and some [other] important districts. (Valdiviezo Sandoval 1998, 9, our translation)

Some municipal elections were more competitive, though before 1995 opposition parties won local races in only two large municipalities and a handful of smaller ones. After 1995 opposition parties had more successes, including mayoral victories in the city of Puebla in 1995 and 2001. But the PRI remains the dominant party, controlling the governorship, the state congress, and most other elected posts.

A weak opposition is part of the explanation for the lack of contestation in Puebla's elections before the mid-1990s. Unlike Baja California and Chihuahua, opposition movements in Puebla had little mass support. Opposition parties were weak and poorly organized, and struggled to maintain a statewide presence. In the 1983 state elections in Puebla, four opposition parties managed to field candidates in all twenty-two state legislative districts. But none could field candidates in all 217 municipalities. The best represented opposition party was the PAN, which ran candidates in just forty of 217 municipalities; the PRI candidate ran entirely unopposed in more than 60 percent of the municipal contests (García García 1998, 83–84).

But even where the opposition was able to organize, the PRI successfully repressed or limited electoral competition. In the run-up to the 1983 election, for instance, the PAN had hopes of winning several municipalities, including the capital city. The election was held just months after the PAN municipal victories in Chihuahua. In Puebla, however, the PRI had little trouble making sure that the vote went in its favor. Preemptively, it charged that the PAN and some affiliated civic groups were preparing to violently disrupt the election, and the governor ordered military and police units to "guard" many of the city's polling stations. During the election, the PRI resorted to a familiar combination of mobilization, intimidation, and fraud (García García 1998). The PAN charged election fraud immediately after the vote, producing evidence of stuffed ballot boxes, burned voting sheets, and intimidated voters. But the state election commission (Comisión Electoral Estatal, CEE), whose members were mostly from the PRI and appointed by the governor, certified the official vote, and opposition appeals to the federal government received no response (García García 1998). The difference in 1983 between Puebla City and Chihuahua City was not that voters defected from the PRI in Chihuahua and stuck with it in Puebla. Voters defected in both elections, but the PRI refused to allow the victory in Puebla.[29]

The trajectory of this story, from mobilization by the opposition, to suspicious electoral activity, charges of fraud, and postelection conflict, is in some ways like the stories of Chihuahua and Baja California. The main difference is that, in Puebla, the opposition response was weak, and the PRI's control of the election process was strong. Even if a substantial proportion of the public supported the opposition, this support could not overcome the obstacles put in place by the state PRI. The combination of a poorly organized opposition and the effective containment of electoral competition produced a lethargic, quiescent electoral arena. Abstention increased steadily in the 1970s and 1980s, peaking in 1989 at 65 percent (Valdiviezo Sandoval 1998, 136–37). This mass apathy was especially notable given the national context: the 1989 Puebla election came just one year after the contentious presidential race between Salinas and Cárdenas, and at the same time as the hotly contested election in Michoacán and other states. Whereas voters in other parts of the country were increasingly mobilized in support of opposition parties, in Puebla they were simply staying away from the polls.

Opposition parties made some headway in the 1995 elections, when the PAN won the mayor's office in the city of Puebla and a few other large municipalities. Competition in the capital city since then has been fierce, and the mayoralty has switched parties between the PAN and the PRI in every election since 1995. Opposition parties compete effectively in many other municipalities as well. But in comparison to the three previous cases, there is relatively little contestation in the state of Puebla even today. Until 2000 the PRI did not lose a single federal congressional district. It retained the governorship in lopsided contests. In the closest gubernatorial election to date, the PRI's Mario Marín Torres won in 2004 with a 14-point margin. And despite increased competition in some municipalities, most remain dominated by the PRI.

The PRI organization in Puebla has avoided the internal reforms that its counterparts have undertaken in many other states. Other than a one-time experiment in 1998 with a party primary, candidates are still chosen via elite negotiations (Cady 2005). The party now pays more attention to its candidates' local popularity, but the selection process is far from transparent. Similarly, elements of the state PRI are unprepared to accept opposition victories. The party certainly has been forced to be more discreet, and it does not always have the power to reject election results it finds displeasing. But even in the late 1990s, the

PRI took advantage of the close relationship between the governor's office and the CEE to deny the opposition victories and to legitimate its own victories when opposition parties claim fraud.

The most famous instance of this is the 1995 municipal election in Huejotzingo (population forty-five thousand). The CEE responded to a PRI petition by selectively disqualifying votes in several ballot boxes, tipping the result from a close PAN victory to the closest of victories for the PRI. That the PRI would resort to such tactics in a relatively unimportant local contest "confirmed the PANistas worst fears about rigged electoral institutions, demonstrated the lengths that local PRI operatives would go to in order to ensure their dominion, and offered the PAN a taste of the PRI-state intolerance usually reserved for the PRD" (Eisenstadt 2004, 190–1). The PRI's motives in Huejotzingo remain obscure, given that it was willing to accept defeat in many other municipal contests. It eventually backed down, consenting in 1996 to the installation of a PAN municipal administration, after the PAN made a national issue out of the case. But the incident (and others like it) demonstrated that the PRI had not fully accepted the new rules of the game in Puebla. Accusations of fraud and formal petitioning of the CEE remain common in Puebla. After municipal elections in 2001, *El Sol de Puebla* reported postelection disputes in thirty-five municipalities (November 17, 2001, p. 1).

The PRI has not foresworn its traditional methods of clientelist mobilization and voter intimidation. Political conflict in Puebla is generally free of the violence seen in Michoacán and some other states in the south. But the calm should be attributed to the low level of contestation in the state, rather than to submission of the main political forces to a democratic framework. Candidate selection procedures remain opaque. The governor dominates the selection process, and aspirants to PRI candidacies work hard to maintain close personal ties with him. Caciques, or local bosses, remain influential in nomination procedures. And it remains common practice for the PRI to threaten voters by claiming that if their neighborhood or town does not vote for the PRI, the government will withhold public services or halt public works projects. During political campaigns parties often charge each other with vote buying or clientelistic gift giving.

These practices are not unique to the PRI. One month before a 2001 election in Huauchinango (population eighty-two thousand), a regional center in the northern part of the state, the PRI accused the PAN's candidate, Carlos Ignacio López, of offering voters microcredits in exchange for their votes.[30] When questioned, Ignacio López admitted that he had made such an offer, but insisted that it was a campaign promise, not an attempt to buy votes. He went on to win the election on November 11 and took office in January 2002.

But his claim that the microcredits comprised a campaign promise was shown to be false when, on November 21, approximately a thousand protesters took control of his campaign headquarters. They had originally come to the city center because, they claimed, Ignacio López had promised to pay them on November 20. When he did not, they overran his headquarters. "We voted for the PAN and they haven't given us the money and the television is already reporting that the money has been made available [by the federal government]," said one of the protesters. If indeed Ignacio López had made such a promise to pay in November, it would be difficult to justify as a campaign promise. The money was to come not from the municipal coffers, but from the federal agency he was working for at the time—the Ministry of Social Development (Secretaría de Desarrollo Social, SEDESOL), which commonly uses microcredits as a poverty relief and development strategy. Even assuming that he would win the election, which he did, he would not have been able to offer microcredits as a municipal policy until he took office in early 2002.[31] Naming the campaign promise as one of "a number of anomalies," the PRI protested Ignacio's election, but the Election Commission rejected the case, and Ignacio López served his full term as municipal president.

This style of politics is not unique to Puebla, and similar stories surely could be told even in the most democratic regions of the country. But the events in Huauchinango indicate a pattern that is more ingrained in Puebla than in Baja California and Chihuahua. Electoral competition came late to Puebla, and still has not penetrated many of its rural areas. Even where elections are competitive and relatively fair, personalism and clientelism are still more common than in more democratic regions. Overt fraud and violence are rare, but vote buying, intimidation, and clientelist inducements are still common. And though leaders of opposing parties have made efforts at reconciliation and compromise in the past few years, interparty relations in the 1980s and 1990s remained conflictual and distrustful. The evidence strongly suggests that democracy is less developed in Puebla than in Baja California, Chihuahua, or Michoacán.

Conclusions

Of the four states we have analyzed, democracy is most advanced in Baja California, where there is by now a long history of multiparty competition. The PRI has fully accepted the new electoral reality and adjusted its strategies to this new reality. The same is true of Chihuahua, except that the PRI remains dominant, especially in the smaller municipalities. The opposition has not fully integrated itself into Chihuahuan civil society, and its social bases remain weak outside of Ciudad Juárez and a few other cities.

Democracy is less advanced in Michoacán and Puebla. Michoacán exhibits a good deal of multiparty competition, and a PRD member currently holds the governor's office. But neither of the two main parties is committed to complying with a democratic electoral framework, and the recent history of their interactions is marred by fraud, clientelism, and violence. Hence the democratic rules of the game maintain only the weakest hold on the major political actors in that state. In Puebla, political competition is less conflict ridden, but most of the state remains a quiescent PRI stronghold. Both the PAN and the PRD have tallied significant victories in a handful of municipal contests, and the capital city has had several party alternations. But in most of the state, elections are uncompetitive, and the style of political mobilization has changed little since the days of national PRI hegemony.

Chapter 3

Regional Variation in the Quality of Democracy in Argentina

TO UNCOVER cross-regional differences in the quality of democracy in Argentina, we draw on provincial and local studies, as well as on our own research. We begin by exploring differences among provinces in patronage and fiscal behavior. We then examine the differences among a subset of regions on a broader set of dimensions: the level of support for political parties and the volatility of this support; the tendency of voters to split their ticket and vote simultaneously for different parties in different races; voters' media exposure and political sophistication; and their willingness to openly discuss their political choices. As in Mexico, we find a consistent set of differences across regions, a pattern that makes us confident in our ranking of these regions according to the quality of democracy in each. These rankings permit us to later analyze the effect of the quality of democracy on regional political cultures.[1]

Statistical comparisons and closer looks at the political dynamics across regions and cities suggest unevenness in the quality of democracy in Argentina. Some provinces are good at maintaining balanced budgets; others are profligate spenders. Some provinces strive to implement good public policy; in others, the governor depicts public assistance as personal charity. Experts deem the Argentine federal budget and the process by which it is written to be far more opaque than in other Latin American countries; yet a handful of mayors have tried to bring community organizations and individuals into the budget process, at least at the local level. In some cities, powerful political and economic actors impose their will on the citizenry; in others, the political leadership has experimented with relatively novel forms of governing, such as the referendum, to give residents a voice in critical collective decisions. These comparisons allow us to posit the following ranking of the regions in which we collected survey data: the highest quality democracy is the district of Mar del Plata, followed in order by the provinces of Buenos Aires, Córdoba, and Misiones.[2]

Cross-Regional Differences in Argentine Politics and Development

Argentina's twenty-three provinces present sharp differences in levels of development, the fiscal behavior of government, tendencies toward patronage and clientelism, and many other respects. On development, some provinces are relatively prosperous, industrialized, politically mobilized, and fiscally sound; others are poor, agricultural, clientelistic, and deeply in debt. The United Nations Development Program (UNDP) has analyzed cross-provincial differences in economic competitiveness and human development and identifies five groups of provinces (2002). The provinces of Buenos Aires, Córdoba, and Santa Fe concentrate "the bulk of national exports, investment in manufacturing sectors, banking, and financial dynamism," and Mendoza "has significant dimensions of investment" (23–24, our translation).[3] Chubut, Neuquén, Santa Cruz and Tierra del Fuego have economies based on nonrenewable resources and relatively small populations. Entre Ríos, La Pampa, Río Negro, Salta, and Tucumán are regions of "intermediate development." Misiones, San Juan, and Jujuy have low levels of human development, according to the UNDP, but also some sectors of economic dynamism. Finally, the regions that are the least competitive and have the lowest levels of human development are Chaco, Corrientes, Formosa, La Rioja, and Santiago del Estero. They lack industrial investment, make a miniscule contribution to national production, and rely on informal sector labor; and their people are relatively poor, ill-educated, and short-lived (see table 3.1 and figure 3.1).[4]

Argentina's provinces differ in their fiscal and economic policies as well as in their levels of development. The UNDP focuses on the provinces' governing capacities, by which it means the capacity to sustain provincial fiscal equilibrium. Some provinces are good at this, others are not. Fiscal conditions range from "healthy fiscal policies in the past and present" in San Luis and the City of Buenos Aires to "a complex fiscal situation and disorderly current fiscal policies" in Mendoza, Salta, Río Negro, and Catamarca (UNDP 2002, 41). The connection between fiscal performance and competitiveness or human development—if there is one—is not explained by the UNDP; nor does it delve deeper into cross-regional differences in political performance.

The Fiscal Behavior of Provincial Governments

Several studies that go more deeply into cross-regional differences emphasize institutional causes of the uneven quality of governance across Argentina. Specifically, they contend that malapportionment of seats in the national legislature, in which small provinces are greatly over-

Table 3.1   Argentina: Provinces by Economic Competitiveness and
Human Development

Provinces	Economic Competitiveness	Human Development
City of Buenos Aires	Urban service economy	High
Buenos Aires, Córdoba, Mendoza, Santa Fe	Large diversified economic structure	Intermediate
Chubut, Neuquén, Santa Cruz, Tierra del Fuego	Productive structure based on intensive use of nonrenewable resources	Intermediate
Entre Ríos, La Pampa, Río Negro, Salta, Tucumán	Intermediate development based on agriculture	Low and intermediate
Jujuy, Misiones, San Juan	Intermediate development with severe rigidities	Low
Corrientes, Chaco, Formosa, La Rioja, Santiago del Estero	Backward productive and business environment	Low

Source: UNDP (2002).
Note: The provinces of San Luis and Catamarca were not classified by UNDP.

represented, explains variation in levels of patronage spending by provincial governments. Provinces with small populations use their disproportionate congressional representation to extract large central government transfers. These provinces therefore rely little on internal sources of revenue, are harder to wean from patronage, and resist fiscal adjustments by the central government.

In their analysis of cross-regional differences in fiscal performance, Remmer and Wibbels (2000) distinguish between the "low-density provinces"—Chubut, La Pampa, Neuquén, Río Negro, Santa Cruz, and Tierra del Fuego—and "the four largest and most developed provinces"—Buenos Aires, Córdoba, Mendoza, and Santa Fe (435). The former provinces' over-representation in the national legislature gives it the leverage to demand heavy transfers from the central government. Remmer and Wibbels note that the low-density provinces were net recipients of transfers from the others, receiving $1,158 of federal transfers per capita in 1995, versus the $277 per capita the industrialized provinces received. These relatively large transfers to the low-density provinces offer "extensive patronage opportunities created by bloated public sectors," which provide "politicians and their clienteles with motives for resisting national pressures for economic reform" (435–36). Remmer and Wibbels operationalize patronage as a province's expenditures on public-sector wages as a proportion of revenues. They find

Figure 3.1   Argentina: Provinces by Gross Provincial Product and Population

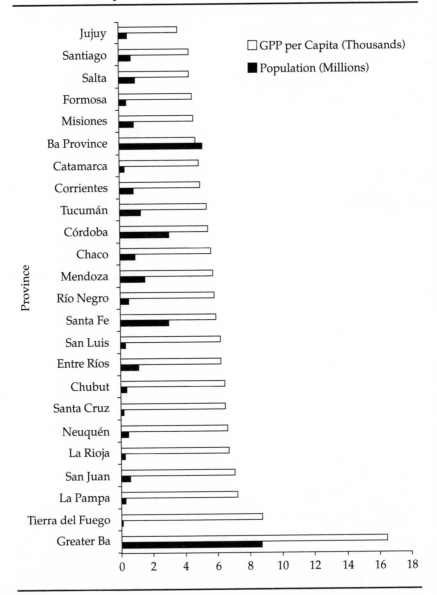

Source: INDEC (2001).
Note: GPP measured in thousands of Argentine pesos per capita; population is from the 2001 census.

that the more a province depends on revenues it raises itself (as opposed to federal transfers), the less it spends on wages (patronage), and that the more competitive a province's elections, the less the provincial government spends on patronage. Heavy spending on patronage, in turn, predicts fiscal indiscipline. Hence their analysis predicts that net-transfer recipients (the low-density provinces listed earlier) will be rife with patronage and will resist the central government's efforts at fiscal adjustment, and that industrialized provinces (and Greater Buenos Aires) will have less patronage and will be more willing to adjust.

In a similar vein, Gibson and Calvo (2000) distinguish between metropolitan and peripheral regions—more specifically, metropolitan and peripheral constituencies of the Peronist Party—to explain how Carlos Menem's administration managed to impose painful economic reforms. Peronist constituencies are "labor-based, economically strategic, and mobilizational in the metropolis, clientelistic, poor, and conservative in the periphery" (34).

Large industrialized cities—Buenos Aires, Córdoba, Rosario, Mendoza—and the provinces that surround them are very different, in Gibson and Calvo's view, than the periphery. This includes impoverished and distant (from Buenos Aires) provinces such as Misiones and Corrientes in the northeast, Catamarca, Santiago del Estero, La Rioja, and Formosa in the north, and sparsely populated southern Patagonian provinces such as Santa Cruz and Chubut. Not only are the peripheral provinces "clientelistic, conservative, and poor," Gibson and Calvo note, they are also over-represented in the national legislature. Their over-representation and their quietism made them strategic for Menem. His administrations granted them targeted benefits in return for their support for the central government's economic adjustment policies.[5]

Ernesto Calvo and María Victoria Murillo (2004) echo these themes. They are most interested in the effect of spending by Peronist Party versus Radical Party provincial governments on the vote share of the two parties in subsequent elections, and find that public employment by Peronists boosts Peronist vote share, but employment by Radicals does not boost the Radical vote share. But they too contend that legislative over-representation of small provinces, which (they claim) tend to be Peronist strongholds, increases the supply of public goods available for redistribution to (Peronist, small-province) constituents. These constituents are more responsive to targeted public resources, in turn, because they are poorer than their Radical counterparts.

To explain one dimension of cross-regional variation in the quality of democracy, then, all these studies describe a causal chain that goes from small provincial population size and over-representation in the national legislature to large transfers from the central government to patronage and fiscal indiscipline. Another research tradition, however,

Table 3.2   Argentina: Provincial Public Employees per Thousand Residents, 1987 to 2000

	Coefficient	Robust Standard Error	t-statistic	p-value
GPP per cap, 000s	0.003	0.007	0.49	0.623
Population (log)	−31.79	5.23	−6.08	0.000
Malapportionment index	2.408	3.953	0.61	0.543
Constant	477.428	67.442	7.08	0.000

Sources: INDEC (2001); authors' compilations.
Notes:
Pooled Time-Series, Fixed-Effects Model, 23 Provinces, 227 Annual Observations
GPP per cap is gross provincial product per capita, in thousands of 1993 pesos.
Population (log) is the natural log of each province's population, interpolated from 1991 and 2001 censuses.
Malapportionment index scores higher the greater the province's overrepresentation in parliament. We are grateful to David Samuels for providing this information.
$F(3,201) = 23.19$
Prob $> F = 0.0000$

links particularistic, targeted spending to voter poverty rather than to legislative over-representation (see, for example, Dixit and Londregan 1996). We therefore would like to further explore the effect of poverty, malapportionment, and population size on levels of provincial public employment.

Multivariate analysis shows that, controlling for each province's logged population, parliamentary over-representation has no effect on the number of employees per capita that a province employed. We analyze provincial data collected by Stokes, Valeria Brusco, and Marcelo Nazareno, which include annual data for the twenty-three provinces spanning the period from 1987 to 2000. The estimation is reported in table 3.2, a fixed-effects GLS model using cross-sectional time-series data. The only factor influencing the size of the provincial public sector per capita was the province's population: the fewer the residents of a province, the larger the number of employees per capita. The explanation may be that provincial governments must employ some minimum threshold number of workers, so that provinces with small populations will automatically have relatively large public sectors. Our findings cast doubt on the standard account by which over-representation leads to fiscal indiscipline.

Just as the fiscal performance of provincial governments varies across regions, so does the budgetary performance of municipal governments. Table 3.3 draws on a database with expenditures on personnel by municipalities in six provinces: Buenos Aires, Córdoba, Misiones, La Pampa, Santa Fe, and Chubut.[6] Most municipalities are

Table 3.3   Argentina: Spending on Personnel as Proportion of Municipal Budgets, 1995 and 1999

	Coefficient	Robust Standard Error	t-statistic	p-value
Buenos Aires	−11.095	1.705	−6.51	0.000
Córdoba	−13.606	1.650	−8.25	0.000
Chubut	−17.208	2.387	−7.21	0.000
La Pampa	−12.071	2.124	−5.68	0.000
Santa Fe	−13.949	1.485	−9.39	0.000
1995	1.555	0.652	2.39	0.017
Peronist	−0.235	1.141	−0.21	0.837
Radical	−0.420	1.149	−0.37	0.715
Margin of victory (lag)	−0.021	0.017	−1.22	0.221
Casa B	−0.057	0.034	−1.70	0.089
Poverty NBI	−0.421	1.149	−0.37	0.715
Total expenditures	−0.0003	0.0004	−0.71	0.477
Population (log)	1.531	0.266	5.769	0.000
Constant	45.081	3.558	12.67	0.000

Sources: INDEC (2001); authors' compilations.
Notes:
1,414 observations.
Buenos Aires, Córdoba, Chubut, La Pampa, and Santa Fe are dummy variables indicating the location of each municipality (data were taken from Misiones as well; this is the base category).
1995 is a dummy for observations for that year (as opposed to 1999).
Peronist is a dummy for municipalities in which the incumbent mayor was a Peronist, Radical for ones in which the incumbent was a Radical.
Margin of victory is the difference in the vote share between the winner and second-place challenger in the previous municipal elections.
Casa B is the proportion of the city or town's population that lived in substandard housing, from the 1991 census.
NBI is the proportion of the population with "unsatisfied basic needs," a measure of poverty.
Total expenditures were expenditures per capita by the municipality.
Population is the natural log of the population of the municipality, according to the 2001 census.

observed twice, in 1995 and in 1999, both election years. The database also contains information that we use as control variables, again measured at the municipal level, such as whether the mayor was a Peronist or a Radical, the margin of victory of the mayor in the previous election, and municipal poverty rates.[7] The total number of observations is 1,414. In table 3.3 we report an OLS regression model of the proportion of the budget spent on personnel.[8] In contrast to our findings at the provincial level, in this sample of municipalities, the higher the poverty rate, if anything, the less was spent on personnel. Also in contrast is that the more populous a municipality, the more it spent on personnel.

Because the model includes dummy variables for each province except Misiones (the base province), we can interpret the coefficients on the province dummies as estimates of each province's expenditures on personnel, in comparison to personnel expenditures in the municipalities of Misiones. All of these coefficients are negative and significant, telling us that expenditures on personnel were significantly higher in municipalities located in the province of Misiones than in those of the five remaining provinces. For instance, all else equal, a Misiones municipality would spend nearly 14 percent more of its budget on personnel than a similar municipality in Córdoba would. To the extent that heavy spending on personnel indicates patronage by city administrations, and to the extent that patronage indicates lower-quality democratic governance, we see here confirmation that democracy on the Argentine periphery is lower quality than in the industrialized heartland.

Cross-Regional Variation in Local Politics

Whether or not small provinces are swamps of patronage, and whether or not congressional malapportionment is at the root of fiscal indiscipline, one might wish to understand variations in the quality of democracy in Argentina from a broader vantage point. The intuition of most observers would be that cross-regional differences in the quality of democracy go beyond matters of the financial behavior of provincial and municipal governments. Observers might also want to consider differences in voting behavior and party strategies, levels of political information and sophistication of the provincial electorates, and the openness of political discussion. Their intuition might well be, furthermore, that the province is not the only relevant unit for making cross-place comparisons; cities and towns have their own institutions, traditions, and quality of democratic life. What's more, cross-provincial variation may manifest itself in variation in the quality of political life at the local level. Perhaps, for instance, the cities and towns of the metropolitan provinces are more responsive to citizen concerns, and those of peripheral provinces rely on clientelism and local patronage.

Partisan orientation is one dimension of cross-municipal and cross-provincial variation worth exploring. There are more than twenty-one hundred municipalities in Argentina. Because Peronists are widely considered the party most prone to patronage and vote-buying (see Auyero 2000; Brusco and colleagues 2004; Calvo and Murillo 2004; and Levitsky 2003), spatial variation in Peronist support is relevant to assessing cross-regional variation in the quality of democracy. Brusco and colleagues (2004), for example, use survey data to show that, even

Table 3.4   Argentina: Peronist and Radical Mayors, 1991 and 1995, by Region

	Peronist Mayors		Radical Mayors	
	1991	1995	1991	1995
Buenos Aires	62% (78)	67% (91)	33% (41)	27% (37)
Córdoba	27% (65)	43% (139)	67% (161)	50% (162)
Santa Fe	60% (180)	53% (173)	40% (119)	47% (156)
Average metropolitan	48% (323)	51% (403)	48% (321)	45% (355)
La Pampa	62% (49)	56% (44)	29% (23)	28% (22)
Misiones	55% (41)	62% (37)	45% (34)	38% (23)
Chubut	38% (10)	38% (10)	38% (10)	38% (10)
Catamarca		50% (17)		50% (17)
Average peripheral	56% (100)	54% (108)	37% (67)	36% (72)

Source: Authors' compilations.
Note: Numbers in parentheses are absolute numbers of mayors from given party in given province.

among low-income voters, those who reported sympathizing with the Peronist Party were more likely than those sympathizing with other parties to have received minor particularistic rewards, such as bags of food or clothing, during an election campaign. Among those sampled who said that a party had distributed such goods in their neighborhood, nearly ten times as many said that the Peronists had done so.

Table 3.4 reports party strength across Argentina's provinces, this time focusing on the local level. It tells us how many local elections produced Peronist rather than Radical mayors in more than eleven hundred municipalities in 1991 and 1995, in seven provinces, three in the industrial heartland (Buenos Aires, Córdoba, and Santa Fe) and four on the periphery (La Pampa, Misiones, Chubut, and Catamarca).[9] The table shows the fallacy of assuming that the bastions of strength of the Peronist Party—the most clientelistic and patronage-prone in the country—lie outside the industrial heartland. In 1995, two-thirds of the mayors elected in Buenos Aires province were Peronists, a higher percentage than in any of the other provinces considered. La Pampa and Misiones also had high percentages of Peronist mayors.

Yet we are interested not only in which party won local elections, but also in regional differences in the volatility of the vote. Volatility sheds light on styles of political mobilization by parties and on the voting calculi of citizens. When voters are relatively free of clientelist ties to parties, we expect their vote to shift more freely from one party to another, from one election to the next.[10] And we shall see that though Peronists occupied more mayors' offices in the province of Buenos

Table 3.5   Absolute Change in Peronist Vote Share, in 1995 to 1991 Elections

	Coefficient	Robust Standard Error	t-statistic	p-value
Buenos Aires	5.980	1.800	3.321	0.001
Córdoba	5.301	1.619	3.274	0.001
La Pampa	3.753	1.804	2.080	0.038
PJ	1.990	0.946	2.103	0.036
Lagged PJ vote	−0.147	0.035	−4.219	0.000
Casa B	0.092	0.028	3.254	0.001
NBI	0.051	0.011	4.696	0.000
Constant	5.979	2.446	2.445	0.015

Sources: INDEC (2001); authors' compilations.
Notes:
Buenos Aires, Córdoba, and La Pampa are province dummies indicating municipalities located in the corresponding province.
PJ is a dummy for municipalities in which the incumbent mayor at the time of the 1995 election was a Peronist.
Lagged PJ vote is the Peronist vote share in the 1991 election.
Casa B is the percentage of low-quality dwellings in the municipality, as measured in the 1991 census.
NBI is the percentage of residents living under the poverty line.
$F(7, 455) = 9.21$
Probability > F = 0.0000
R-squared = 0.1241

Aires, the Peronist vote share was also more volatile in the cities of Buenos Aires province and in Córdoba, the other province of the industrial heartland for which we have data. It was least volatile in the peripheral province of Misiones.

Table 3.5 is a model of volatility of the Peronist vote in local elections in 1995 across the provinces of Buenos Aires, Córdoba, La Pampa, and Misiones. The dependent variable in this OLS estimation is the absolute change in the Peronist vote share in 1995 with regard to 1991. The model includes dummy variables for municipalities in three of the four provinces, with Misiones as the base category; hence the coefficients on the other province dummies indicate the volatility of the vote in that province in comparison to Misiones. Indeed, this volatility was significantly greater in Buenos Aires, Córdoba, and La Pampa than in Misiones, as indicated by the positive and statistically significant coefficients on dummy variables corresponding to the first three provinces. The province effects hold up in the presence of controls for poverty (Casa B and NBI), the percentage of the Peronist vote in the earlier election (Lagged PJ), and the presence of a Peronist incumbent mayor (PJ). The same was true of the change in the Peronist vote share from 1995 to 1999 elections (not shown). This greater volatility suggests that

Figure 3.2   Argentina: Political Behaviors by Region

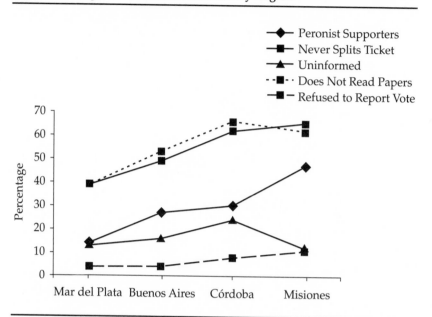

Source: Authors' compilations.

voters in the heartland, though just as Peronist as voters in the periphery, are less hemmed in by clientelist relations with the Peronists.

Notice also that the smaller the Peronist vote share in 1991, the more volatile the party's vote share in 1995 with regard to 1991. The variable Lagged PJ is the share of the vote going to the Peronist Party (PJ) in the 1991 election. The negative and significant coefficient relating this variable to change in the Peronist vote tells us that less strongly Peronist municipalities were also ones where people shifted more freely toward and away from the Peronists. The same was true in 1999 with regard to 1995 (not shown). If one is willing to accept the assumption that stability of the vote indicates clientelism, then this result indicates greater clientelism in Peronist enclaves.

Varying levels of democracy also appear in the contrasting political behavior and modes of participation of voters across Argentina's provinces. Figure 3.2 draws from our surveys (which we discuss later) in the district of Mar del Plata, in the rest of Buenos Aires province, and in the provinces of Córdoba and Misiones. (Figure 3.3 is a map indicating the location of these four regions.) It shows a monotonic increase in the proportion of survey respondents who supported the Peronist Party across the four regions. It also shows a monotonic increase in the

Figure 3.3   Map of Argentina

Source: Generated by the authors using ArcGIS 8.0.

percentages of people in the regions who said they never split their tickets and always voted for the same party, from a low of 39 percent in Mar del Plata to a high of 65 percent in Misiones. People who never split their ticket tend to be more enmeshed in clientelistic ties to a party and are less likely to use their votes to hold incumbents to account. The figure also shows the number in each region who described themselves as politically uninformed, a subjective measure of political sophistication. Here the trend as we move across the four regions is not monotonic. The number of uninformed citizens increases from Mar del Plata to the rest of Buenos Aires province to Córdoba, but then drops abruptly in Misiones. The numbers of respondents who report getting their political information from newspapers, another sign of political sophistication, declines sharply over the regions, with a drop of 23 percent between Mar del Plata and Misiones (though here again the decline is not strictly monotonic: a somewhat larger number of people in Misiones than in Córdoba reported reading the papers). Finally, the figure shows the percentage of people who refused to reveal their electoral choice in the 1999 presidential race. We follow Almond and Verba (1963, 115–18) in using this as an indicator of how safe people felt in talking about politics: they should feel more safe in more democratic regions, where parties are less intrusive and less likely to punish people for making the "wrong" choices. The numbers rise monotonically here too, and nearly three times as many respondents in Misiones as in Mar del Plata chose not to reveal their vote. These cross-regional differences strongly suggest differences in the quality of democracy.

The statistical comparisons we made earlier across provinces and municipalities suggest variation in patronage (as measured by levels of public employment) and clientelism (as measured by levels and stability of support for the Peronist Party). These comparisons lend support to the general notion that Argentina's new democracy functions better in the industrial heartland than in the poor periphery. Yet all of these measures are potentially ambiguous. Perhaps provinces offer public employment as a way of responding to job losses in the private economy. Presumably also some level of public employment is desirable and necessary: states have to provide goods and services and hence need to employ people. Perhaps the Peronist Party in Argentina enjoys high levels of support in some areas because it is responsive to popular needs and has performed well in office. Perhaps the greater stability of Peronist support in cities and towns of the periphery reflects freely chosen citizen support for the party rather than entanglement in Peronist clientelist networks. Given these ambiguities, we delve deeper into regional variations in democracy.

Qualitative Assessments of Cross-Regional Variation

To get a better feel for the varying texture of democracy across Argentina's regions, we turn to a rich qualitative literature. The case study literature assessing politics in Argentina's towns, cities, and provinces gives us a feel for patronage, clientelism, and graft, as well as for more encouraging developments in Argentine democracy.

Reports of problematic democratic practices by no means emerge only from the periphery. Indeed, leading recent studies of political clientelism in Argentina have drawn principally on field research in Greater Buenos Aires, by far the most industrialized and densely populated area of the country (Auyero 2000; Levitsky 2003; Szwarcberg 2001). Still, the most lurid accounts of clientelism, patronage, and personalism emerge from the periphery.

One province that has produced a rich case study literature is Misiones. Misiones is a semitropical province that takes its name from the eighteenth-century Jesuit missions that dot its landscape. It lies in the northeast corner of the country, on a spit of land jutting into Brazil and Paraguay. About one million people live in Misiones, a quarter of them in the capital city, Posadas. The Iguazú Falls, which lie on the border with Brazil, attract tourism; but tourist flights go directly to Iguazú, so the impact elsewhere in the province is minimal. Posadas is a tidy, sleepy city, where awnings and trees protect pedestrians from the midday heat. There are other small cities, such as Eldorado and Oberá, each with populations of about fifty-five thousand; but much of the province's population lives in small towns and hamlets. Agriculture is the principal economic activity, dominated by tea and mate plantations. Logging is also important. Some towns were founded in the nineteenth and early twentieth centuries by European immigrants, mainly Germans, Swiss, and Czechs. Others are populated by more recent Latin American immigrants, especially from Paraguay, many of whom live in fourth-world conditions. The post-democratic-transition history of Misiones is dominated by the Peronists, who have won all but one gubernatorial election since the transition to democracy in 1983.

Political anthropologists who have studied towns and cities in Misiones have found them to be less than civics book examples of local democracy. Yolanda Urquiza (2002) examined the dominance of a local magnate over the political life of one of Misiones's cities, which she does not identify. The magnate owned a major provincial trucking company, a chain of gas stations, and various local businesses. Because of the extent of his economic power there, Urquiza jokingly referred to him as el dueño del pueblo (the owner of the town). His wealth and that of his family members were palpable; his home and those of his children were powered by private generators and remained lit when the rest of the town suffered power outages. The dueño belonged to the Radical Party—the Unión Cívica Radical (UCR). With the dueño's support, a fellow Radical became the town's mayor in 1995. But the mayor became too independent; when he ran for reelection in 1999, the dueño supported another Radical candidate. Even though, Urquiza reports, the mayor was popular, the dueño's candidate beat him. Urquiza reports that townspeople feared losing their jobs and losing access to services that the dueño controlled if they voted against his candidate.

Another peripheral Argentine province is San Luis, which lies to the west of Buenos Aires and directly east of Mendoza, and has a population of four hundred thousand. Traditionally it is an agricultural province, but the provincial government in the 1980s and 1990s used tax incentives to attract industry. San Luis has also engaged in major public employment projects. Because of its industrial growth and relatively low unemployment, the UNDP lists San Luis as making gains in economic competitiveness and human development. Since the return to democracy in 1983, the province has been governed by the Rodríguez Saá family, preeminent local Peronists. Adolfo Rodríguez Saá—known locally as el Adolfo—was governor from 1983 until 2002, when he stepped down to serve the briefest of terms as president of the Argentine Republic. His brother, Alberto Rodríguez Saá (known, inevitably if less affectionately, as el Alberto), was elected to replace Adolfo as governor in 2002. But Adolfo remained the beloved leader, his presidential inauguration portrait hanging on the walls of Peronist mayors and grassroots activists.

San Luis is known in Argentina for the personalism of its politics, a personalism that rotates around the Rodríguez Saás. María Trocello (2003) describes the relation between the governor and constituents as involving "multiple symbolic actions" that gloss government beneficence as personal charity. The governor personally gives out "keys to [public] housing, school supplies, blankets for future babies, a decree authorizing a scholarship, etc." (16–17). The Rodríguez Saás ritualize their personal responsiveness to voters through a practice known as "the handing over of the letter" (la entrega de la carta). When the governor attends a public event, common people or neighborhood leaders approach him and personally hand him a letter. The letter contains a description of some personal or neighborhood problem and requests his help in solving it. Trocello interviewed a puntera, or grassroots Peronist operative, who described the practice:

> I've brought him letters that people in the barrio have written, sometimes they haven't even had enough [money] for an envelope, and I hand it to him, folded in half, so as not to see their intimate details. . . . I have carried the letters to Mr. Governor (Sr. Gobernador), and he has received them and answered them . . . right away he sends his card, recording that he received the letter, and after 15, 20 days he's solved the problem. Maybe he's sent financial support (un subsidio), building materials for the house, or perhaps he sends a receipt with details of everything that's been paid for, or it might be food. And so he solves some problems. (2003, 17, our translation)

The extreme personalism of politics in San Luis, where public assistance appears as personal gifts from the governor, seems designed to persuade citizens that their political leaders are personally caring and trustworthy.

Yet by no means does politics everywhere in Argentina revolve around such putative relations of personal trust. Especially in the first years of the new century, when the country suffered a devastating economic depression, in many regions a politics of confrontation became the norm. Among the most salient social figures since 2000 has been the piquetero (picketer), the unemployed man or woman who joins a street rally, blocks roads and highways, and, in one instance, helps bring about the fall of a national government (see Auyero 2003).[11]

In other places we see the emergence of a politics not of personal trust, nor of mobilized confrontation, but of institutionalized account-ability. A symptom of the rise of accountability is the experimentation by a few cities with participatory budgeting (presupuestos participativos), which was pioneered in 1989 in the Brazilian city of Porto Alegre and spread since then to dozens of other cities in Brazil, Chile, Mexico, Venezuela, and to a handful of cities in Argentina (see Abers 1998; Santos 1998). In participatory budgeting, organizations and individuals take part, through a series of pubic meetings and forums, in formulating local budgetary priorities and in monitoring municipal expenditures. Participatory budgeting has been announced or implemented in cities of the industrialized provinces: Rosario in the province of Santa Fe, and the Federal District of Buenos Aires and Mar del Plata in the province of Buenos Aires.

Participatory budgeting never really got off the ground, however, in Mar del Plata. As several of our interviews in that city made clear, municipal officials who tried to implement it found little public interest or willingness to attend the required meetings. The fate of participatory budgeting there is consistent with our findings in chapter 5, that people in Mar del Plata participated less in civic associations than their counterparts in less democratic regions.

We now explore in greater depth an episode in the politics of local finance in a district where democratic consolidation has progressed especially far. Municipal officials invited citizens to make a major decision about their taxes and the future course of municipal development through a referendum.[12] Their actions testify to an unusually healthy local democratic life.

Democracy and Accountability in Mar del Plata

Mar del Plata, a city of six hundred thousand, sits on the Atlantic coast in the southeast of the province of Buenos Aires. Outside of Greater Buenos Aires, Mar del Plata is the province's second-largest city after La Plata, and in the summer months its population swells to over one million. Mar del Plata began in the nineteenth century as a community of fishermen, and remains Argentina's leading exporter of haddock. Textiles and other manufacturing industries were established there in the middle decades of the twentieth century, but the leading industry today is tourism. Originally, wealthy porteños, as people from Buenos Aires are called, summered in Mar del Plata. Later the city developed infrastructure to attract a wider range of tourists. In the 1930s, Route 2—a two-lane road that winds gracefully along the coast—opened. In the 1940s, the federal government built a set of hulking casinos on the beachfront. Today Mar del Plata is a top destination for Argentine tourists, including many of the middle-class from Greater Buenos Aires. The city attracts more than six million visitors a year.

Although Mar del Plata's profile as a major tourist destination sets it apart from most Argentine cities, it has not escaped many of the social trends and problems that have plagued other cities since the end of military rule in 1983. With its large service sector and smaller industrial sector, it has attracted large influxes of migrants from rural parts of the province of Buenos Aires, as well as from other cities and towns. As of October 2001, 30 percent of Mar del Plata's residents lived below the poverty line, not much below the national average of 38 percent (Instituto Nacional de Estadística y Censos 2001). Industrial decline in textiles and commercial fishing left the city with an unemployment rate in 2002 of 20 percent, one of the highest in the nation.

Perhaps as distinctive as Mar del Plata's economic development into a tourist destination were its politics. The city had a strong socialist tradition through the middle decades of the twentieth century, electing mayors from the Social Democratic Party (Partido Socialista Democrático). During the military regime of the 1970s and early 1980s, a leading local socialist served as appointed mayor (intendente). This association with the dictatorship tarnished the party's image. Since the transition to democracy in 1983 the city's preeminent party has been the Radical Party. The Peronist Party has dominated local labor unions, but it has never won control over city government. Municipal elections returned the Radicals to power in 1983, 1987, 1995, 1999, and 2003. In 1991, residents elected a mayor and city-council (Consejo Deliberante) party list from the center-right Alianza Marplatense.

Mar del Plata is not unique in Argentina. But its relatively healthy local democratic life makes it distinctive, and the distinctiveness of the events in the mid- and late 1990s drew national attention to the city. Political actors in other cities and regions have introduced innovations and sometimes enlivened local democracy. But the innovations introduced in Mar del Plata came earlier and were more homegrown than those of these other cities. Nowhere else in Argentina has a municipal government used a referendum to raise taxes for particular projects (and this was the first referendum for any purpose ever held in Mar del Plata). In contrast to the democratic innovation of Mar del Plata, the more typical experience of local government in these difficult years was of incompetence, clientelism, and a lack of transparency in local finances.

The Popular Consultation as an Instrument of Democracy in Mar del Plata

In 1995, Mar del Plata residents chose as their mayor Elio Aprile, a professor of philosophy at the National University of Mar del Plata and member of the Radical Party. In early April 1996, a time of national economic downturn and uncertainty, Mayor Aprile announced that he would sponsor a referendum, or Popular Consultation.[13] Aprile had not offered concrete proposals for public works in the campaign that brought him to office. The campaign emphasized instead his personal honesty in contrast to the perceived graft of the outgoing Alianza Marplatense administration. The proposed referendum would allow residents to cast votes in favor of or against the mayor's proposal for a special tax to finance a program of improvements to the city's infrastructure. Aprile titled the program Mar del Plata 2000.[14] Households would pay three or four pesos per month, for eight years to finance twenty-five public works projects.[15] In the decree announcing the referendum, the mayor described in detail, down to the precise city blocks involved, the twenty-five public works programs to be financed by the special tax. They included widening and paving streets; installing lighting on streets and beaches; installing pavement, lighting, and drainage systems in an industrial park; planting trees and greenery; and installing sewers. The decree included the chronological order in which the projects would be carried out.

The referendum, scheduled for May 12, 1996, was unusual in several respects. The city had never held one, and Aprile's legal counsel found few precedents in the province of Buenos Aires.[16] As mayor, Aprile had the legal authority to carry out public works programs and to finance them with a special tax without public approval in a referendum if he so desired. His move to generate a mandate for Mar del Plata 2000 was politically, not legally, motivated. The referendum would allow him to carry out an aggressive program with broad public support—assuming, of course, that his proposal prevailed.

Aprile's design for the election itself showed that this was a departure from politics as usual in Argentina. Voting would be voluntary, not (as in other elections) compulsory. The usual registration rolls (padrones) were set aside and instead anyone who could show proper documentation would be allowed to vote. Foreigners who resided in the city (most of them immigrants from Paraguay or from Andean countries) who could produce identity cards and proof of residency would also be permitted to vote. In normal Argentine elections, men and women are sorted into separate voting tables (mesas); the referendum dispensed with sex-segregated voting.

The referendum was a bold move not just in motivation or design but also in what people in an economically volatile developing country were being asked to do: agree to pay a special tax (sobretasa), regularly, over a long period. Veterans of efforts to pass bond issues in advanced industrial countries will appreciate the difficulty of the challenge facing the Aprile administration and the boldness of the campaign. The municipality predicted that the special tax would bring in 65 million pesos in the first four years, those corresponding with Mayor Aprile's term. It would cost households up to 48 pesos per year, or more than 300 pesos over the full eight years of the program. For many families this was not an insignificant sum. In our survey, the average reported household income was between 300 and 500 pesos per month. Thus, over the course of the entire Mar del Plata 2000 program, the average family could expect to pay almost the equivalent of one month's household income.

Argentina in the mid-1990s was not a country where one would expect people to be especially trusting of public officials or especially happy to turn over extra resources to any governmental entity. They might well have been distrustful both of the competence of these officials and of their honesty. On competence, Argentines in the 1980s and early 1990s had observed national governments flit from one economic program to the next as the economy succumbed to hyperinflation and rioters filled the streets. On honesty, by 1996 the national government under Carlos Menem had already suffered from some embarrassing and highly publicized corruption scandals, involving, for example, kickbacks from privatization schemes. Provincial and local authorities in many parts of the country had also given Argentines reasons to be skeptical of the political leadership. We might well expect Argentines to have been leery of voluntarily placing more of their money—which, during the recession of the late 1990s, they had less of—into the hands of possibly incompetent and possibly corrupt public officials. In our survey, we asked whether the then current economic crisis (more acute in 2001 than in 1996) was due to politicians pursuing bad policies or to politicians being corrupt. Eighty-two percent believed that corruption caused the crisis. With the public perception of politicians as incompetent and corrupt, little wonder that Mar del Plata's mayor, trying to drum up support for his referendum, repeatedly spelled out—as reported in the *Diario el Atlantico* of April 16, 1996—his "fundamental premises: honesty and efficiency" (cited in Albo and colleagues 2000, 6).

We will offer evidence in chapter 4 that people in Mar del Plata are more prone than other Argentines to see political accountability and good government as matters of institutional design, rather than as depending on the personal qualities of office-holders. Yet the story of Mar del Plata 2000 shows that, even in that city, personal qualities of the mayor played a key role in the public's willingness to place additional resources at the city's disposal.

The administration's private polling a few weeks before the referendum indicated that it would fail. Aprile's associates, including a public-relations firm hired to promote the Yes campaign (as it came to be known) therefore decided that they had to personalize their appeal to the voters. As Mayor Aprile explained the referendum campaign during a February 25, 2004 interview:

> At first I refused to campaign personally. I said, "here, the only thing that we should do is give information, explain to people: these are the public works, these are the periods in which they'll be completed, these are the costs." And the people, with their intelligence, will perceive that this is good, or not. But as the campaign advanced, the polls showed that the "No" was winning. Only when I went out personally to speak to the people did it turn around. And with that I saw again, trust, no? [people said to themselves,] "I trust him" . . . . [Voting Yes in the referendum] was an act of confidence, it was to say, "I know that this man isn't going to steal the money, at least."

Describing the effect of a new television commercial, part of the effort to link Mar del Plata 2000 with Aprile's personal honesty, he remarked:

> We made an ad, a two-minute message [with me] speaking to the people. That was on the weekend. Monday we took a poll and already the 'Yes' was winning. . . . [In the ad] we said the same things we had been saying impersonally, and technically. Then I said it affably.

Aprile added wistfully, "Well, later they didn't believe in me so much, but, in any case, in that moment there was a gesture of personal trust." The personalizing of the campaign came out in a new Aprile slogan, reported in *Diario la Capital* on April 20, 1996: "lend me some pesos, and I'll give them back in works" (préstenme unos pesos, y los devuelvo en obras) (cited in Albo and colleagues 2000, 2). Again implicitly pointing to the mayor's personal trustworthiness as a reason to support the plan, the newspaper *Diario la Capital* reported on May 7, 1996, the union of municipal workers declaring, "Mar del Plata needs a reactivation in all dimensions . . . it's for all of these reasons that we have our *confidence deposited in the Mayor*" (cited in Albo and colleagues 2000, 7, emphasis added).[17]

It is hard to review the debate that the announcement of the referendum unleashed without feeling that democracy was alive and well in Mar del Plata—at least democracy in the sense of a system that encourages broad-ranging debates about community affairs.[18] The debate embraced a number of themes: whether Mar del Plata 2000 would achieve its stated goals of increasing productivity, improving the quality of life, and attracting tourism; whether the tax increase would depress the local economy; whether the distribution of the costs and the benefits was fair and sufficiently progressive; whether changing the location of some of the proposed public works would better promote community development; whether the process of choosing the particular projects included in the plan had been fair and democratic; whether the sequencing of the work would be fair to people in poor, outlying barrios; whether official estimates of the number of jobs the program would create were inflated;[19] whether a referendum was an appropriate way to make community decisions; whether the voting would be clean; what level of turnout would legitimize the results; and whether the city government, if it prevailed in the referendum, would make appropriate and transparent use of the funds that the special tax would generate.

There is much that is remarkable about this story of local democracy in Mar del Plata. Mayor Aprile's proposals were bold, as was his use of a novel form of a referendum, an instrument that has the political benefit of producing a mandate and the democratic benefit of allowing people a direct choice on crucial community matters. The debate that the proposals and the referendum set off was rich. Perhaps most remarkable of all is that the Yes vote prevailed. On Sunday, May 12, 1996, despite the recession, despite widespread suspicion about the probity of politicians, and despite serious challenges raised against Mar del Plata 2000, almost half of Mar del Plata's eligible voters turned out at the polls, 54 percent of them voted in favor of raising their own taxes.

The Grupo de Análisis Político of the National University of Mar del Plata has studied the distribution of Yes and No votes by electoral circuito (similar to a city precinct in the United States) and by neighborhood or barrio. Among the eight circuitos and the eighty barrios, they find little evidence that the income level of a circuito or barrio's residents, the stance that community leaders in a particular neighborhood took vis-à-vis the consultation, or the planned location of public works affected levels of support for the mayor's plan. Mayor Aprile and his allies seem to have persuaded a majority of those who were willing to vote to "deposit their confidence" in the local government, and that if they lent "a few pesos," these would indeed be returned "in public works."

Epilogue: The Fall of Mayor Aprile

The story of Mar del Plata in the late 1990s is one of political creativity, of a deepening of democratic practices, and of policy success. Yet the epilogue, as we move into the new century, is darker. There are at least two morals. First, policy successes are fragile in democracies rocked by huge economic volatility. Second, the personal trust that the public has in politicians matters, even in regions where democratic life is relatively vigorous. Yet the personality traits of politicians that matter are not always the ones on which the public is led to focus.

From the vantage point of 1999, when Mayor Aprile ran for reelection, Mar del Plata 2000 was a resounding success. Between mid-1996 and 2000, compliance with payment of the extra tax was at the same level as payment of other local taxes, around 60 percent. All of the twenty-five public works projects were completed, some ahead of schedule. Several additional projects had been completed, and several of the projects in the original plan, such as road construction and repair, had been expanded to cover more ground. Policy success led to political success for the Radical Party leadership, a success made clear by election returns. Aprile had won the mayoralty in 1995 with 38 percent of the vote. In 1996, when half of the city council seats were up for election, the Radical Party list received 54 percent of the vote, and in 1997, 52 percent. In 1999, Mayor Aprile "strolled to victory," as one of his associates put it, with 62 percent of the vote. Yet in 2001 the Radical vote share fell to a stinging 16 percent. The final denouement came in February 2002, when Aprile resigned.

The initial factor leading to the debacle was the city's worsening finances as the national recession deepened in 1999. Because of the recession, ever fewer people paid their property taxes, including the special tax. Local officials we interviewed estimated that tax compliance fell in the first years of the new century from more than 60 percent to between 30 and 40 percent. Total tax receipts fell from nearly 70 million pesos in 1996 to just under 48 million in 2000 (Folcher and colleagues 2002, 13). Another factor working against compliance with the special tax was the quick pace of the program. By late 1999, Mar del Plata 2000 projects were completed. The special tax was therefore not providing funding for ongoing Mar del Plata 2000 projects, but was being used instead to repay municipal debt that the city had incurred to pay for the projects—debt that it was able to secure, mainly from the Bank of the Province of Buenos Aires, on the promise of future tax receipts. Some of Aprile's close associates in interviews expressed the view that the fast pace at which Mar del Plata 2000 projects were completed became a political liability. That the building and improvements had already been completed while people still paid the extra tax broke the link in people's minds between the extra payments and the projects.

Even before the economic crisis deepened and tax receipts fell, the Aprile administration's enthusiasm for infrastructure projects was leading to less than sound financing. In an interview, Oscar Pagni, who was the president of the city council during the first Aprile administration, recalled that whenever the city received a competitive bid below the amount it had budgeted for a project, it rolled over the savings into additional projects or into an expansion of the one originally planned. At the end of the 1990s, the fund for Mar del Plata 2000 increasingly ran in the red and had to be periodically supplemented out of the general city budget. According to our interviews, never was there a misappropriation of Mar del Plata 2000 funds, just excessive enthusiasm and less than conservative budgeting.

Another factor leading to the debacle was Mayor Aprile's decision-making as he began his second term. The lesson Aprile drew from the political success of his first term was that he had to keep promoting public works. The predicament was how to finance them in tight fiscal circumstances. One option would have been to treat his 1999 reelection campaign as an opportunity to build a mandate for a second stage of Mar del Plata 2000. Aprile and his advisors preferred, however, to highlight past success, rather than discuss the future, in his "stroll to victory." Another option would have been to hold a second referendum, asking residents to extend the special tax beyond its initial eight years to fund a second stage of projects. But, according to Aprile's associates and members of his entorno (inner circle), he believed that a second referendum would fail, and therefore rejected the idea. A third option would have been to hold off on more building until the economy improved. But weighing against this option was Aprile's belief that his political success up to this point lay in his active city development program. And so he chose a fourth option, one that seemed to contradict everything that the first consulta popular (referendum) stood for. In early 2000, he proposed, and the city council approved, an indefinite extension of the special tax.

In our interview with the former mayor he spoke publicly about this period for the first time. Of the decision to extend the special tax, he said during our February 25, 2004, interview: "I believe it was a mistake. I believe another referendum should have been called. I should have had faith in myself in that." All of his former colleagues agree that the extension was a mistake. The Radical Party bloc of the city council voted unanimously in favor of the extension, although with misgivings; the one exception was council member Daniel Katz, who would succeed Aprile after the mayor resigned, and was elected in his own right in 2003. As council member Luis Rech put it, the referendum was a contract and the extension of the tax violated that contract. Of course, the referendum was (by provincial law) nonbinding. That is, there was no contract in a literal sense. But in a political sense the contract was very real, and Aprile was to suffer dire consequences from breaking it.

Contributing to the debacle were social disturbances nationwide, disturbances that took the form of piqueteros blocking roads and highways, middle-class housewives marching on the streets of Buenos Aires banging pots, widespread looting, and strikes and sit-ins in public and private institutions. In Mar del Plata the disturbances were less severe than elsewhere, a relative calm that local political actors attribute to the city's tradition of negotiation and deliberation. But in early 2002 the municipal workers' union, protesting the fact that their members were owed months of back pay, went on strike and occupied city hall. The political and psychological pressure on the city's leadership was intense; in many interviews leaders recalled arriving and leaving work through side passageways, attempting to avoid the angry crowds. Mayor Aprile, according to his political associates, became isolated, failing to appear at city hall or at local shops or restaurants, and instead shutting himself in his home.

The mayor's disappearance coincided with rumors that he had embezzled city funds. He and his former colleagues insist that it was a well-orchestrated smear campaign by political opponents. In our interview, Aprile bitterly recalled rumors that he had invested in hotels and lavish mansions in Italy. No evidence was ever produced of graft. But employees in a firm doing business with the city publicly accused officials of mishandling a city contract, and the timing contributed to a spreading public perception of official corruption. One can only speculate that the mayor's extension of the special tax eroded his reputation for honesty and created the conditions in which later accusations, even spurious ones, stuck. Crushed by the dual pressures of the municipal strike and what he describes as "attacks on his honor," in late February 2002 Aprile abruptly resigned.

The public mood in Argentina at the time, as nearly everyone we interviewed volunteered, was "que se vayan todos" (get rid of all the politicians). But Aprile's erstwhile colleagues insist that his resignation was unnecessary, that he took the accusations of corruption too personally, and that he lacked a certain toughness in putting up with striking workers. Public discontent with the mayor who violated the agreement on the special tax, and with a chaotic state of affairs in the country and in the city, was easily translated into the idiom of corruption. Mar del Plata residents were not wrong to care about the personal traits of their mayor, but ironically they worried about the wrong traits. Rather than doubting his personal honesty, as they were led to, they should have been concerned about his judgment and durability under pressure.[20]

In our interview, former Mayor Aprile reflected on the importance of a personal rapport or "affection" (afecto) between governors and the governed—a trust that helped his administration "turn the city around," in his words, during his first term. But the loss of this trust helped to bring him down early in his second term:

> I have always believed that at the root of politics is affect (lo afectivo). I'm convinced that if there is not a relation of affection between government and the governed, and in the personal relations on both sides, it's difficult to construct things. I believe that the referendum was achieved out of trust (la confianza), which is a kind of affection.

Conclusions

To summarize, statistical comparisons and qualitative case studies demonstrate that democracy works better in some regions of Argentina than in others. This variation comes out in the fiscal behavior of provincial governments and of municipalities, in the openness of the budgeting process, in the governing style of leaders and their inventiveness in experimenting with the institutions of local democracy. Drawing on these comparisons, we rank Mar del Plata as the highest quality democracy and Misiones as the lowest, with the provinces of Buenos Aires and Córdoba falling between.

One district that we studied in detail, Mar del Plata, stood out for the quality and inventiveness of local democracy. Yet, as we have just seen, local democracy was not immune from national crises or the shortcomings of local leaders. We will now present evidence that the people in this small region think about politics differently than those in other parts of Argentina. These differences, we will argue, amount to distinctive regional cultures of democracy.

PART III

TESTING HYPOTHESES ABOUT DEMOCRACY AND POLITICAL CULTURE

Chapter 4

Political Culture and the Quality of Democracy

E ARLIER WE found no compelling theoretical link between democracy and personal trust. We identified flaws in the propositions that if citizens trust each other, and if citizens personally trust politicians, democracy works better. If trust and democracy are related, the deepening of democracy should induce a shift from personal to institutional trust, from clientelism to accountability. The political culture of democracy, we argue, should be one of skepticism, not of trust.

Here we probe these propositions empirically by seeking answers to a number of questions. Do citizens in less democratic regions display personal trust in politicians, and do those in more democratic regions display institutional trust? Do voters expect their fellow citizens to hold parties accountable, and does the pervasiveness of this expectation also vary across regions with different levels of democracy? Are voters in more democratic regions especially likely to believe that their neighbors pay attention to the past performance of governments in making their voting decisions, or are they just as likely as their counterparts from less democratic regions to expect their neighbors to be bought off by private inducements? In more democratic regions, is the belief particularly widespread that one's neighbors pay attention to parties' programmatic appeals rather than individual inducements?

We also want to learn about how clientelism works in different regions. Does the degree of clientelism covary with the level of democracy? Do voters who are "clients" personally trust politicians more than nonclients? Are nonclients more attuned to accountability and institutional trust? If so, this would support our claim that democratic consolidation entails a shift away from personal trust, and toward institutional trust and accountability. Finally, are cross-regional differences in democracy associated with differences in people's postures toward the rule of law? If the quality of democracy is reflected in changes in political culture, one might expect a greater proceduralism—a belief that one ought to act in ways consistent with laws and with social norms—in regions where democracy has achieved a greater consolidation.

To answer these questions we turn to a set of surveys that we conducted in four regions of Argentina and in four states in Mexico. In Argentina, in late 2001 and early 2002, we instructed the polling firm Consultores en Políticas Públicas to conduct face-to-face interviews with 480 adults in the provinces of Buenos Aires, Córdoba, and Misiones, and with a separate sample of 480 adults from the district of General Pueyrredón, B.A., which contains the city of Mar del Plata. To select the sample, we used clustered random sampling. Buenos Aires is Argentina's most developed and industrialized province, and encompasses 135 municipalities, some of them in the area of Greater Buenos Aires. Córdoba is another relatively industrialized province to the northwest of Buenos Aires, but one with significant agricultural regions as well. Misiones is a poorer and more rural province in the northeast, bordering Brazil and Paraguay. By drawing a large random sample from the city of Mar del Plata and the surrounding district we are able to conduct a systematic analysis of public opinion in a city that, as explained in chapter 3, had introduced innovative democratic reforms.[1]

In Mexico, we instructed the polling firm Parametría to conduct face-to-face interviews with 400 adults in each of the four states of Baja California Norte, Chihuahua, Michoacán, and Puebla, using a clustered random-sample selection method with standard procedures for randomizing gender, age, and location.[2] As in Argentina, we drew representative samples of each state's adult population (but not a representative national sample), samples that allow us to make cross-state comparisons. And, as in Argentina, the surveys were timed to follow elections. Baja California and Chihuahua held state elections in July 2001; Michoacán and Puebla held them in November of the same year. In each state we conducted the surveys two weeks after the election.

Trust in Institutions and Trust in Politicians

We distinguished conceptually in chapter 1 between personal and institutional trust. To investigate political trust empirically, we designed a series of questions that forced respondents to choose between plausible reasons that politicians sometimes perform well. We asserted, for instance, that governments sometimes provide good public services (variable name, Services) and are efficient (Efficient), and that politicians sometimes pay attention to the opinions of constituents (Attention). The questions then asked people to choose between alternative explanations for this good performance. In each case, one option attributed good performance to the personal qualities of politicians ("they are committed people," "they care about constituents' opinions"), the other to mechanisms of accountability ("they're under the watch of the courts," "they'll lose the next election").[3]

Argentina

In our full Argentine sample, the accountability or institutional trust answer was the one most frequently chosen (see table 4.1). The institutional trust answer was, after all, also the answer most in line with a skeptical view of politicians. Recall that this was the era of the slogan "que se vayan todos" (they—the politicians—should all go). We should not be surprised that Argentines would assert that when municipal governments perform efficiently, they do so because local officeholders fear losing the next election, or that when these same officeholders pay attention to constituents, they do so because they want to curry favor with the next election in mind. (Table 4.2, below, shows that institutional trust responses dominated in Mexico as well, but less so than in Argentina.)

Argentines' perceptions of the motivations animating politicians, and of the institutional constraints politicians are under, map onto cross-regional differences in democracy. The number of people offering an institutional trust answer to the first three questions in table 4.1 is highest in our most democratic region and then trends downward. For example, 65 percent of our Mar del Plata sample attributed good services to institutional monitoring, versus only 40 percent of our Misiones sample.[4] In many cases, institutional trust declines monotonically as the quality of democracy declines.

But there are other differences among regions that might explain differences in political trust. Misiones is not only the least democratic region, but also the poorest, and poverty (or some other confounding factor) might explain lower levels of institutional trust in that province. To find out, we estimated multivariate models of responses to these questions (see table 4A.1 in the appendix at the end of this chapter).[5]

These estimations show that, if anything, people with higher incomes were more personally trusting of politicians and less trusting of institutions. In turn, younger people were more skeptical of politicians and more likely to ascribe good performance to institutional constraints. Women were more likely to ascribe good government to the characters of politicians, men to their fear of losing votes. Peronist supporters evinced personal rather than institutional trust. But regional differences persist. Respondents from the least democratic region (Misiones) tended more than others to believe that the personal qualities of politicians, rather than institutional constraints, explained good government

Table 4.1 Argentina: Responses to Questions About Political Trust by Region

	Mar del Plata	Buenos Aires	Córdoba	Misiones	Total
Services					
When governments provide good services to the people, is this because					
They are under the watch of the courts, congress, or the press	65% (311)	56% (268)	48% (232)	40% (192)	52% (1003)
They are good, committed people	30% (142)	40% (192)	40% (194)	53% (256)	41% (784)
No answer	6% (27)	4% (20)	11% (54)	7% (32)	7% (133)
Efficient					
When governments function efficiently, is this because					
They know if they don't, people won't vote for them in the next election	71% (340)	75% (362)	68% (326)	67% (321)	70% (1349)
The people governing are good, committed people	24% (116)	22% (106)	26% (125)	29% (140)	25% (487)
No answer	5% (24)	3% (12)	6% (29)	4% (19)	4% (84)
Attention					
When politicians really pay attention to people like you, is this because					
They want to be reelected	85% (410)	80% (386)	78% (375)	78% (375)	81% (1546)
They really care	11% (55)	17% (83)	16% (76)	18% (87)	16% (301)
No answer	3% (15)	2% (11)	6% (29)	4% (18)	4% (73)

Trustpol

Of the people who hold public office, how many are trustworthy without being watched?

All or a majority	2%	6%	10%	9%	7%
	(11)	(29)	(50)	(45)	(135)
A minority	59%	59%	47%	68%	58%
	(284)	(281)	(224)	(325)	(1114)
None	38%	35%	37%	20%	32%
	(183)	(166)	(177)	(96)	(622)
No answer	0.4%	1%	6%	3%	3%
	(2)	(4)	(29)	(14)	(49)

Bribe

When a politician takes a bribe, how likely is it that he'll get caught?

Very likely	24%	33%	22%	30%	27%
	(115)	(156)	(107)	(142)	(520)
Not likely	55%	47%	43%	41%	46%
	(262)	(227)	(205)	(195)	(889)
Impossible (nada probable)	20%	19%	33%	24%	24%
	(97)	(93)	(160)	(115)	(465)
No answer	1%	1%	2%	6%	2%
	(6)	(4)	(8)	(28)	(46)

Source: Authors' compilations.
Note: Total number of responses in parentheses.

Figure 4.1   Argentina: Simulated Expected Probabilities of Answer, Governments Provide Good Services When They Are Monitored, by Region

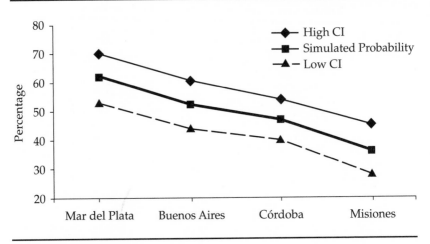

Source: Authors' compilations.
Note: Clarify simulations, see note 6. Figure reports 95 percent confidence intervals.

performance. Respondents from Misiones were the least likely to say that governments provide services when they are under the watch of the courts, the congress, and the press, and most likely to say that good public services come from good politicians. Our Misiones sample was significantly less likely than that from the rest of the province of Buenos Aires, and somewhat less likely than those from Mar del Plata and Córdoba to believe that efficient governments are ones that fear losing office. The Misiones sample was also significantly more likely than the Mar del Plata one to say that when politicians pay attention, they do so because they are good people, not simply because they want to be reelected.

For a sense of how much of a difference region makes in institutional trust, consider a typical respondent in our sample, one with a median household income, education level, and quality of housing, and who lived in a city of median size. Simulations in figure 4.1 show that if she lived in Mar del Plata, this typical respondent had a 62-percent chance of saying that governments provide good services "because they are monitored" rather than because "they are good people." But if she lived in Misiones the chance dropped to 36 percent.[6] This is roughly the difference in the bivariate analysis, suggesting that variation in responses is driven by region and not income, education, or partisanship.

We have seen that, in our high-quality regional democracy, one is likely to encounter the skeptical view that good government performance is the product of strong controlling institutions. In our low-quality democracy, one is likely to encounter the view that good performance is the product of trustworthy officeholders.

Not only do we find distinct cross-regional beliefs about the likely sources of good governance, we also find direct evidence that people in low-quality democratic regions believe that politicians actually are personally trustworthy. Argentines were skeptical about the inherent trustworthiness of politicians. We asked: "Thinking about people who hold public office, in general how many of them are trustworthy and will behave well even without being monitored?" (Trustpol, table 4.1). The modal answer was a pessimistic "a minority" (58 percent), followed by the outright skeptical "none" (32 percent); only a smattering thought that "all" (2 percent) or "a majority" (5 percent) were trustworthy. In short, Argentines in all four regions were more prone to trust institutions than, as a breed, politicians.

The exception was beliefs about what would happen to venal politicians. Argentines trusted institutions less to deal with corrupt officials than to induce efficiency and responsiveness. When asked, "When a politician accepts a bribe, how likely is it that he or she will be caught by the press or by the authorities?" (Bribe), only about one-quarter said it was "very likely."

One can think of the responses to the question "How many politicians can be trusted without being monitored?" as a measure of personal trust in politicians. We scored answers to this question as a four-point ordinal indicator (from "none" through "all"), with higher values indicating more personal trust in officeholders.

People from the least democratic region in Argentina were more personally trusting of politicians than were people from our other three regions (for multivariate analysis, see table 4A.1, model 4, in the appendix at the end of this chapter).[7] These differences held up even when we controlled for respondents' perceptions of official corruption (Bribe). We included Bribe as an independent variable to account for the possibility that, in more democratic regions, the press might cover corruption more aggressively and hence give residents there a sense that corruption was widespread. This perception might then feed a general distrust of politicians.[8] Even when we control for perceived levels of corruption, people from low-quality democratic regions displayed greater personal trust in politicians.

Simulations give an intuitive feel for regional differences in political trust. If a typical respondent lived in Misiones she had a 20-percent chance of responding that no politicians are trustworthy. But if she lived in Buenos Aires or Mar del Plata, she had a 30-percent chance, and if she lived in Córdoba she had a 32-percent chance.[9] Personal trust in politicians was most widespread in Misiones and significantly less prevalent in the other three regions.

The deeper the roots of democracy across our Argentine regions, the more likely its residents were to believe that venal politicians would be discovered and held to account—another form of institutional trust. Recall that we asked, "When a politician takes a bribe, how likely is it that he or she will be caught?" (Bribe, table 4.1). Multivariate analysis clarifies a relationship between Bribe and region that is difficult to see in table 4.1. It reveals a greater prevalence of trust in institutional safeguards against corruption in our more democratic regions. Trust in institutions to catch official venality is most prevalent in our pair of more democratic regions, less prevalent in our pair of less democratic regions, but the ordered ranking of region by levels of institutional trust is reversed in both pairs. We shall see that, in Mexico, democratic consolidation has quite a different effect on trust that institutions will catch venal politicians.

Our central finding thus far is that, when forced in the abstract to explain good government performance, residents of our more democratic regions disproportionately attributed it to institutional controls; they exhibited institutional trust. And when asked whether politicians actually are trustworthy, residents of our less democratic regions disproportionately believed that politicians can be trusted; they expressed personal trust in politicians.

Mexico

Mexicans in general tended to believe that institutional constraints were more effective than politicians' personal characters in forcing governments to be accountable. In all four states we surveyed, respondents chose the institutional answer to each question more frequently than the personalist answer (see table 4.2). As in Argentina, Mexicans were more likely to attribute good behavior to mechanisms of accountability, such as a desire for reelection or a fear of being exposed by the courts or press, than to the personal qualities of politicians. But those we sampled were decidedly less institutionally trusting than Argentines were. Fifty-two percent of Argentines, versus only 47 percent of Mexicans, believed that institutional mechanisms of accountability explained good government performance. Seventy percent of Argentines, versus only 52 percent of Mexicans, thought that municipal governments were efficient when they feared losing the next election and not when they were staffed by committed people. And 81 percent of Argentines, versus only 63 percent of Mexicans, believed that politicians pay attention to constituents because they want to be reelected, not because they really care about constituents' points of view.

The biggest differences were between our Mexican and Argentine samples' assessments of electoral mechanisms of accountability. Mexicans have good institutional reasons to have doubts about the existence of an "electoral connection." Term limits prevent all Mexican incumbents, in national, state, and local governments, from running for reelection. (Most Mexican politicians, however, run for more than one office during their career, and citizens still perceive politicians as reelection-minded; see Cleary 2004). Argentine politicians face far less severe term limits.[10] The greater severity of term limits in Mexico may explain the large gaps between our two samples on these questions.

Institutional trust, in Mexico as in Argentina, prevailed most strongly over trust in politicians in the more democratic states. In response to our question: "Why do some governments provide good services?" our Baja California sample was almost twice as likely to appeal to accountability mechanisms as it was to the personal qualities of those in government. Our Michoacán and Puebla samples were only slightly more likely to do so. In answering all three questions about responsiveness and efficiency, Baja Californian and Chihuahuan samples were more likely to express institutional trust than their counterparts from Michoacán and Puebla.

Multivariate analysis sustains these findings (see table 4A.2). Respondents in Baja California were significantly more likely than those in Chihuahua and Michoacán to attribute municipal government efficiency to reelection concerns. They were also slightly more likely to offer this answer than respondents from Puebla, but this difference was not statistically significant. They were significantly more likely than respondents from Michoacán to attribute the responsiveness of municipal officeholders to reelection pressures. The results do not fit our expectation of a neat ordering from Baja California, to Chihuahua, to Michoacán, and finally to Puebla, from most to least institutionally trusting. Still, in every case, our Baja California sample expressed the highest levels of institutional trust; in most cases, our Michoacán and Puebla samples expressed the lowest levels.

As in Argentina, we asked two additional questions to elicit Mexicans' views of accountability. In response to the question whether public officials who were not monitored could be trusted, we found striking differences between the Argentine and Mexican samples: four times as many Mexicans as Argentines believed one could trust the majority of politicians. The difference may reflect the timing of the Argentine surveys, which coincided with the 2001 economic crisis and hence with a spike in the public's skepticism about politicians.

In Mexico, we find clear cross-state differences in levels of personal trust in politicians. Contrary to arguments about the importance of personal trust in democracy, but in line with our own expectations, people

Table 4.2 Mexico: Responses to Questions About Political Trust, by State

	Baja California	Chihuahua	Michoacán	Puebla	Total
Services					
Some governments provide good services to the people, others do not. In your opinion, for those that provide good services, why do they do it?					
Because they are under the watch of the courts, congress, or the press	57% (227)	47% (189)	44% (174)	40% (158)	47% (748)
Because they are honorable people	30% (121)	40% (158)	30% (120)	40% (157)	35% (556)
No answer	13% (52)	13% (51)	27% (106)	21% (85)	18% (294)
Efficient					
When municipal governments function efficiently, is this because					
They know if they don't work hard the people won't vote for them	63% (253)	50% (200)	45% (180)	49% (197)	52% (830)
The people governing are committed people	28% (113)	39% (155)	30% (118)	28% (112)	31% (498)
No answer	9% (34)	11% (43)	26% (102)	23% (91)	17% (270)
Attention					
When politicians really pay attention to people like you, is this because					
They want to be reelected	73% (290)	71% (282)	49% (195)	62% (247)	63% (1014)

They really care	19% (76)	23% (92)	36% (144)	19% (76)	24% (388)
No answer	9% (34)	6% (24)	15% (61)	19% (77)	12% (196)

Trustpol

Of the people who hold public office, how many are trustworthy without being watched?

All or the majority	20% (80)	29% (116)	37% (149)	36% (143)	31% (488)
A minority	60% (238)	47% (189)	27% (108)	37% (148)	43% (683)
None	17% (68)	17% (66)	20% (81)	15% (60)	17% (275)
No answer	4% (14)	7% (27)	16% (62)	12% (49)	10% (152)

Bribe

When a politician takes a bribe, how likely is it that he'll get caught?

Very likely	20% (79)	19% (77)	26% (105)	25% (100)	23% (361)
Not likely	52% (206)	37% (149)	43% (171)	47% (189)	45% (715)
Impossible (nada probable)	23% (91)	38% (152)	18% (71)	22% (86)	25% (400)
No answer	6% (24)	5% (20)	13% (53)	6% (25)	8% (122)

Source: Authors' compilations.
Note: Total number of responses in parentheses.

Figure 4.2   Mexico: Personal Trust in Politicians, by State

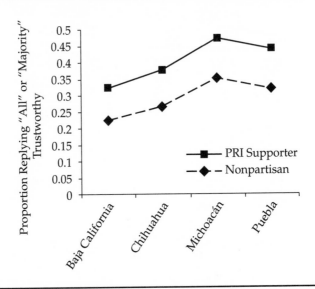

Source: Authors' compilations.
Note: Clarify simulations. All other independent variables are held at their sample medians.

in our Baja California and Chihuahua samples were less likely to believe that unmonitored politicians were trustworthy. Only 20 percent of those surveyed in Baja California thought that "all" or "a majority" of officeholders were personally trustworthy. Nearly twice as many respondents in Michoacán (37 percent) and Puebla (36 percent) thought so. In the presence of statistical controls, respondents in Michoacán and Puebla were significantly more personally trusting of politicians than were respondents in Baja California (see table 4A.2).[11] The ranking of states in ascending order of personal trust in politicians was Baja California, Chihuahua, Puebla, and Michoacán.

Figure 4.2 shows simulated predicted probabilities that a respondent would believe that all or a majority of politicians are trustworthy, depending on the state in which he or she lived. A hypothetical median citizen, a forty-year-old middle-class woman, was less likely to trust most politicians if she lived Baja California (22 percent) than if she lived in Michoacán or Puebla (36 percent and 33 percent, respectively). The figure also illustrates the effect of partisanship. Compared to our hypothetical citizen (whom we assume to be a nonpartisan), a PRI supporter was about 12 percent more likely to trust most politicians. Partisans of the three main parties were all more trusting of politicians than were nonpartisans.

Figure 4.3   Mexico: State-Level Democracy and Clean Elections

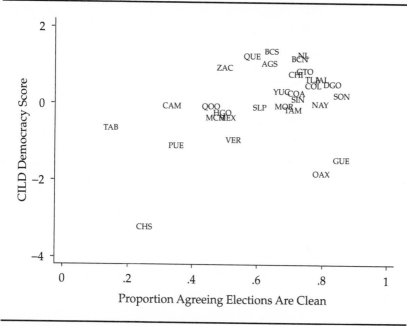

Sources: Hernández Valdez (2000); Lawson and colleagues (2002).
Notes: N = 31, correlation coefficient rho = .40.

Data from the Mexico 2000 Panel Study (Lawson and colleagues 2002) allow another test of the hypothesis that people in more democratic regions display more institutional trust. A consortium of scholars designed this panel survey and implemented it in four phases before and after the 2000 Mexican federal elections, collecting responses from a national sample of twenty-four hundred citizens. The researchers designed the survey to study political behavior, vote choice, and media effects. But they asked one question that sheds light on Mexicans' levels of institutional trust. In February of 2000 they asked how clean respondents expected the upcoming national elections to be.[12] Fifty-five percent of Mexicans believed the upcoming elections would be "totally" or "more or less" clean, and 36 percent that they would be "not very" or "not at all" clean.

Our hypothesis about institutional trust leads us to predict that people in Mexico's more democratic states have more confidence that elections are clean. And we find that trust in elections is indeed more widespread in states that are more democratic. For each state, we calculated the percentage of respondents who thought that the upcoming national election would be "totally" or "more or less" clean.[13] Figure 4.3 plots this percentage against Hernández Valdez's (2000) CILD score, the measure of state-level democracy introduced in chapter 2. Notwithstanding some outliers, such as Guerrero and Oaxaca, confidence in elections was moderately correlated with level of democracy (correlation coefficient = 0.40; p = 0.026). Citizens who live in states that are more democratic have more confidence in electoral institutions.

As in Argentina, we asked our Mexican respondents how likely it would be for a politician to be caught if he or she took a bribe (Bribe). Overall, they were skeptical of this possibility, their expectations resonating with the common perception that Mexican politics remains corrupt. Only about one-quarter of respondents in Mexico declared it "very likely" that a venal politician would be caught, a number comparable to the one we found in Argentina. But in contrast to Argentina, where the level of democracy was associated with more trust in institutional mechanisms to detect and punish corruption, the opposite was true in Mexico. People in Baja California and Chihuahua were more skeptical about the possibility of venal politicians being caught and hence displayed less institutional trust. This finding is clarified by multivariate analysis (see table 4A.2, model 5), which shows that institutional trust is most widespread in Michoacán, followed by Puebla, Baja California, and Chihuahua (but not all differences are statistically significant). The simulated probability that a typical Chihuahuan believes that bribe takers will not be caught is 47 percent. But if the same respondent lives in Michoacán the probability drops to 26 percent, and if she lives in Puebla it drops to 30 percent.[14]

We can only speculate about why Mexicans in the most democratic regions distrust institutional mechanisms to catch venal politicians, whereas Argentines in the most democratic regions trust them. Contrasting regional expectations may reflect real difference in levels of corruption across regions in each country. It is also possible that they reflect differences in perceptions about how widespread corruption is across the Mexican states, perceptions that in turn reflect how often the regional press exposes corruption. Ironically, respondents in Michoacán and Puebla may believe that corrupt officials would be caught because they read little about corruption in the press and infer that anticorruption institutions work efficiently. We lack data on levels of corruption and media coverage, and these explanations therefore remain speculative.

On balance, still, our evidence is that in the more democratic Mexican states, people have a stronger sense of the power of institutions to constrain politicians. No single piece of evidence is conclusive. But, combined, the evidence supports our hypothesis that democratization in Mexico entails a shift from personal to institutional trust. Citizens in more-democratic states, such as Baja California and Chihuahua, were more likely to believe that politicians behave well when they are constrained by judicial oversight, the watchful eye of the press, or an electoral threat. They were more likely to believe that electoral institutions are fair. And they were less likely to believe that politicians are personally trustworthy. They may remain skeptical about the motives of those who govern, and the government's ability to combat corruption. But it is a healthy skepticism, matched by a weak form of institutional trust that blossoms when institutions function well enough to warrant it.

Elections, Trust, and Accountability

One form of institutional trust is the belief that elections force politicians to be responsive to voters. To believe that elections have this effect, one must expect other voters to consider politicians' past performance or proposals for the future in deciding how to vote. One must believe that other voters will not be bought off by minor handouts and favors. We asked people which party was most widely supported in their neighborhood, and then asked a series of questions that invited them to explain this support. Did it arise from minor favors? From the party's proposals? Its universal concern for voters? Tables 4.3 and 4.4 report two of these questions and responses across our four regions in Argentina and in Mexico.

Argentina

In Argentina (as in Mexico) we asked people's neighbors if they supported the party that was most popular locally "because it has the best program" or "because it gave things out in the campaign" (Handout). And we asked whether people supported this party "because it's concerned for everyone" or "because it did them a favor" (Favor). Residents of the more democratic regions of Argentina expected their fellow citizens to use voting decision rules consistent with accountability. People from Mar del Plata were seven times more likely to attribute a party's popularity to its program than to its handing out campaign favors. In contrast, in Misiones, people were equally split between these two explanations for the party's popularity. And very few in Mar del Plata believed that other voters were swayed by favors, whereas those from the other three regions perceived clientelism as pervasive.

Multivariate analysis reinforces the conclusion that residents of more democratic regions, and especially of Mar del Plata, were more likely to see other voters as behaving in a manner that enforced accountability (see table 4A.3). That is, they were more likely to see other voters as responding to parties' programs and universalistic concerns, than were respondents from less democratic regions. And region of residence, not

Table 4.3   Argentina: Responses to Questions About Voting, by Region

	Mar del Plata	Buenos Aires	Córdoba	Misiones	Total
Handout					
Do people in your neighborhood support the [locally most important party] because					
It gave out favors during the campaign	10% (46)	36% (171)	28% (136)	40% (191)	28% (544)
It has the best program	67% (323)	49% (234)	52% (248)	43% (205)	53% (1010)
No answer	23% (111)	16% (75)	20% (96)	18% (84)	19% (366)
Favor					
Do people support this party because					
It has done them some favor	16% (77)	45% (215)	36% (175)	35% (166)	33% (663)
It is concerned for everyone	52% (250)	42% (200)	43% (204)	45% (217)	45% (871)
No answer	32% (153)	14% (65)	21% (101)	20% (97)	22% (416)

Source: Authors' compilations.
Note: Total number of responses in parentheses.

economic or demographic factors, explained variation in expectations of accountability.

Mexico

In Mexico we also found substantial cross-state differences in expectations of accountability. Table 4.4 shows the Mexican responses to these same two questions (Handout and Favor). The results are consistent with what we found in Argentina, although the magnitude of the cross-state differences was smaller. Baja Californians were less likely than respondents from other states to see popular support for parties as a response to personal favors or campaign handouts.[15]

The only anomaly is that our Chihuahua and Michoacán samples were more likely than our Baja California sample to link a party's support to its "concern for people." But in fact responses to this question support our hypothesized link between weak trust and democracy: given a forced choice between "favors" and a "concern for people," Baja Californians were more likely to reject both possibilities. Baja Cali-

Table 4.4   Mexico: Responses to Questions About Voting, by State

	Baja California	Chihuahua	Michoacán	Puebla	Total
Handout					
Thinking about the most important political party in this area, would you say that people support it because					
It gave out things during the campaign	17% (66)	34% (134)	36% (144)	21% (85)	27% (429)
It has a better program	53% (211)	50% (200)	39% (157)	45% (181)	47% (749)
No answer	31% (123)	16% (64)	25% (99)	34% (134)	26% (420)
Favor					
Do people support the party because					
It has done them a favor	20% (78)	33% (130)	29% (114)	36% (143)	29% (465)
It is concerned for people	47% (188)	56% (222)	51% (203)	36% (145)	47% (758)
No answer	34% (134)	12% (46)	21% (83)	28% (112)	23% (375)

Source: Authors' compilations.
Note: Total number of responses in parentheses.

fornians rejected both answers and refused to respond to the question at a much higher rate (34 percent) than was true in the three other states. This was one of the few questions for which Baja Californians had the highest rate of nonresponse.[16]

Multivariate analysis shows that these results are robust to statistical controls: respondents in the other three states were more likely than Baja Californians to believe that favors and campaign handouts drive popular support (see table 4A.3).[17]

bThe results do not match our expectations perfectly; multivariate models do not show that expectations of accountability declined monotonically across the states, from the most to the least democratic. What the results do show is that the most democratic state (Baja California) was also the one in which institutional-trust responses were the most widespread. Thus, as in Argentina, in high-quality democratic regions, we find the belief that good performance in office and programmatic positions, rather than the distribution of favors and campaign handouts, lie behind popular support for political parties.

Personal Trust and Clientelism

In chapter 1 we hypothesized that clientelist parties cultivate personal relations of friendship and trust between clients and their patrons. If this hypothesis is correct, we should find: first, that clientelism is more widespread in low- than in high-quality democratic regions; second, that personal trust in politicians is more prevalent in regions where clientelism is widespread; and, third, that clients, wherever they live, are especially prone to personally trust politicians.

Our surveys included a series of questions designed to find out whether a respondent was involved in patron-client relations with political parties: how enmeshed he or she was in personalized relations with parties, and whether he or she would typically receive a flow of minor material support, a flow that would intensify in the run-up to elections. In both countries we asked respondents to identify the most politically prominent person in their neighborhood and then asked, "In the past few years, have you turned to this person to resolve some problem?" We asked whether they knew an operative from a political party (Know Party), and whether they had turned to an operative for help in the past year (Party Help). We asked whether, in the event that the head of the respondent's household lost his or her job, the respondent would turn to a party operative for help (Job). We asked whether, during the previous election campaign, a political party had distributed items in their neighborhood (Party Give), and whether they had received anything in the campaign (Gift). In Argentina we asked recipients of gifts whether the gift influenced his or her vote (Influence).

Argentina

The distribution of clientelist responses by region gives some indication that clientelism is less prevalent in the more democratic regions (see table 4.5). The percentages of people who turned to a patron for help (Patron) and who would turn to a party operative for help in case of unemployment (Job) increase monotonically as we move from most to least democratic region, and the differences are often quite large. People in Misiones were about four times as likely as people from Mar del Plata, and twice as likely as people from Buenos Aires, to have gone to a prominent politician for help. People from Misiones and Córdoba were almost twice as likely as those from Mar del Plata to imagine turning to a party if they (hypothetically) lost their job. The percentages

Table 4.5 Argentina: Responses to Questions About Clientelism, by Region

	Mar del Plata	Buenos Aires	Córdoba	Misiones	Total
Patron					
In recent years, have you turned to [most important local political person] to resolve some problem?					
Yes	5%	9%	13%	20%	12%
	(23)	(44)	(64)	(95)	(226)
No	94%	90%	86%	80%	88%
	(352)	(280)	(150)	(222)	(1004)
No answer	1%	1%	1%	1%	1%
	(4)	(4)	(2)	(3)	(13)
Know party					
Do you know a representative of a political party in your neighborhood?					
Yes	14%	36%	30%	37%	29%
	(66)	(175)	(144)	(179)	(564)
No	86%	63%	68%	61%	69%
	(412)	(301)	(325)	(292)	(1330)
No answer	0.5%	1%	2%	2%	1%
	(2)	(4)	(11)	(9)	(26)
Party help					
In recent years, have you turned to the representative of a political party for help with a problem?					
Yes	5%	10%	8%	13%	9%
	(23)	(46)	(38)	(62)	(169)

(Table continues on p. 102.)

Table 4.5 *Continued*

	Mar del Plata	Buenos Aires	Córdoba	Misiones	Total
No	94%	90%	90%	85%	90%
	(453)	(430)	(430)	(408)	(1721)
No answer	1%	1%	3%	2%	2%
	(4)	(4)	(12)	(10)	(30)
Job					
If the head of your family lost his/her job and the family needed help, would you turn to the representative of a political party?					
Yes	24%	37%	40%	41%	36%
	(117)	(177)	(191)	(198)	(683)
No	74%	62%	55%	54%	61%
	(354)	(297)	(262)	(260)	(1173)
No answer	2%	1%	6%	5%	3%
	(9)	(6)	(27)	(22)	(64)
Party give					
During the campaign, did a candidate or party distribute things to people?					
Yes	40%	36%	47%	52%	44%
	(194)	(173)	(224)	(248)	(839)
No	52%	60%	48%	39%	50%
	(250)	(288)	(230)	(189)	(957)
No answer	8%	4%	5%	9%	6%
	(36)	(19)	(26)	(43)	(124)

Gift

Did you receive something from a party or candidate?

Yes	4% (20)	5% (26)	10% (50)	9% (45)	7% (141)
No	94% (453)	94% (450)	88% (423)	90% (432)	92% (1758)
No answer	1% (7)	1% (4)	1% (7)	1% (3)	1% (21)

Influence

Did receiving this good influence your vote?

Yes	0.2% (1)	1% (3)	3% (14)	2% (10)	2% (28)
No	3% (12)	7% (33)	11% (51)	10% (47)	7% (143)
Didn't receive anything or no answer	97% (467)	92% (444)	86% (415)	88% (423)	91% (1749)

Source: Authors' compilations.

Notes: Patron and Party Help were follow-up questions; respondents were first asked whether they knew the most important local politician and a party representative (respectively), and those who answered "yes" were then asked if they had gone to this person for help. Here we include those who reported no knowledge of the politician or party representative as having said "no" to the follow-up questions. Total number of responses in parentheses.

who knew a party operative (Know Party), had turned to a party representative for help (Party Help), in whose neighborhoods goods had been given out during campaigns (Party Give), and who themselves received an item (Gift) trended upward as the level of democracy declined, although not monotonically. In several of these cases the cross-regional differences are large, with clientelist responses two or three times as common in Misiones as in Mar del Plata.

Most, but not all, of these regional differences are robust to multivariate controls for income and other socioeconomic factors[18] (see table 4A.4). In table 4.5 we saw that more than twice as many respondents from Misiones as from Mar del Plata received handouts (forty-five versus twenty). In multivariate analysis, apparent regional differences wash out: the lower income of our Misiones respondents rather than region per se explained the larger number of them who received handouts. But when we turn to the question not of whether one merely received a handout but also whether the handout influenced one's vote (Influence), the results come closer to meeting our expectations. Even controlling for income, education, and housing quality, people in Mar del Plata were the least likely to shift their vote in response to clientelistic "gifts" (although Córdoba stands out as the most clientelistic province). People from Mar del Plata were also somewhat less likely to imagine turning to a party for help in securing a job than were those from Buenos Aires province and from Misiones, and significantly less likely than those from Córdoba.

Thus our expectation that the deepening of democracy involved the waning of clientelism was only partially confirmed. Parties in our most democratic region eschewed clientelism. But it remained an attractive strategy in Córdoba, another region where, in other respects, democracy works better than in our least democratic case, Misiones. Yet recall that, when we probed clientelism not by asking people whether they had received handouts but by asking them whether their neighbors had, we found that clientelism increased monotonically as one moved from more to less democratic regions.

Does clientelism increase trust? If so, people whose votes were influenced by handouts should trust politicians. This turns out to be the case (see table 4A.5). A person who received a gift that influenced her vote had a 12-percent chance of saying that no politicians can be trusted, whereas someone who did not had a 22-percent chance. Someone who received nothing had a 3-percent chance of saying that all politicians could be trusted, whereas someone who was influenced by a gift had a 7-percent chance.[19]

Clientelism does not, however, swamp the effect of region—and hence of democratization—on trust in politicians. Figure 4.4 shows that both clientelism and region influence levels of trust in politicians. The figure presents simulated expected probabilities of the response "No

Figure 4.4   Argentina: Probability of Response, "No Officeholders Are Trustworthy," by Region

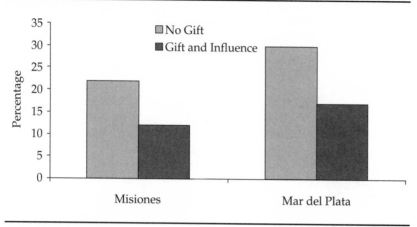

Source: Authors' compilations.
Note: Clarify simulations. All other independent variables are held at their sample medians.

officeholders are trustworthy if unmonitored." In all cases, we assume a female Peronist supporter who is in every other way at the median for the sample. The two bars on the left represent expected responses for people who live in Misiones, those on the right for people who live in Mar del Plata. In both regions, a person whose vote was influenced by a gift was more likely to trust politicians than a person who received no gift. At the same time, those influenced by gifts were more trusting if they lived in Misiones than in Mar del Plata, and those who received no gift in Misiones were more trusting than their counterparts in Mar del Plata. Hence clientelism is one source of personal trust. But other features of less democratic regions also foster personal trust in politicians.[20]

Mexico

By some measures, clientelism appears less prevalent in our Mexican samples than in Argentina. For example, fewer Mexicans (28 percent) than Argentines (36 percent) said they would turn to a party representative for help if the head of household lost his or her job (see table 4.6). By other measures, clientelism was more widespread in Mexico. Twice the number of Mexicans as Argentines said they had received a handout during the previous campaign (14 percent versus 7 percent). Paradoxically, more Argentines (44 percent) than Mexicans (26 percent) said that parties gave things out in their neighborhoods during the campaign. The difference was partly that more Mexicans said that parties did not give out goods in their neighborhoods (56 percent versus 50 percent). But it was also partly that Mexicans were simply more

Table 4.6 Mexico: Responses to Questions About Clientelism, by State

	Baja California	Chihuahua	Michoacán	Puebla	Total
Patron					
In recent years, have you turned to [most important local political person] to resolve some problem?					
Yes	7% (26)	11% (44)	9% (34)	8% (30)	8% (134)
No	93% (181)	89% (214)	90% (129)	91% (119)	90% (643)
No answer	1% (4)	0% (1)	2% (7)	2% (6)	12% (18)
Know party					
Do you know a representative of a political party in your neighborhood?					
Yes	17% (69)	26% (102)	23% (93)	27% (107)	23% (371)
No	81% (322)	72% (287)	70% (281)	67% (269)	73% (1159)
No answer	2% (9)	2% (9)	7% (26)	6% (24)	4% (68)
Party help					
In recent years, have you turned to the representative of a political party for help with a problem?					
Yes	5% (20)	8% (31)	9% (37)	8% (32)	8% (120)
No	92% (368)	89% (356)	83% (332)	84% (335)	87% (1391)
No answer	3% (12)	3% (11)	8% (31)	8% (33)	5% (87)
Job					
If the head of your family lost his/her job and the family needed help, would you turn to the representative of a political party?					
Yes	17% (68)	45% (180)	28% (113)	21% (82)	28% (443)
No	73% (292)	49% (196)	56% (223)	67% (267)	61% (978)
	10%	6%	16%	12%	11%

Party give

During the campaign, did a candidate or party distribute things to people?

Yes	22% (87)	25% (101)	30% (120)	26% (102)	26% (410)
No	65% (260)	62% (245)	47% (188)	52% (207)	56% (900)
No answer	13% (53)	13% (52)	23% (92)	23% (91)	18% (288)

Gift

Did you receive something from a party or candidate?

Yes	9% (37)	14% (56)	15% (60)	19% (75)	14% (228)
No	85% (338)	83% (329)	72% (288)	69% (274)	77% (1229)
No answer	6% (25)	3% (13)	13% (52)	13% (51)	9% (141)

Does obligate

Do families that receive help from the representative of a political party feel obligated to vote for that party?

Yes	33% (133)	38% (153)	38% (150)	39% (154)	37% (590)
No	63% (252)	60% (239)	52% (207)	50% (198)	56% (896)
No answer	4% (15)	2% (6)	11% (43)	12% (48)	7% (112)

Should obligate

Should families that receive help from the representative of a political party feel obligated to vote for that party?

Yes	11% (44)	22% (88)	19% (77)	21% (84)	18% (293)
No	86% (342)	74% (294)	67% (269)	60% (239)	72% (1144)
No answer	4% (14)	4% (16)	14% (54)	19% (77)	10% (161)

Source: Authors' compilations.
Note: Total number of responses in parentheses.

reluctant to answer this question: the Mexican nonresponse rate was 18 percent, the Argentine, 7 percent. This higher nonresponse rate may mean that Mexicans were more reluctant to acknowledge clientelism— they also failed to offer responses to the question "Did you receive something?" at a much higher rate than Argentines (9 percent versus 1 percent).[21]

Our surveys show that parties forged fewer personal links with voters in Baja California, the most democratic state among those we studied, than in the other Mexican states. And clientelism was a more pervasive political force in Michoacán and Puebla than in Baja California and Chihuahua. Table 4.6 lists the responses to several survey questions, broken down by state. The results do not entirely match our expectations: the frequency of clientelist responses did not always increase monotonically from the most to the least democratic state. But Baja Californians tended to offer fewer clientelist responses. They were significantly less likely than respondents from the other three states to know a party representative or to have received something during the campaign (see Know Party and Gift). And they were less likely than respondents from Chihuahua and Michoacán to consider going to a party for help with employment (Job).[22]

Turning to campaign handouts, we asked whether parties had distributed goods in the respondent's neighborhood during the campaign (Gift), and whether receiving these goods obliged citizens to support the party at the polls (Does Obligate). (Recall that our surveys were conducted about two weeks after state elections in all four states.) Across the full sample, 26 percent said that the parties did distribute goods, and 14 percent reported having received something personally. Again, we find significant differences across states. In response to both questions, Baja Californians were least likely to report clientelist activity, and people from Puebla were most likely to report it. As in Argentina, where twice as many people in our least democratic region received handouts as in our most democratic region, Puebla residents received goods at more than twice the rate of Baja Californians.[23]

The Mexican patterns stand up to multivariate analysis (see table 4A.6). In the presence of controls for income, education, and other factors on which our state samples differ, we still find that Baja California has low levels of personalism. Respondents from Chihuahua, Michoacán, and Puebla were more likely than those from Baja California to know a party operative and to consider going to one for help finding a job. Responses to the questions about a job did not fall into the order we would have predicted: respondents from Chihuahua were more likely than those from the less democratic states of Michoacán and Puebla to consider going to a party representative for help finding a job. But in other respects the pattern was as we would expect, with those from Michoacán and Puebla showing higher levels of person-alism.[24]

The most powerful determinant of clientelism was region. All else equal, residents of Chihuahua, Michoacán, and Puebla were more likely than ones from Baja California to have received clientelist goods before the election. Baja Californians were also least likely to think that recipients of clientelist handouts do or should feel obliged to vote for the donor party. Simulations show that the typical resident of Baja California has a 10-percent chance of agreeing that gifts should obligate reciprocity in the form of a vote. But a similar person residing in one of the other three states is roughly twice as likely to offer such a re-sponse (from 17 percent for Michoacán to 21 percent for Puebla).[25] (Re-spondents who received gifts during the campaign were significantly more likely to say that gifts do and should obligate the recipient to offer his vote in return.) Clearly, personalized political networks were less prevalent in Baja California than in the other three states. This sup-ports our expectation that the political culture in regions where democ-racy functions less well will feature both more clientelism and more personal trust in politicians.

Did clientelism and personal contacts with politicians increase politi-cal trust in Mexico? We find strong evidence that it did. People in our sample who knew a party representative personally, said they would turn to a party for help securing a job, observed gifts being distributed in their neighborhoods leading up to elections, or said that they them-selves received gifts, were more likely to offer personal trust rather than institutional trust answers on a range of questions. Additionally, those who received handouts were more likely to say that the handouts do and should obligate people to reciprocate with their votes. As in Argentina, then, clientelism in Mexico appears to generate personal trust in politicians.

Democracy, Contingent Consent, and the Rule of Law

Our findings to this point show a general consistency between Mexico and Argentina and consistency with our theoretical expectations. Peo-ple in the more democratic regions of both countries display beliefs consistent with our theory, which links the deepening of democracy to a shift from personal to institutional trust. Another dimension of re-gional political cultures we study is postures toward the rule of law. One expectation is that as a region becomes more democratic, citizens will conform increasingly to what we call proceduralism: an adherence to laws and publicly sanctioned informal rules.

In Mexico, as we will see, the political culture of more democratic regions was more proceduralist than in less democratic regions. In Argentina, people in more democratic regions were less likely to advocate flouting laws across the board. Yet on some issues, rather than unconditional support for laws and rules, Argentines in more democratic regions adhered to what might be called contingent consent: the idea that one should comply with laws and rules only when they are fair (see Levi 1988, 1997). Comparing residents of relatively democratic regions in the two countries, then, in Mexico these people were simply more law and rule abiding, or at least more prone to say that laws should be obeyed. In Argentina, people from relatively consolidated regions were also in a sense more law abiding: they were less prone than others to sanctify the regular violation of laws. But they were also more sensitive to the contingencies that can justify violating the law. These cross-national differences surprised us, and we speculate later about why they appear.

We asked people in both countries whether it was always, sometimes, or never justified for someone to do the following things: evade taxes (Taxes), claim public goods and services that they did not deserve (Claim), avoid military service (Military), buy stolen goods (Stolen), and for a politician to accept a bribe (Corrupt). In Mexico we asked whether it was justified for someone to avoid paying a bus fare (Fare); in Argentina we asked whether it was justified not to pay admission to a public event (Admission). We also asked some follow-up questions, meant to probe further the conditions under which people saw violating laws as justified. We asked whether evading taxes was justified under the circumstance that "many others don't pay" ("dado que mucha gente no paga"—Tax Many), whether one could claim undeserved public goods if others were doing so (Claim Many), and whether dodging military service was justified if others were also dodging (Military Many).[26]

Mexico

Table 4.7 lists the percentage of respondents in each state who said that each type of violation was "never justified" or "unfair." In every case, the percentage of proceduralist answers trends downward—often monotonically—as the level of democracy decreases, from Baja California to Puebla. Respondents in Michoacán, and especially in Puebla, were less likely to say that violations are never justified, exhibiting either more ambiguity in their moral outlooks or a greater willingness to flout the laws. Respondents in Chihuahua and, especially, in Baja California were more likely to categorically condemn violations and thus offered more rigid views of rules and norms.

These differences persist even when we asked the respondents whether it is justified to violate laws if many others also violate them.

Table 4.7 Mexico: Responses to Questions About Proceduralism, by State

			Percentage Saying "Never Justified"		
	Baja California	Chihuahua	Michoacán	Puebla	Total
Question: Is it always, sometimes, or never justified . . .					
To avoid paying taxes that one owes (Taxes)	65%	52%	33%	33%	45%
	(258)	(206)	(131)	(130)	(725)
If many people didn't pay taxes, is it justified? Percentage answering "no" (Taxes Many)	88%	68%	56%	60%	68%
	(351)	(272)	(222)	(238)	(1083)
To claim public goods or services that one does not deserve (Claim)	52%	53%	36%	34%	43%
	(208)	(210)	(142)	(135)	(695)
If many people claim goods or services they don't deserve, is it justified? Percentage answering "no" (Claim Many)	75%	62%	62%	57%	64%
	(301)	(245)	(247)	(228)	(1021)
To avoid military service (Military)	61%	56%	37%	34%	47%
	(242)	(224)	(147)	(135)	(748)
To avoid service if many others avoided it (Military Many)	84%	66%	64%	60%	68%
	(337)	(261)	(255)	(238)	(1091)
To buy stolen goods (Stolen)	72%	67%	56%	50%	61%
	(286)	(268)	(224)	(201)	(979)
For a functionary to accept a bribe (Corrupt)	88%	69%	58%	56%	68%
	(351)	(274)	(233)	(224)	(1082)
To not pay the fare for public transportation (Fare)	67%	62%	53%	40%	56%
	(268)	(246)	(212)	(161)	(887)

Source: Authors' compilations.
Note: Total number of responses in parentheses.

When we asked whether evading taxes would be justified if many others didn't pay, respondents in Baja California and Chihuahua were still more likely to say that tax evasion was unjustified. Our Michoacán and Puebla samples were more swayed by the rule breaking of others.[27] Eighty-eight percent of our Baja California sample believed that tax evasion was unjustified even if others were evading. This number dropped to 68 percent in Chihuahua, 56 percent in Michoacán, and 60 percent in Puebla. Citizens of Baja California and Chihuahua remained committed to proceduralism even when others were breaking the law.[28]

Multivariate analysis shows that these cross-state differences are not simply a function of socioeconomic or demographic differences among the states (see table 4A.7). Income and social class both have significant effects on the responses. Oddly, higher income predicts stricter proceduralism (that is, a greater probability of the "never justified" response), whereas higher self-reported social class predicts the opposite.[29] Partisanship also had a modest effect, with PRI supporters tending to be less proceduralist.

But large differences across the four states persist even when we control for socioeconomic effects. People in Baja California always show the strongest commitment to the rule of law, followed by respondents from Chihuahua, Michoacán, and Puebla.[30] Furthermore, the largest difference is in the gap between Chihuahua, ranked second, and Michoacán, ranked third. Here again the gap between our most democratic pair of states (Baja California and Chihuahua) and our least democratic pair (Michoacán and Puebla) is larger than the difference between the states within each pair.

We simulated the probability that a respondent would say it is never justified to evade taxes and that it is never justified to avoid paying the fare for public transportation (see figure 4.5). (Both estimations draw on the multivariate models in table 4A.7, and hold all other variables at their median values.) Consider a hypothetical middle-class, forty-year-old, female high school graduate living in an urban area. If she lives in Baja California, her chance of saying that tax evasion is never justified is 68 percent. Move her to Puebla, and the probability falls to 41 percent. The probability that she will frown upon someone not paying a bus fare is 71 percent if she lives in Baja California, but only 50 percent if she lives in Puebla.

To summarize, proceduralism was another feature of political culture that varied from more to less democratic states. People in Baja California and Chihuahua were more legalistic, whereas people in Puebla and Michoacán were less committed to the rule of law. The ranking of the four states on proceduralism also exactly matches the ranking on democracy that we derived in chapter 2.

Figure 4.5   Mexico: Proceduralist Responses, by State

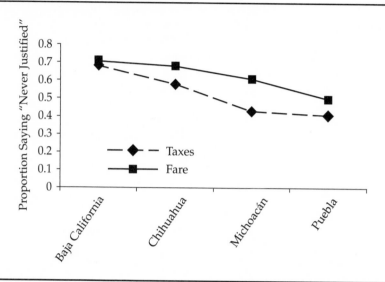

Source: Authors' compilations.
Note: Clarify simulations, holding other independent variables at their sample median values.

Argentina

In Argentina, people from the most democratic region were more likely to evince proceduralism in only a limited sense. They were less likely to believe that breaking laws was always justified. But instead of being unambiguously committed to the rule of law, they were often more likely to embrace a conditional perspective, believing that one is some-times justified in breaking the law.

Consider, for instance, the matter of paying taxes. Our evaluation of democratic performance in Argentina in chapter 3 focused on the fiscal behavior of provincial governments and on one district's remarkable story of self-taxation. But the reader will recall that the epilogue to the story of local democracy in Mar del Plata was not a happy one. With the growing national economic crisis, the city's residents started evad-ing taxes more and more, the municipality's revenues fell, and its debt rose. The mayor who had gotten residents to raise their own taxes left office before the end of his term. Levi (1988, 1997) has linked fairness in the structure and application of tax codes to citizens' contingent con-sent to pay taxes, and to a broader democratization of some Western societies. We might then expect our region of relatively healthy democracy to be one of contingent consent to taxation: people there would comply only when taxes were levied fairly and when governments made good use of revenues.

Indeed, according to Mar del Plata's political leadership, tax compliance in their region was, by Argentine standards, high.[31] But, in the leadership's view, their constituents' attitude toward taxation was transactional, its willingness to pay contingent on its belief that it obtained good services in return. In a February 2004 interview with Fernando Folcher and Susan Stokes, Walter Malagutti, Mar del Plata's secretary of education under Mayor Aprile, explained this attitude:

> Here the culture of paying doesn't run too deep, the idea that you have to pay because you have to pay. No. Here, in general, some pay and others don't pay. And those who pay, they pay if they believe that they are receiving something in return. If not, they don't pay.

Malagutti's view was echoed by Luis Rech, another city official, in another interview the same month:

> In accordance with how the government is responding to my demands, I pay or I don't pay, with no criterion of solidarity, of how it's responding to the demands of others. It's almost as though it were a kind of vote, of permanent voting, a person doesn't wait two years to change [the government] but instead, already right now, he withdraws support. And, in withdrawing support, they feel like they're paying too much in taxes.[32]

The results of our surveys paint a picture of Mar del Plata's residents that is consistent with Malagutti and Rech's description. Residents of our high-quality democracy believed that, under some circumstances, a person is justified in not paying taxes. We see in table 4.8 that fewer people in the high-quality democratic regions said that one is never justified in evading than in the low-quality democratic region—the opposite of the Mexican pattern. One can think of this question as producing an ordinal measure of commitment to compliance with taxation, going from the view that one is "always" justified in evading (scored 1), to "sometimes" justified (scored 2), to "never" justified (scored 3). In the presence of controls, people in Mar del Plata scored significantly lower on this measure than did those from Misiones, and somewhat lower (though not significantly so) than people from elsewhere in Buenos Aires and from Córdoba (see table 4A.8). Standing alone, this analysis would lead us to conclude that the effect of democratic consolidation in Argentina was to reduce commitment to the rule of law.

But another way to think about postures toward the rule of law is that people can fall into several categories. Those who favor regularly breaking the law are law flouters. Those who always favor obeying

Table 4.8 Argentina: Responses to Questions About Proceduralism, by Region

	Percentage Saying "Never Justified"				
	Mar del Plata	Buenos Aires	Córdoba	Misiones	Total
Question: Is it always, sometimes, or never justified . . .					
To avoid paying taxes that one owes (Taxes)	40% (191)	41% (199)	48% (231)	49% (236)	45% (857)
If many people didn't pay taxes (and knowing that this would reduce services), is it justified (percentage "no") (Taxes Many)	75% (359)	75% (362)	70% (338)	75% (360)	74% (1419)
To claim public goods or services that one does not deserve (Claim)	73% (349)	72% (345)	67% (321)	63% (304)	69% (1319)
If many people claim goods or services they don't deserve, is it justified? (percentage "no") (Claim Many)	88% (423)	83% (399)	79% (380)	73% (352)	81% (1554)
To avoid military service (Military)	14% (68)	13% (64)	15% (74)	18% (85)	15% (291)
If many people avoided military service, was it justified? (percentage "no") (Military Many)	75% (359)	86% (411)	70% (338)	81% (387)	78% (1495)
To buy stolen goods (Stolen)	87% (418)	87% (416)	86% (412)	80% (386)	85% (1632)
For a functionary to accept a bribe (Corrupt)	97% (466)	98% (468)	94% (449)	94% (451)	96% (1834)
To not pay admission to a public event (Admission)	75% (358)	86% (415)	74% (356)	77% (371)	78% (1500)

Source: Authors' compilations.
Note: Total number of responses in parentheses.

the law are law abiders. Those who favor sometimes obeying it and sometimes violating it, depending on the circumstances, are contingent consenters. To understand the factors pushing people into one category or another, we need to know more than just whether changes in the value of explanatory factors cause the index we described earlier to go up (toward "never") or down (toward "always"). We would also like to know whether changes in the explanatory variables change the probability that a person will say that it is "sometimes" justifiable to break the law, at the expense of both "always" and "never" answers. The statistical analysis that follows shows that shifts in some explanatory variables, and in particular the shift from living in a less to a more democratic region, increased the probability that a person would be a contingent consenter. Regional differences in the prevalence of contingent consent distinguish Argentina from Mexico.

Multinomial logit regressions show several significant effects (see table 4A.9). On the tax question, men were less likely than women to answer that evasion was "always" justified, and to answer that it was "never" justified. Men were hence more prone to be contingent consenters. Also, a person who lived in Mar del Plata was more likely to acquiesce to paying taxes only conditionally than were those from Córdoba and Misiones. Following the broader logic of the chapter, the consolidation of democracy in Argentina encouraged a political culture of contingent consent to taxation, whereas in Mexico consolidation simply encouraged tax compliance.

We simulate the effect of region on proceduralist postures toward taxation and military service. Figure 4.6 simulates responses to the tax question. Drawing on the multinomial logit regressions, it assumes a typical respondent (the values of other independent variables are held at their median values) and varies the region in which she lives. The figure illustrates that moving our hypothetical respondent from Mar del Plata to other parts of Buenos Aires province has little effect on her views of tax evasion. In either case, she is almost twice as likely to say that evasion is sometimes justified than that it is never justified. Whether she lives in Mar del Plata or elsewhere in the province of Buenos Aires, she has only about a 10-percent chance of saying that evasion is always justified. If one moves her to Córdoba or to Misiones, she is about equally likely to say that evasion is sometimes or never justifiable. Hence the line representing "sometimes" slopes downward as one moves from left to right, whereas the line representing "never" slopes upward, indicating a dropping off of contingent consent in Córdoba and Misiones.

Turning to military service, if we conceptualize people's views as sorting them into distinct types—law flouters, contingent consenters, and law abiders—we find regional differences. The simulations in fig-

Figure 4.6   Argentina: Simulated Expected Probabilities of Responses on Justifiability of Evading Taxes, by Region

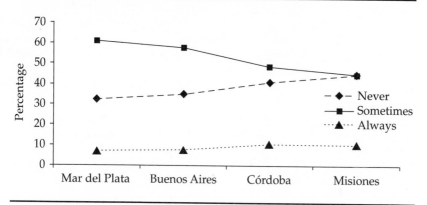

Source: Authors' compilations.
Note: Clarify simulations. All other independent variables are held at their sample means.

ure 4.7 illustrate regional effects. A Misiones resident is more likely than a Mar del Plata resident to say that avoiding service is never justified, but less likely to say it is sometimes justified.[33] In this sense, our Argentine results are the opposite of the Mexican: in Mexico, people from the most consolidated region were law abiders, but in Argentina, with regard to military service, they were law flouters.

Figure 4.7   Argentina: Simulated Expected Probabilities of Responses on Justifiability of Avoiding Military Service, by Region

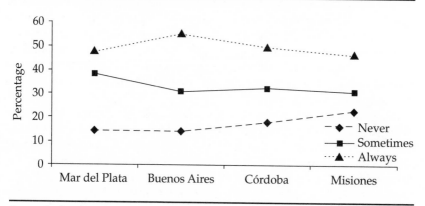

Source: Authors' compilations.
Note: Clarify simulations, holding other explanatory variables at their sample means.

Table 4.9   Argentina: Prevalence of Contingent Consent, Law-Flouting, and Law-Abiding Postures, by Region

Compared to Mar del Plata:	Taxation	Gate-Crashing	Military Service
Buenos Aires	No difference	More law-abiding	More law-flouting
Córdoba	Less contingent consent	No difference	No difference
Misiones	Less contingent consent	More law-abiding	More law-abiding

Source: Authors' compilations.
Notes:
Taxation: "Do you believe that not paying taxes is always, sometimes, or never justified?"
Gate-crashing: "Do you believe that not paying admission to a public event is always, sometimes, or never justified?"
Military service: "Until recently obligatory military service existed. Do you believe that not complying with military service in that era was always, sometimes, or never justified?"

We summarize in table 4.9 the effect of region on proceduralism in Argentina. The table reveals that contingent consent in Mar del Plata is centered on taxation. Comparing our Mar del Plata and our Misiones samples, people in Misiones were simply more law abiding when it came to paying admission to a public event and to military service. But on taxation, the difference between our Misiones and our Mar del Plata samples was that the latter contained more contingent consenters, people who said that one was sometimes justified in not paying taxes. There were also more contingent consenters on taxes in Mar del Plata than in Córdoba. On military service, people in Misiones were more law abiding than those in Mar del Plata and Buenos Aires, where people were prone to believe that one was always justified in evading military service.

We can only speculate about why regional democratization in Mexico brings with it an unambiguous proceduralism, whereas in Argentina it brings a more nuanced contingent consent. One explanation is that Argentines lived fairly recently under an abusive military dictatorship that followed its own rules and laws. By contrast, the legal structure was sound in the long era of Mexican soft authoritarianism, but the authorities broke the laws. In Argentina, the rule of law meant the rule of bad laws. In Mexico, it meant forcing the authorities to submit to the rule of good laws.

To summarize, in Argentina and Mexico the deepening of democracy entailed a shift from personal trust in politicians to institutional trust in government. It also involved a heightened proceduralism or contingent consent. These shifts did not always go in the predicted direction. People in more democratized regions of Mexico, for instance, were less trusting of institutions to catch venal politicians. Still, the distinctiveness of regional political cultures of democracy is striking. In both countries, democratic deepening encouraged the belief that governments provide good services when they are under the watch of other agents. It deepened the belief that municipal governments are efficient when they fear losing office in the next election. In both countries, citizens in the less democratic regions believed governments provide good services and are efficient when they are staffed by good people. In both countries, respondents from the least democratic regions believed that you can trust politicians even when you cannot monitor them. People in these less consolidated regions were more enmeshed in clientelism and in personalistic politics. And clientelism increased people's personal trust in politicians.

Appendix

Table 4A.1   Argentina: Models of Institutional Trust Responses

Dependent Variable	(1) Service	(2) Efficient	(3) Attention	(4) Trustpol	(5) Bribe
Model	Logit	Logit	Logit	Ordered logit	Ordered logit
Income	−0.057	0.005	−0.105	**0.097**	0.005
	(0.043)	(0.038)	(0.054)	(0.034)	(0.033)
Education	0.041	−0.073	−0.060	0.016	−0.042
	(0.037)	(0.038)	(0.043)	(0.029)	(0.027)
Housing	−0.006	−0.065	0.018	−0.082	0.067
	(0.076)	(0.089)	(0.094)	(0.068)	(0.074)
Gender	**−0.318**	−0.014	−0.062	0.095	**0.189**
	(0.102)	(0.103)	(0.119)	(0.095)	(0.094)
Age	**−0.013**	**−0.017**	−0.006	0.004	0.001
	(0.004)	(0.004)	(0.004)	(0.004)	(0.003)
Peronist supporter	**−0.230**	0.049	**−0.420**	**0.520**	**0.357**
	(0.116)	(0.127)	(0.150)	(0.128)	(0.108)
Radical supporter	−0.058	−0.036	0.045	**0.360**	0.180
	(0.144)	(0.142)	(0.226)	(0.159)	(0.102)
Interpersonal trust				**0.544**	
				(0.088)	
Bribe				**0.346**	
				(0.075)	
Log population	0.006	0.040	0.031	**−0.123**	−0.059
	(0.037)	(0.046)	(0.046)	(0.037)	(0.034)
Buenos Aires	**−0.408**	0.081	**−0.438**	−0.014	0.143
	(0.184)	(0.190)	(0.214)	(0.166)	(0.142)
Córdoba	**−0.618**	−0.115	−0.313	−0.113	**−0.546**
	(0.187)	(0.224)	(0.255)	(0.199)	(0.176)
Misiones	**−1.080**	−0.384	**−0.517**	**0.495**	−0.192
	(0.229)	(0.222)	(0.247)	(0.190)	(0.199)

Table 4A.1 *Continued*

Dependent Variable	(1) Service	(2) Efficient	(3) Attention	(4) Trustpol	(5) Bribe
Constant	**1.605** (0.528)	**1.881** (0.697)	**2.664** (0.742)		
Cut 1				0.337 (0.606)	**−1.715** (0.553)
Cut 2				**3.838** (0.623)	0.402 (0.555)
Cut 3				**5.102** (0.656)	

Source: Authors' compilations.

Notes: Standard errors in parentheses. Boldface indicates coefficient is statistically significant at $p < .05$. $N = 1,920$.

We coded answers to Services, Efficient, and Attention questions as dummy variables for "institutional-trust" answers. For example, if a person answered "when municipal governments are efficient, this is because otherwise people won't vote for them in the next election," we scored this person 1 on the dummy variable Efficient. We then estimated logit regression models of these institutional-trust answers.

These and all subsequent regressions draw on five datasets with imputed values for missing data. To generate the imputed datasets we used the Amelia program described in King et al. (2001) and implemented in Honaker et al. (2001).

We report robust standard errors designed to account for the possibility of correlated errors, due to the clustered sample design of the survey.

Explanation of variables:

Service: Dummy for response, "Governments provide good services when they're under the watch of the courts, congress, and the press."

Efficient: Dummy for response, "When municipal governments are efficient, this is because they know otherwise people won't vote for them."

Attention: Dummy for response, "When politicians pay attention to people like me, this is because they want to be reelected."

Trustpol: "Thinking about people who hold public office, how many of them do you think are trustworthy (confiables) and will behave well without being watched? (1) None, (2) a minority, (3) a majority, or (4) all."

Bribe: "When a politician takes a bribe, is it not at all likely (scored 1), somewhat likely (2), or very likely (3) that he'll get caught."

Income: Self-reported by respondent, 9-level scale of family income.

Education: 9-level scale, from no formal education to university.

Housing: Assessed by interviewer, 5-level scale (1 = poorest quality, 5 = highest quality), based on assessment of building materials, flooring, and presence or absence of consumer durables.

Gender: male = 0, female = 1.

Peronist supporter: coded 1 for respondents who said, independent of how they voted, that they liked the Peronist Party more than others, 0 otherwise.

Radical supporter: coded 1 for respondents who said, independent of how they voted, that they liked the Radical Party more than others, 0 otherwise.

Interpersonal trust: responses no one (coded 1), a minority (2), or a majority (3) of people can be trusted.

Log population: natural log of the number of inhabitants, according to 2001 census, residing in the municipality where the respondent lived.

Buenos Aires: Dummy variable for respondents who live in Buenos Aires.

Córdoba: Dummy variable for respondents who live in Córdoba.

Misiones: Dummy variable for respondents who live in Misiones.

Table 4A.2   Mexico: Models of Institutional Trust Responses

Dependent Variable	(1) Services	(2) Efficient	(3) Attention	(4) Trustpol	(5) Bribe
Model	Logit	Logit	Logit	Ordered logit	Ordered logit
Income	0.076	0.028	0.119	0.075	0.047
	(0.070)	(0.053)	(0.070)	(0.057)	(0.056)
Education	−0.018	−0.023	−0.058	−0.001	**−0.116**
	(0.057)	(0.066)	(0.059)	(0.053)	(0.051)
Class	−0.092	**−0.349**	**−0.558**	**0.249**	**0.494**
	(0.091)	(0.129)	(0.124)	(0.096)	(0.091)
Gender	−0.120	−0.135	−0.180	0.097	−0.060
	(0.122)	(0.114)	(0.126)	(0.108)	(0.093)
Age	0.040	−0.064	−0.043	0.071	**−0.105**
	(0.046)	(0.057)	(0.052)	(0.037)	(0.040)
PRI supporter	**−0.412**	**−0.450**	**−0.945**	**0.518**	**0.535**
	(0.176)	(0.178)	(0.222)	(0.148)	(0.151)
PAN supporter	−0.038	−0.290	**−0.671**	**0.344**	**0.543**
	(0.186)	(0.177)	(0.205)	(0.154)	(0.159)
PRD supporter	−0.208	0.405	−0.171	0.281	**0.484**
	(0.263)	(0.276)	(0.297)	(0.265)	(0.199)
Interpersonal trust				**0.618**	
				(0.080)	
Bribe				**0.365**	
				(0.088)	
Rural	−0.150	0.094	0.046	−0.003	0.047
	(0.102)	(0.109)	(0.109)	(0.096)	(0.121)
Chihuahua	−0.298	**−0.466**	−0.111	0.228	**−0.524**
	(0.214)	(0.206)	(0.228)	(0.152)	(0.228)
Michoacán	−0.171	**−0.500**	**−1.098**	**0.626**	**0.406**
	(0.199)	(0.204)	(0.251)	(0.210)	(0.206)
Puebla	**−0.457**	−0.195	−0.097	**0.493**	0.226
	(0.205)	(0.188)	(0.258)	(0.176)	(0.240)
Constant	**0.881**	**1.607**	**2.869**		
	(0.416)	(0.441)	(0.462)		
Cut 1				**1.928**	−0.203
				(0.418)	(0.366)
Cut 2				**4.234**	**2.035**
				(0.446)	(0.372)
Cut 3				**6.170**	
				(0.472)	

Source: Authors' compilations.
Notes: Standard errors in parentheses (see 4A.1). Boldface indicates coefficient is statistically significant at $p < .05$.   N = 1,598.
In each model, the dependent variable is coded 1 for the response that invokes accountability mechanisms, and 0 otherwise. The models draw on five datasets with imputed values for missing data; see note to Table 4A.1.
Explanation of variables: For Service, Efficient, and Attention, see note to Table 4A.1.

Table 4A.2   *Continued*

Income: self-reported family income on a six-point scale.
Education: self-reported level of education on a six-point scale.
Class: self-reported social class, 1 = lower, 2 = middle, 3 = upper.
Gender: 1 = male, 2 = female.
Age: self-reported age, on a five-point scale.
Rural: surveyor's coding of whether the neighborhood was urban (0), mixed (1), or rural (2).
PRI supporter, PAN supporter, and PRD supporter are dummy variables for people who report supporting each respective party. Chihuahua, Michoacán, and Puebla are dummy variables for people living in each state, respectively.

Table 4A.3   **Models of Institutional Responses to Questions About Voting**

Argentina (N = 1,920)			Mexico (N = 1,598)		
Dependent Variable	(1) Handout	(2) Favor	Dependent Variable	(3) Handout	(4) Favor
Model	Logit	Logit	Model	Logit	Logit
Income	−0.056 (0.038)	−0.051 (0.040)	Income	−0.064 (0.065)	0.084 (0.057)
Education	0.039 (0.041)	0.017 (0.034)	Education	−0.016 (0.062)	**0.143** (0.060)
Housing	−0.009 (0.102)	0.059 (0.086)	Class	0.202 (0.106)	−0.200 (0.113)
Gender	0.013 (0.107)	0.032 (0.102)	Gender	0.131 (0.107)	−0.094 (0.115)
Age	−0.001 (0.004)	**−0.014** (0.004)	Age	−0.023 (0.045)	0.075 (0.047)
Peronist	**−0.557** (0.156)	**−0.782** (0.149)	PRI supporter	−0.118 (0.202)	**−0.769** (0.199)
Radical	**−0.671** (0.186)	−0.122 (0.177)	PAN supporter	**−0.313** (0.179)	**−0.758** (0.214)
			PRD supporter	0.325 (0.225)	−0.612 (0.318)
Log population	−0.030 (0.041)	**0.122** (0.043)	Rural	**−0.260** (0.102)	−0.157 (0.124)
Buenos Aires	**1.387** (0.216)	**1.239** (0.195)	Chihuahua	**0.458** (0.228)	0.299 (0.197)
Córdoba	**1.100** (0.257)	**1.124** (0.197)	Michoacán	**0.637** (0.220)	0.152 (0.222)
Misiones	**1.746** (0.258)	**1.343** (0.237)	Puebla	0.263 (0.191)	**0.588** (0.206)
Constant	−0.975 (0.595)	**−1.908** (0.623)	Constant	−0.562 (0.427)	−0.391 (0.384)

Source: Authors' compilations.
Notes: Standard errors in parentheses. Boldface indicates coefficient is statistically significant at p < .05.
Handout: coded 1 for "it gave out favors during the campaign," 0 for "it has the best program."
Favor: coded 1 for "it has done them some favor," 0 for "it is concerned for everyone."

Table 4A.4   Argentina: Regression Models of Responses to Questions About Clientelism

Dependent Variable	(1) Job	(2) Party Give	(3) Gift	(4) Influence	(5) Does Obligate
Model	Logit	Logit	Logit	Ordered logit	Logit
Income	−0.068	−0.002	**−0.211**	**−0.206**	0.028
	(0.037)	(0.038)	(0.060)	(0.060)	(0.036)
Education	**−0.198**	0.015	**−0.179**	**−0.220**	0.031
	(0.033)	(0.035)	(0.080)	(0.076)	(0.031)
Housing	−0.151	**0.180**	**−0.297**	**−0.358**	0.037
	(0.087)	(0.088)	(0.127)	(0.126)	(0.083)
Gender	**0.209**	−0.076	−0.091	0.118	−0.011
	(0.099)	(0.089)	(0.170)	(0.160)	(0.087)
Age	**−0.022**	−0.006	**−0.014**	**−0.017**	**0.009**
	(0.004)	(0.004)	(0.006)	(0.006)	(0.003)
Peronist	**0.715**	−0.077	**0.875**	**0.782**	**−0.296**
	(0.126)	(0.125)	(0.213)	(0.208)	(0.113)
Radical	0.149	−0.033	−0.190	0.167	0.039
	(0.169)	(0.173)	(0.361)	(0.304)	(0.153)
Log population	−0.007	**−0.252**	−0.071	−0.055	**0.081**
	(0.037)	(0.049)	(0.058)	(0.066)	(0.032)
Buenos Aires	0.326	**−0.416**	−0.194	0.562	0.217
	(0.177)	(0.195)	(0.359)	(0.380)	(0.182)
Córdoba	**0.543**	−0.229	0.495	**1.224**	−0.217
	(0.203)	(0.244)	(0.343)	(0.436)	(0.176)
Misiones	0.113	0.029	−0.281	0.369	**−0.490**
	(0.226)	(0.237)	(0.388)	(0.462)	(0.210)
Received goods					**−0.564**
					(0.208)
Constant	**1.395**	**2.818**	0.782		**−1.371**
	(0.534)	(0.727)	(0.873)		(0.517)
Cut 1				−0.498	
				(1.050)	
Cut 2				1.501	
				(1.006)	

Source: Authors' compilations.

Notes: Standard errors in parentheses. Boldface indicates coefficient is statistically significant at p < .05. N = 1,920.

Job: coded 1 if respondent would go to party representative for help with a job.

Party Give: coded 1 if the respondent reported that parties "distributed things" during the campaign.

Gift: coded 1 if the respondent reported receiving something personally.

Table 4A.5   Argentina: Model of Responses to Question, "How Many Politicians Can You Trust Without Their Being Monitored"

Dependent Variable	(1) Trustpol
Model	Ordered logit
Income	**0.116** (0.033)
Education	0.035 (0.028)
Housing	−0.079 (0.068)
Gender	0.078 (0.095)
Age	0.005 (0.004)
Peronist	**0.566** (0.126)
Radical	**0.404** (0.154)
Log population	**−0.127** (0.035)
Buenos Aires	0.049 (0.165)
Córdoba	−0.216 (0.194)
Misiones	**0.428** (0.187)
Clientelist influence	**0.384** (0.168)
Cut 1	−0.829 (0.586)
Cut 2	**2.581** (0.599)
Cut 3	**3.833** (0.632)

Source: Authors' compilations.
Notes: Standard errors are in parentheses. Boldface indicates coefficient is statistically significant at $p < .05$. N = 1,920.

Table 4A.6   Mexico: Models of Responses to Clientelism Questions

Dependent Variable	(1) Know Party	(2) Party Help	(3) Job	(4) Party Give	(5) Gift	(6) Does Obligate	(7) Should Obligate
Model	Logit	Logit	Logit	Logit	Logit	Logit	Logit
Income	0.059	0.031	−0.110	−0.036	−0.122	−0.082	−0.069
	(0.074)	(0.121)	(0.058)	(0.064)	(0.079)	(0.070)	(0.072)
Education	−0.062	−0.015	0.043	0.105	0.126	0.079	−0.059
	(0.081)	(0.148)	(0.073)	(0.064)	(0.083)	(0.058)	(0.062)
Class	**0.415**	**0.834**	**0.434**	0.011	0.172	0.175	**0.339**
	(0.111)	(0.171)	(0.108)	(0.111)	(0.154)	(0.107)	(0.124)
Gender	−0.109	0.210	−0.163	−0.055	−0.126	0.078	0.156
	(0.122)	(0.195)	(0.122)	(0.122)	(0.165)	(0.123)	(0.129)
Age	0.027	0.132	0.063	−0.007	0.072	0.034	0.019
	(0.048)	(0.084)	(0.049)	(0.049)	(0.060)	(0.043)	(0.057)
PRI supporter	**0.884**	**1.122**	**0.727**	0.175	**0.499**	**0.404**	0.260
	(0.193)	(0.374)	(0.204)	(0.183)	(0.254)	(0.198)	(0.220)
PAN supporter	**0.412**	**0.806**	**0.743**	0.024	0.400	0.296	0.208
	(0.210)	(0.366)	(0.220)	(0.190)	(0.277)	(0.200)	(0.203)
PRD supporter	0.314	0.663	−0.180	**−0.805**	−0.716	0.499	**0.610**
	(0.290)	(0.474)	(0.304)	(0.294)	(0.390)	(0.271)	(0.294)
Rural	−0.041	0.059	0.041	−0.204	−0.117	0.052	0.159
	(0.138)	(0.202)	(0.121)	(0.120)	(0.160)	(0.115)	(0.108)
Chihuahua	0.402	0.362	**1.256**	0.175	0.401	0.128	**0.765**
	(0.234)	(0.351)	(0.254)	(0.242)	(0.285)	(0.214)	(0.259)
Michoacán	**0.548**	**0.841**	**0.942**	**0.672**	**0.762**	0.254	**0.680**
	(0.275)	(0.383)	(0.245)	(0.237)	(0.307)	(0.220)	(0.263)
Puebla	**0.614**	0.605	0.271	0.328	**0.821**	0.287	**0.915**
	(0.240)	(0.383)	(0.278)	(0.243)	(0.336)	(0.188)	(0.235)
Received goods						0.551	0.829
						(0.166)	(0.194)
Constant	−2.714	−5.852	−2.682	−1.051	−2.808	−1.474	−2.944
	(0.479)	(0.725)	(0.531)	(0.363)	(0.574)	(0.395)	(0.504)

Source: Authors' compilations.
Notes: Standard errors in parentheses. Boldface indicates coefficient is statistically significant at p < .05. N = 1,598.
The dependent variables are coded 1 for affirmative answers that suggest personalism and clientelism, and 0 for negative answers.

Table 4A.7   Mexico: Models of Proceduralism Responses

Dependent Variable	(1) Taxes	(2) Claim	(3) Military	(4) Stolen	(5) Corrupt	(6) Fare
Model	Ordered logit	Ordered logit	Ordered logit	Ordered logit	Ordered logit	Ordered logit
Income	0.056	0.070	0.085	**0.208**	**0.204**	**0.185**
	(0.058)	(0.065)	(0.070)	(0.061)	(0.068)	(0.074)
Education	0.026	−0.019	−0.013	−0.069	−0.064	−0.101
	(0.054)	(0.051)	(0.057)	(0.062)	(0.064)	(0.057)
Class	**−0.294**	**−0.247**	**−0.367**	**−0.582**	**−0.860**	**−0.543**
	(0.101)	(0.105)	(0.117)	(0.122)	(0.122)	(0.127)
Gender	−0.031	0.110	−0.048	−0.056	0.062	0.060
	(0.108)	(0.105)	(0.115)	(0.100)	(0.114)	(0.103)
Age	0.072	0.004	0.021	−0.038	0.016	0.084
	(0.041)	(0.039)	(0.046)	(0.052)	(0.052)	(0.051)
PRI supporter	**−0.326**	**−0.342**	−0.237	−0.069	**−0.443**	−0.124
	(0.161)	(0.149)	(0.170)	(0.175)	(0.216)	(0.180)
PAN supporter	−0.217	**−0.287**	−0.189	−0.209	−0.338	−0.173
	(0.158)	(0.137)	(0.153)	(0.179)	(0.226)	(0.191)
PRD supporter	−0.118	−0.205	−0.157	0.122	−0.264	−0.034
	(0.221)	(0.219)	(0.248)	(0.236)	(0.280)	(0.231)
Rural	0.018	0.103	−0.001	−0.025	−0.050	−0.019
	(0.107)	(0.090)	(0.098)	(0.143)	(0.170)	(0.143)
Chihuahua	**−0.433**	0.133	−0.173	−0.065	**−0.967**	−0.127
	(0.220)	(0.217)	(0.196)	(0.257)	(0.282)	(0.252)
Michoacán	**−1.058**	**−0.469**	**−0.753**	**−0.642**	**−1.520**	**−0.420**
	(0.208)	(0.213)	(0.186)	(0.285)	(0.294)	(0.273)
Puebla	**−1.121**	**−0.572**	**−0.902**	**−0.853**	**−1.745**	**−0.914**
	(0.198)	(0.210)	(0.191)	(0.264)	(0.273)	(0.232)
Cut 1	**−2.921**	**−2.359**	**−2.958**	**−4.209**	**−5.228**	**−3.537**
	(0.451)	(0.421)	(0.383)	(0.545)	(0.591)	(0.522)
Cut 2	**−0.895**	**−0.442**	**−1.110**	**−1.975**	**−3.423**	**−1.432**
	(0.435)	(0.429)	(0.376)	(0.579)	(0.597)	(0.523)

Source: Authors' compilations.
Notes: Standard errors in parentheses. Boldface indicates coefficient is statistically significant at $p < .05$. N = 1,598.
Each dependent variable is coded on a 3-point ordinal scale according to whether the person responded that a violation was "always," "sometimes," or "never" justified. Thus, increasing values on the dependent variables indicate greater proceduralism.

Table 4A.8   Argentina: Models of Proceduralism Responses

Dependent Variable	(1) Taxes	(2) Claim	(3) Military	(4) Stolen	(5) Corrupt	(6) Admission
Model	Ordered logit	Ordered logit	Ordered logit	Ordered logit	Ordered logit	Ordered logit
Income	**0.089**	**0.110**	−0.031	0.083	0.041	0.049
	(0.036)	(0.040)	(0.030)	(0.054)	(0.092)	(0.046)
Education	0.017	0.050	0.039	0.019	0.113	0.013
	(0.031)	(0.035)	(0.031)	(0.046)	(0.078)	(0.041)
Housing	−0.034	0.017	**0.198**	0.001	**0.382**	0.033
	(0.086)	(0.086)	(0.076)	(0.098)	(0.181)	(0.104)
Gender	−0.043	−0.003	0.148	**0.512**	0.110	0.084
	(0.092)	(0.109)	(0.090)	(0.135)	(0.249)	(0.108)
Age	**0.015**	**0.018**	−0.012	**0.043**	**0.034**	**0.027**
	(0.003)	(0.003)	(0.003)	(0.006)	(0.009)	(0.005)
Peronist supporter	−0.172	**−0.369**	−0.131	−0.293	−0.512	−0.227
	(0.121)	(0.132)	(0.120)	(0.174)	(0.330)	(0.131)
Radical supporter	0.130	−0.281	−0.144	−0.071	−0.128	0.333
	(0.168)	(0.158)	(0.162)	(0.223)	(0.442)	(0.227)
Log population	**−0.071**	**−0.117**	0.022	−0.072	0.000	−0.018
	(0.036)	(0.041)	(0.046)	(0.050)	(0.072)	(0.050)
Buenos Aires	0.056	0.033	−0.240	0.057	0.429	**0.921**
	(0.174)	(0.188)	(0.150)	(0.246)	(0.471)	(0.215)
Córdoba	0.205	−0.295	−0.002	0.157	−0.385	0.162
	(0.204)	(0.190)	(0.173)	(0.285)	(0.427)	(0.221)
Misiones	0.354	−0.269	0.170	−0.176	−0.003	0.429
	(0.231)	(0.204)	(0.238)	(0.270)	(0.474)	(0.251)
Cut 1	**−2.115**	**−2.856**	0.404	**−2.337**	−1.784	**−2.108**
	(0.530)	(0.636)	(0.681)	(0.753)	(1.149)	(0.749)
Cut 2	20.474	−1.079	**2.019**	−0.431	−0.412	0.281
	(0.530)	(0.639)	(0.686)	(0.755)	(1.170)	(0.698)

Source: Authors' compilations.
Notes: Standard errors in parentheses. Boldface indicates coefficient is statistically significant at $p < .05$. N = 1,920.

Table 4A.9 Argentina: Multinomial Logit Models of Responses on Taxes, Gate-Crashing, and Military Service

Dependent Variable	(1) Is It Justified to Evade Taxes? (Compared with "Sometimes")		(2) To Enter an Event Without Paying? (Compared with "Sometimes")		(3) To Avoid [Compulsory] Military Service? (Compared with "Sometimes")	
	Always	Never	Always	Never	Always	Never
Income	−0.091	0.075	0.080	0.063	0.017	−0.031
	(0.065)	(0.039)	(0.127)	(0.051)	(0.039)	(0.051)
Education	−0.073	−0.007	−0.101	−0.001	**−0.071**	−0.046
	(0.060)	(0.032)	(0.113)	(0.044)	(0.036)	(0.048)
Housing	−0.227	−0.111	−0.270	−0.012	−0.163	0.096
	(0.134)	(0.091)	(0.241)	(0.104)	(0.085)	(0.129)
Gender	**−0.489**	**−0.201**	0.091	0.111	**−0.282**	−0.212
	(0.171)	(0.098)	(0.313)	(0.113)	(0.121)	(0.158)
Age	−0.000	**0.016**	−0.014	**0.026**	**0.014**	0.003
	(0.006)	(0.003)	(0.016)	(0.005)	(0.004)	(0.005)
Peronist supporter	0.159	−0.130	0.130	−0.214	0.171	0.049
	(0.228)	(0.126)	(0.354)	(0.142)	(0.142)	(0.188)
Radical supporter	0.111	0.172	0.208	0.354	0.178	0.034
	(0.269)	(0.177)	(0.593)	(0.222)	(0.181)	(0.226)
Log population	**0.190**	−0.013	−0.077	−0.028	0.019	0.077
	(0.056)	(0.039)	(0.097)	(0.049)	(0.041)	(0.080)
Buenos Aires	0.177	0.127	−0.139	**0.915**	**0.368**	0.208
	(0.315)	(0.194)	(0.598)	(0.222)	(0.167)	(0.239)
Córdoba	**0.681**	**0.480**	0.101	0.180	0.219	0.392
	(0.296)	(0.223)	(0.564)	(0.226)	(0.204)	(0.289)
Misiones	**0.720**	**0.631**	0.625	**0.557**	0.200	**0.686**
	(0.349)	(0.239)	(0.502)	(0.256)	(0.240)	(0.350)
Constant	**−2.929**	−0.757	−0.164	0.100	0.187	−1.887
	(0.901)	(0.593)	(1.431)	(0.686)	(0.619)	(1.136)

Source: Authors' compilations.
Notes: Standard errors in parentheses. Boldface indicates coefficient is statistically significant at $p < .05$. N = 1,920.
The coefficients relate the probabilities of "always" and "never" responses to the baseline category of "sometimes," conditional on values of the independent variables. When both "always" and "never" responses are statistically significant and carry the same sign, this indicates that a change in the explanatory variable either increases or decreases the probability of a person being a contingent consenter, relative to being either a law flouter or a law abider.

Chapter 5

Trust and Democratization

IN AN effort to explain why the pace of democratization and of the deepening of democracy has been quick in some regions of Mexico and Argentina and slow in others, we begin by testing the social capital approach. Does a richer civic culture produce the differences we have observed in political culture and in the quality of democracy across regions? Finding scant support for social capital theory, we then turn to other propositions. For decades, theorists have posited that economic development encourages countries to democratize. Does it also encourage a deepening of regional democracies within countries? If so, why? Our discussion in chapter 1 identified the following sort of scenario. In a poor and unequal region of a democratic country, parties deploy the strategy of political clientelism to win votes. That is, they trade minor individualized payments as quid pro quos for political support. As the region undergoes economic development and as the middle class grows, clientelism becomes a decreasingly viable strategy. It becomes too expensive for parties to proffer individualized payments to middle-class constituents, and the clientelist equilibrium collapses. But the political class discovers that building bonds of accountability with citizens enhances the power and scope of the state. Hence, if development occurs, it encourages practices and a culture of accountability.

Here we look for evidence that a process like this stylized one actually explains the differing pace of democratization across regions in Mexico and Argentina.

Does Social Capital Improve Democracy?

If the social capital theory of democracy is right, the following propositions should be sustained by our data:

- In regions where democracy works best, people should be more involved in civic associations.

- People involved in civic associations should evince greater interpersonal trust of their fellow citizens.

- People involved in civic associations should show greater institutional trust in government.

- People involved in civic associations should be more willing to comply with burdensome demands of the government, such as paying taxes or complying with military service.

We asked survey respondents a range of questions about their involvement in civic associations (see tables 5.1 and 5.2). We asked whether they had, in the past twelve months, attended any meetings about a problem in their community, neighborhood, or school (Meet). In a separate question, we read a list of kinds of associations and asked which, if any, the respondent belonged to. We asked a general question about how many associations the participant belonged to (Belong). We asked how much time, summed over the past twelve months, the respondent had spent on the activities of this association (Time).[1] We asked: "During the past twelve months, have you collaborated with people who are not family members to solve a common problem?" (Comprob). We asked: "Aside from work duties, during the past 12 months did you collaborate with people with whom you work to solve a common problem?" (Workprob). We also asked how many times each month the respondent attended mass or other religious services (Religion).

Democracy and Civic Participation

Argentina   Twenty-four percent of respondents participated in at least one organization (Belong). The participation rate was higher when our sample listened to a list of kinds of associations: 26 percent said they belonged to some association (not shown). To those who did belong, we asked how much time they spent on the activities of these associations (Time). Those who did participate participated heavily: by far the largest number said they spent more than a quarter of the year in these activities. The most frequently mentioned association, in the land of Maradona, was the sports club (Sport).[2] In response to our question, "During the past twelve months, have you collaborated with people who are not family members to solve a common problem?" 43 percent said they had, 56 percent that they had not (Comprob). In response

Table 5.1 Argentina: Responses to Questions About Participation, by Region

	Mar del Plata	Buenos Aires	Córdoba	Misiones	Total
Meet					
During the past twelve months, did you attend a meeting about a problem in your community or school?					
Yes	16%	19%	20%	21%	20%
	(76)	(91)	(95)	(129)	(391)
No	83%	80%	79%	73%	79%
	(400)	(382)	(377)	(350)	(1509)
No answer	1%	2%	2%	0.2%	1%
	(4)	(7)	(8)	(1)	(20)
Belong					
How many organizations do you belong to?					
None	75%	81%	71%	77%	76%
	(358)	(387)	(339)	(371)	(1455)
One	19%	14%	22%	17%	18%
	(92)	(66)	(103)	(79)	(340)
Two to three	5%	4%	7%	6%	6%
	(25)	(21)	(31)	(28)	(105)
More than three	1%	1%	1%	0.4%	1%
	(5)	(6)	(6)	(2)	(19)
No answer	0%	0%	0.2%	0%	0.1%
	(0)	(0)	(1)	(0)	(1)

(Table continues on p. 132.)

Table 5.1 *Continued*

	Mar del Plata	Buenos Aires	Córdoba	Misiones	Total
Time					
During the past twelve months, how much time did you dedicate to these organizations?					
One day	7%	8%	4%	3%	6%
	(9)	(8)	(6)	(3)	(26)
One week	19%	9%	11%	7%	12%
	(23)	(9)	(16)	(8)	(56)
Two to three weeks	14%	10%	20%	23%	17%
	(17)	(10)	(28)	(25)	(80)
One to two months	15%	13%	15%	10%	13%
	(19)	(12)	(21)	(11)	(63)
Three or more months	38%	55%	47%	54%	48%
	(47)	(53)	(67)	(59)	(226)
No answer	7%	4%	4%	3%	5%
	(9)	(4)	(5)	(3)	(21)
Comprob					
During the past twelve months, have you collaborated with a nonrelative to solve a problem that your community faces?					
Yes	36%	40%	45%	51%	43%
	(171)	(194)	(215)	(244)	(824)
No	64%	59%	55%	47%	56%
	(306)	(283)	(262)	(227)	(1078)
No answer	1%	1%	1%	2%	1%
	(3)	(3)	(3)	(9)	(124)

Workprob

During the past twelve months, have you collaborated with someone from work to solve a common problem?

Yes	35%	29%	42%	36%	34%
	(678)	(141)	(202)	(171)	(164)
No	63%	70%	54%	62%	65%
	(1207)	(336)	(261)	(298)	(312)
No answer	2%	1%	4%	2%	1%
	(35)	(3)	(17)	(11)	(4)

Religion

How many times per month do you attend mass or other religious services?

None	45%	24%	47%	58%	53%
	(871)	(115)	(224)	(277)	(255)
One or two	32%	42%	31%	27%	29%
	(617)	(199)	(150)	(128)	(140)
Three or four	11%	17%	13%	8%	7%
	(212)	(82)	(61)	(37)	(32)
More than four	11%	17%	9%	8%	10%
	(207)	(82)	(42)	(38)	(47)
No answer	1%	1%	1%	0%	1%
	(13)	(4)	(3)	(0)	(6)

Source: Authors' compilations.
Note: Total number of responses in parentheses.

Table 5.2 Mexico: Responses to Questions About Participation, by Region

	Baja California	Chihuahua	Michoacán	Puebla	Total
Meet					
During the last twelve months, have you attended an assembly or meeting about a problem in your community or school?					
Yes	15%	31%	26%	22%	23%
	(60)	(122)	(105)	(86)	(373)
No	81%	65%	64%	73%	71%
	(324)	(259)	(257)	(290)	(1130)
No answer	4%	4%	10%	6%	6%
	(16)	(17)	(38)	(24)	(95)
Belong					
At this moment, to how many organizations do you belong?					
None	85%	82%	73%	79%	80%
	(340)	(326)	(293)	(315)	(1274)
One	11%	14%	15%	11%	13%
	(44)	(54)	(61)	(43)	(202)
Two	2%	3%	4%	2%	2%
	(6)	(11)	(14)	(8)	(39)
Three or more	1%	1%	2%	1%	1%
	(4)	(2)	(7)	(2)	(15)
No answer	2%	1%	6%	8%	4%
	(6)	(5)	(25)	(32)	(68)

Time

During the last twelve months, about how many hours per week on average have you dedicated to activities of these organizations?

One to two	45%	42%	36%	27%	36%
	(27)	(30)	(37)	(23)	(117)
Three to five	13%	31%	17%	29%	23%
	(8)	(22)	(18)	(25)	(73)
Six to eight	18%	11%	7%	0%	8%
	(11)	(8)	(8)	(0)	(27)
More than eight	12%	11%	15%	5%	11%
	(7)	(8)	(16)	(4)	(35)
No answer	12%	6%	26%	39%	22%
	(7)	(4)	(28)	(33)	(72)

Comprob

During the last twelve months, have you collaborated with other people who are not your relatives to try to resolve some problem in your community?

Yes	25%	29%	25%	21%	25%
	(100)	(116)	(100)	(85)	(401)
No	73%	66%	69%	71%	70%
	(292)	(263)	(274)	(284)	(1113)
No answer	2%	5%	7%	8%	5%
	(8)	(19)	(26)	(31)	(84)

(Table continues on p. 136.)

Table 5.2 *Continued*

	Baja California	Chihuahua	Michoacán	Puebla	Total
Workprob Other than work duties, during the past twelve months have you collaborated with people you work with to try to resolve a common problem?					
Yes	28% (111)	27% (109)	24% (97)	29% (117)	27% (434)
No	71% (284)	67% (268)	68% (271)	62% (248)	67% (1071)
No answer	1% (5)	5% (21)	8% (32)	9% (35)	6% (93)
Religion About how many times per month do you attend mass or another religious service?					
None	33% (130)	25% (100)	18% (71)	19% (74)	23% (375)
One to two	37% (146)	42% (166)	38% (151)	37% (146)	38% (609)
Three to four	18% (71)	26% (103)	32% (127)	29% (115)	26% (416)
More than four	13% (53)	7% (27)	13% (50)	13% (51)	11% (181)
No answer	0% (0)	1% (2)	0% (1)	4% (14)	1% (17)

Source: Authors' compilations.
Notes: Total number of responses in parentheses.

to our question, "Aside from work duties, during the past twelve months did you collaborate with people with whom you work to solve a common problem?", 35 percent answered yes, 63 percent no (Work-prob). In response to our question about church attendance, 45 percent responded that they never attend, 32 percent that they attend once or twice per month, and 11 percent each responded that they attended three or four times, or more than four times, per month.

Was the associational life of people in more democratic regions especially rich? Cross-tabulations indicate that, if anything, the opposite was true. The number of people participating to solve a common problem rose monotonically across the four regions, from 171 in Mar del Plata to 244 in Misiones. Among those who said they belonged, people in Mar del Plata dedicated less time to their associations than did people in Misiones (Time). In Mar del Plata, among those who participated, 38 percent dedicated three to four months to their organization over the space of a year; the corresponding figure for Misiones was 54 percent. Multivariate analysis (not shown) confirms these trends. The only kind of association that Mar del Plata residents participated in more than people from other regions was sports clubs. In the presence of controls, people in Misiones participated in "other" associations—ones not included in our list—significantly more frequently than people from other regions. Misiones residents also worked with neighbors to solve a common problem significantly more frequently than did people from other regions. To the extent, then, that we find regional differences in community participation, they run against the grain of the social capital theory of democracy.

Misiones residents were also more churchgoing than residents of the other three regions. They were half as likely as those from Mar del Plata or Buenos Aires to say that they never went to church, and twice as likely as those from the other three regions to attend services weekly. The greater church attendance of Misiones residents holds up to statistical controls (see table 5A.1 in the appendix at the end of this chapter). Our results counter the view that modernization reduces religiosity: socioeconomic status had no effect on religious attendance. In contrast, gender, age, and region explained much of the variation in levels of religious attendance. The simulated expected probability that a young man from Mar del Plata would never attend a religious service was 72 percent. The probability that an elderly woman from Misiones would never attend was a mere 9 percent. The young male Mar del Plata resident had only a 3 percent chance of attending more than four services per month; the elderly female Misiones resident had a 47 percent chance. But the critical point is that religious associational life, like secular associational life, was richer in regions where democracy worked badly.

Mexico   The effect of cross-regional differences in democracy on civic participation was roughly the same in Mexico as in Argentina. Twenty-five percent of our full sample belonged to at least one of the associations we listed, although, in a separate question, the participation rate fell below 20 percent (see table 5.2, Belong). Most of those who did participate spent less than five hours per week on association activities. About one-quarter of the sample had attended a community meeting (23 percent), or collaborated with others in their community (25 percent) or workplace (27 percent). For most forms of participation, we find no strong cross-state differences. But where we do find differences, they were that people in Baja California, our most democratic state, participated less in civic associations, not more.

Even among people from the same income strata and of the same ages and genders, those from Baja California were less likely to have attended a meeting than were those from the other three states (see table 5A.2 in the appendix at the end of this chapter). People from Chihuahua and Michoacán were more likely than those from Baja California to have worked with others to solve a common problem. Our Chihuahua, Michoacán, and Puebla samples also all had higher incidences of group membership than did our Baja California Norte sample, although the difference was only statistically significant in the case of Michoacán. Clearly, the evidence does not support the proposition that more democratic regions are places denser in social capital.

Civic Associations and Interpersonal Trust

Do people who participate in civic associations trust other citizens more? To find out, we asked a series of questions to gauge levels of interpersonal trust (that is, trust in other people, as opposed to trust in politicians). We asked: "If you go away on a trip, do you have any neighbors whom you could trust to take care of your house?" (Neighbor); "Do you believe that most people would take advantage of you if they had a chance?" (Advantage); and "Which statement is closest to your way of thinking: You can trust a majority of people, you can only trust a minority of people, or I don't trust anyone?" (Trust).[3]

Argentina   Table 5.3 reports responses to these questions. Multivariate analysis (see table 5A.3) shows that wealthier people, men, older people, and (in one model) residents of smaller towns and cities were more personally trusting. People from Misiones were less willing than those from Mar del Plata and Córdoba to trust their house to a neighbor's care. Hence we fail to find strong relationships between region and

Table 5.3   Argentina: Responses to Questions About Interpersonal Trust, by Region

	Mar del Plata	Buenos Aires	Córdoba	Misiones	Total
Neighbor If you go away on a trip, do you have a neighbor whom you could trust to care for your house?					
Yes	75%	80%	75%	68%	75%
	(360)	(383)	(359)	(328)	(1430)
No	25%	20%	24%	30%	25%
	(113)	(97)	(117)	(146)	(473)
No answer	2%	0%	1%	1%	1%
	(7)	(0)	(4)	(6)	(17)
Advantage Do you believe most people would take advantage of you if they had the chance?					
Yes	55%	53%	50%	57%	54%
	(263)	(254)	(241)	(272)	(1030)
No	42%	45%	45%	37%	42%
	(203)	(215)	(214)	(178)	(810)
No answer	3%	2%	5%	6%	4%
	(14)	(11)	(25)	(30)	(80)
Trust Which is closest to your way of thinking?					
You can trust a majority of people	20%	26%	23%	18%	22%
	(96)	(123)	(111)	(84)	(414)
You can only trust a minority	61%	61%	56%	59%	59%
	(294)	(291)	(271)	(284)	(1140)
I don't trust anyone	18%	13%	20%	22%	18%
	(87)	(64)	(95)	(105)	(351)
No answer	1%	0.4%	1%	2%	1%
	(3)	(2)	(3)	(7)	(15)

Source: Authors' compilations.
Note: Total number of responses in parentheses.

interpersonal trust; if our evidence speaks to a relationship, it is that less democratic regions are less interpersonally trusting.

Do people who participate in civic associations trust others more? We find some evidence that they do. Multivariate analysis (see table

5A.3) confirms that people who worked with others to solve problems in their neighborhoods (Comprob) were significantly more likely to trust a majority of people and to be willing to entrust their house to a neighbor and to express generalized interpersonal trust. The effects of participation on trust are nonnegligible. Compare, for instance, social capital effects with class effects. Shifting from a poor to a wealthy person increased the probability of the response, "you can trust a majority of people" only modestly, from 13 percent to 20 percent. Shifting from a person who does not participate to one who participates at the highest level has a much larger effect, increasing the probability of the trusting response from 15 percent to 40 percent.[4]

The direction of causality is open to debate: do people join civic associations because they trust people or do they trust people because they belong to associations? Whichever is true, we can conclude that, in Argentina, people who were active in civic associations tended to be especially trusting.

Mexico   In Mexico as well, we find that civic involvement increases interpersonal trust (or, perhaps, that personal trust increases civic involvement). We report answers to our trust question broken down by region in table 5.4. The first panel of the table shows a moderate relationship between trust and region: respondents in the more democratic states are more likely to say that they would trust a neighbor to watch their house (Neighbor). But the other two questions do not reveal any cross-regional pattern, and multivariate analysis (see table 5A.4) indicates that the pattern for the Neighbor variable in table 5.4 is not robust.

As with Argentina, the multivariate analysis does offer some evidence to support the proposition that people who collaborated with neighbors to solve a common problem also, in significantly higher numbers, trusted their neighbors and believed that most people were trustworthy. Those in our sample who belonged to at least one civic organization were slightly more trusting, though the estimated effect is only weakly significant.

Civic Associations and Institutional Trust

What we really care about are the political implications of social capital. Hence a crucial question is whether civic involvement had any effect on institutional trust. The claim of Robert Putnam (1993, 2000) and others is that social capital and the interpersonal trust that comes with it make government work better: it allows people to be confident

Table 5.4   Mexico: Responses to Questions About Interpersonal Trust, by State

	Baja California	Chihuahua	Michoacán	Puebla	Total
Neighbor					
If you were to go away on a trip, do you have a neighbor whom you could trust to care for your house?					
Yes	54%	55%	42%	43%	49%
	(216)	(220)	(166)	(173)	(775)
No	41%	41%	43%	44%	42%
	(165)	(162)	(170)	(177)	(674)
No answer	5%	4%	16%	13%	9%
	(19)	(16)	(64)	(50)	(149)
Advantage					
Do you believe most people would take advantage of you if they had the chance?					
Yes	45%	53%	39%	36%	43%
	(180)	(210)	(157)	(142)	(689)
No	43%	42%	41%	44%	42%
	(171)	(167)	(164)	(176)	(678)
No answer	12%	5%	20%	21%	14%
	(49)	(21)	(79)	(82)	(231)
Trust					
Which is closest to your way of thinking?					
You can trust a majority of people	24%	29%	24%	30%	27%
	(94)	(115)	(96)	(119)	(424)
You can only trust a minority	48%	54%	35%	38%	43%
	(193)	(213)	(139)	(150)	(695)
I don't trust anyone	24%	13%	24%	21%	21%
	(94)	(52)	(97)	(85)	(328)
No answer	5%	5%	17%	12%	9%
	(19)	(18)	(68)	(46)	(151)

Source: Authors' compilations.
Note: Total number of responses in parentheses.

that others are doing their part to monitor the government. Did Argentine and Mexican respondents who were active in civic associations trust other voters and third parties to monitor the government?

Argentina   The Argentine findings could scarcely depart more sharply from the predictions of the social capital theory of democracy. In Argentina, social capital discouraged institutional trust, and it did not reduce personal trust in politicians. The more organizations a respondent belonged to, the less likely he or she was to interpret good government performance as induced by institutional constraints. And respondents who worked with their neighbors to resolve a common problem were also less prone to trust institutions and were equally prone to personally trust politicians. Recall that Services is a dummy for people who said that governments behave responsively when they are under the watchful eye of other institutions, and Efficient is a dummy for people who said that, when municipalities offer efficient public services, this is because they want to be reelected, not because they are staffed by good people. In the regression models in table 5.5, the effect of participation on dampening institutional trust is revealed by the negative and significant coefficients relating Belong, a measure of how many organizations the respondent belonged to, and Comprob, a dummy for people who said they had joined with others to try to solve a common problem, to Services and Efficient.[5]

Figure 5.1 illustrates the capacity of civic involvement to dampen institutional trust. A Misiones resident, someone otherwise typical of our sample, had a 55-percent chance of attributing good government service to electoral constraints (Service) if she belonged to no organizations and did not in the past year collaborate with others to solve a common problem. The chance drops to 32 percent if she belonged to more than three organizations and did collaborate.[6]

A critical part of the social capital theory of democracy is that people heavily endowed with social capital trust each other to hold governments accountable. But in Argentina we find no such effect. Active and collaborative respondents were no more inclined than the inactive and the isolated to say that their fellow voters paid attention to programs rather than to special favors in deciding which party to support. Active participants were also no more likely to say that their fellow voters supported parties that showed concern for all rather than ones that gave out gifts. Churchgoers were no more likely to believe that their neighbors would hold politicians accountable. People who were active and, by a range of measures, richly endowed with social capital, were no more likely to perceive their neighbors as using performance criteria to evaluate incumbent politicians. We simply find scant evidence that social capital produced the belief that one's fellow citizens will hold government accountable.[7]

Mexico   Our Mexican samples on the whole—like our Argentine ones—failed to confirm the prediction that social capital encourages

Table 5.5   Argentina: The Impact of Social Capital on Political Trust

Dependent Variable	(1) Services	(2) Efficient	(3) Trustpol
Model	Logit	Logit	Ordered logit
Income	−0.043	0.018	**0.099**
	(0.044)	(0.039)	(0.034)
Education	0.069	−0.048	0.011
	(0.038)	(0.038)	(0.029)
Housing	0.004	−0.050	−0.100
	(0.075)	(0.089)	(0.069)
Gender	**−0.350**	−0.037	0.102
	(0.103)	(0.104)	(0.094)
Age	**−0.012**	**−0.016**	0.004
	(0.004)	(0.004)	(0.004)
Peronist	−0.204	0.068	**0.585**
	(0.116)	(0.126)	(0.125)
Radical	−0.053	−0.046	**0.402**
	(0.144)	(0.143)	(0.155)
Log population	0.000	0.033	**−0.125**
	(0.037)	(0.047)	(0.036)
Buenos Aires	**−0.404**	0.101	0.055
	(0.183)	(0.187)	(0.161)
Córdoba	**−0.594**	−0.080	−0.201
	(0.185)	(0.221)	(0.192)
Misiones	**−1.029**	−0.298	**0.389**
	(0.180)	(0.221)	(0.183)
Belong	**−0.230**	−0.129	**0.191**
	(0.088)	(0.089)	(0.092)
Comprob	**−0.275**	**−0.411**	0.171
	(0.112)	(0.119)	(0.115)
Constant	**1.610**	**1.917**	
	(0.538)	(0.700)	
Cut 1			**−1.368**
			(0.568)
Cut 2			**2.044**
			(0.579)
Cut 3			**3.294**
			(0.621)

Source: Authors' compilations.
Notes: Standard errors in parentheses. Boldface indicates coefficient is statistically significant at $p < .05$. N = 1,920.

Figure 5.1   Argentina: Simulated Expected Effect of Civic Participation on Institutional Trust

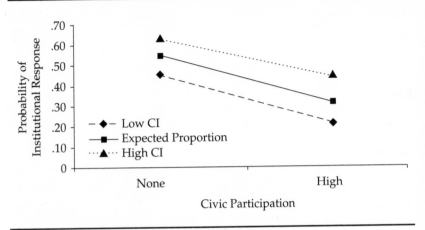

Source: Authors' compilations.
Notes: Simulated expected percentages of response, "governments provide good services when they are under the watch of the courts, congress, or the press." *Clarify* simulations, holding other explanatory variables at their sample means. "None" means lowest score on Belong and Comprob variables; "High" means highest score on each.

institutional trust. The only evidence that it does is that participants in civic associations were significantly less likely to believe that their fellow voters are swayed by campaign handouts (analysis not shown). But those who collaborated with neighbors were less likely to offer an institutional trust answer to the questions about service provision and government efficiency and more likely to say the politicians were personally trustworthy (see table 5.6). Thus the balance of the evidence contradicts the hypothesis that social capital encourages institutional trust in Mexico.

Civic Associations and the Rule of Law

Perhaps, as Boix and Posner (1998) have explained, social capital helps democracy work better by giving participants more optimistic expectations about others' compliance with burdensome rules and laws. Our questions about proceduralism do not allow us to test this proposition directly. But they do allow us to answer the question, "Are people who are especially active in civic associations themselves more likely to support compliance?"

The short answer is, no. People who belonged to associations or at least met with others to solve problems were not more likely to express

Table 5.6 Mexico: The Impact of Social Capital on Political Trust

Dependent Variable	(1) Services	(2) Efficient	(3) Trustpol
Model	Logit	Logit	Ordered logit
Income	0.073	0.031	0.059
	(0.070)	(0.053)	(0.055)
Education	−0.015	0.042	0.001
	(0.058)	(0.066)	(0.052)
Class	−0.064	**−0.297**	**0.288**
	(0.090)	(0.128)	(0.098)
Gender	−0.122	−0.155	0.053
	(0.122)	(0.118)	(0.104)
Age	0.045	−0.055	0.055
	(0.046)	(0.057)	(0.035)
PRI supporter	**−0.390**	**−0.406**	**0.562**
	(0.180)	(0.181)	(0.148)
PAN supporter	−0.020	−0.258	**0.469**
	(0.189)	(0.179)	(0.158)
PRD supporter	−0.217	0.397	0.414
	(0.265)	(0.279)	(0.250)
Rural	−0.154	0.100	−0.006
	(0.101)	(0.109)	(0.097)
Chihuahua	−0.282	**−0.432**	0.226
	(0.215)	(0.201)	(0.152)
Michoacán	−0.166	**−0.455**	**0.659**
	(0.198)	(0.201)	(0.224)
Puebla	**−0.467**	−0.201	**0.577**
	(0.203)	(0.185)	(0.188)
Belong	0.061	−0.188	−0.081
	(0.114)	(0.124)	(0.115)
Comprob	**−0.367**	**−0.540**	**0.642**
	(0.144)	(0.129)	(0.123)
Constant	**0.898**	**1.581**	
	(0.415)	(0.441)	
Cut 1			0.211
			(0.389)
Cut 2			**2.423**
			(0.406)
Cut 3			**4.302**
			(0.421)

Source: Authors' compilations.
Notes: Standard errors in parentheses. Boldface indicates coefficient is statistically significant at p < .05. N = 1,598.

support for paying taxes, foregoing undeserved services and benefits, or complying with military service; nor did they expect their neighbors to support parties that emphasized program or universalism over particularistic favors.[8] In Mexico, the results are even less propitious for social capital theory. Mexicans who were active in civic associations were less likely to comply and to expect their neighbors to comply. They were significantly less likely, for instance, to say that they would forgo undeserved goods or services or always pay their bus fares (see tables 5A.5 and 5A.6).

Causes of Variation in the Consolidation of Democracy

If social capital does little to improve the quality of democracy, or to lead people to expect accountable government, what alternative theoretical approach do our data support? Here, we explore two possibilities.

Economic Development Enhances Democracy

A venerable line of thinking in comparative politics is that economic development makes democracy more likely to appear and, once it has appeared, more stable. Does the relationship between development and democratization extend to regional democratization within countries?

Argentina   The first hypothesis we test is that individuals with high incomes hold beliefs more consistent with a culture of democracy. In chapter 4 we considered income as a control variable in the analysis of democratic consolidation and institutional trust, because we knew that the regions where democracy is more consolidated are also regions where incomes are higher. Here we take a fresh look at income as a variable of interest, testing the hypothesis that wealth produces prodemocratic beliefs.

Table 5.7 shows striking differences in self-reported family income by region. The proportion of the sample reporting low incomes rises monotonically as we move from more to less consolidated regions, and middle incomes decrease sharply (though not monotonically). Particularly noteworthy is the gap between Misiones and the rest: 23 percent more respondents in Misiones than in Córdoba (the next poorest province) reported low incomes, and 14 percent more people in Córdoba than in Misiones reported middle incomes. (These differences are confirmed by regression estimations of income, where, holding other factors constant, Misiones residents had substantially lower incomes.)

Table 5.7   Argentina: Self-Reported Family Income, by Region

	Mar del Plata	Buenos Aires	Córdoba	Misiones
Low income	27%	33%	34%	57%
Middle income	59	51	53	39
High income	14	16	12	5
Total	101%	100%	99%	101%

Source: Authors' compilation.
Notes: Low: up to 300 pesos per month.
Middle: 301 to 1,000 pesos per month.
High: More than 1,001 pesos per month.
Columns do not sum to 100 percent due to rounding.

Given the correlation of regional income and consolidation, we must consider the possibility that the beliefs we have studied are unrelated to democratic consolidation and are instead related to wealth.

In fact, wealthier Argentines tended to personally trust politicians more than poor ones did.[9] We can only speculate about why this is true. As in most democracies, in Argentina the political class is drawn from among lawyers, professionals, and business elites. Citizens with higher incomes may simply be more likely to know some officeholders personally or to feel that these are people like themselves and hence can be trusted. For whatever reason, far from personal wealth predicting institutional trust, it had the opposite effect.

Furthermore, in the presence of controls for income, regional differences remain. Simulations show that regional effects are stronger than income effects. We compare the simulated expected probabilities that wealthy versus poor people, and that people from Mar del Plata versus Misiones, would believe that "governments provides good services" when they are "under the watch of the courts, the congress, or the press," and not because they are staffed by "good, committed people." Assume first a man from Mar del Plata with a reported household income of zero (that is, all adult family members were unemployed). His probability of the institutional answer is 78 percent. If his household income were to rise to more than 1,000 pesos per month, the probability of an institutional answer would fall to 70 percent. Then take the same man and set his income at the median for the sample. If he resides in Mar del Plata, his probability of offering an institutional answer is 74 percent. If he resides in Misiones, it falls to 49 percent (see figure 5.2). Both income and region make a difference, but region makes the larger difference. And economic development, as reflected in higher incomes, did not cause a democratization of people's political beliefs.

In another way, however, increasing wealth did favor the consolidation of democracy: it undermined clientelism. We can see this by ex-

Figure 5.2   Simulated Expected Probability of an Institutional Explanation for Why Governments Provide Good Services, by Income and Region

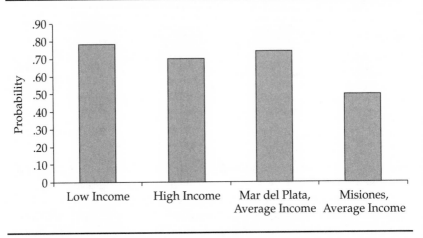

Source: Authors' compilations.
Note: Clarify simulation. We hold education level, quality of housing, and size of respondent's municipality at the sample median.

ploring how the income level of individuals shaped their links to political parties. Poorer and less educated people had stronger ties to parties. People who lived in low-quality housing were more likely than were their better-housed fellow citizens to have turned to a party representative for help in the past year, and they were more likely to imagine doing so if they lost their job. People with low incomes, little education, and low-quality housing were especially likely to have accepted a handout during the previous campaign and to have allowed the handout to influence their vote (see table 4A.4). Our interpretation is that, given diminishing marginal utility of income—the lower a person's income, the more he or she values a political "gift" of the same value— clientelist parties get more bang for their buck by targeting poor people (see Dixit and Londregan 1996; Calvo and Murillo 2004; Stokes 2005).

In chapter 4 we studied people's postures toward the rule of law. Economic development may encourage a democratic culture by instilling among citizens a respect for the rule of law. These citizens might themselves become more law abiding and might expect the same of their fellow citizens and of their leaders. Indeed we find some tendency toward proceduralism among wealthier Argentines. People with higher incomes were more in favor of paying taxes and of claiming government goods and services only when one truly deserves them (see table

4A.8). Also, people who lived in higher-quality housing were more in favor of complying with compulsory military service and more resentful of corrupt officials.[10]

Perhaps, however, it is not individuals' incomes but the level of development of communities that shapes democracy-promoting beliefs. We test this hypothesis by estimating the effect of municipal economic development on the beliefs of respondents who live there. Our measure of economic development is municipal expenditures per capita averaged over the two years 1998 and 1999, the period closest to the time of the survey (from late 2001 to early 2002) for which we have data. Our assumption is that the wealthier the municipality, the more revenues it can raise locally, and thus the more it can spend.[11] Our measure is not perfect: a municipality's revenues are partly a function of residents' resources, but also a function of the revenue-raising efforts of municipalities, as the Mar del Plata 2000 experience testifies.

In many respects, community economic development (as captured by municipal spending) did not appreciably influence beliefs about the trustworthiness of politicians, about how constrained politicians are by institutions, or about other voters' decision rules. But there are some hints of municipal development contributing to democratic consolidation by undermining clientelism. Independent of their personal incomes, the wealthier the community in which people lived, the more likely they were to perceive their neighbors as having supported the most locally popular party, because it was concerned about everyone and not because it had granted particularistic favors (see table 5.8). (In both cases, people in a Misiones municipality at the same level of economic development as Mar del Plata's remained more likely than residents of Mar del Plata to say that parties were popular because they gave out favors, and less likely to attribute responsiveness to reelection pressures.) In general, however, the absence of any effect of community wealth on other indicators of institutional trust makes us wary of making strong claims that economic development in itself promoted a democratic culture of skepticism in Argentina.

In sum, the incomes and socioeconomic status of individuals played a surprisingly small part in shaping democratic political culture in Argentina, as reflected in institutional trust in politicians. To the extent that income had an effect, it sometimes went against the modernization prediction that development promotes a democratic culture. The exceptions were the effect of development on the strategies of political parties. Development discouraged parties from practicing political clientelism. Development also encouraged commitment to the rule of law. But neither individual wealth nor community development effaced the impact of region, which remained to large degree irreducible to cross-regional economic differences.

Table 5.8   **Argentina: Effect of Municipal Economic
Development on Clientelism**

Dependent Variable	(1) Favor
Model	Logit
Income	−0.046
	(0.041)
Education	0.013
	(0.034)
Housing	0.081
	(0.087)
Gender	0.019
	(0.102)
Age	**−0.014**
	(0.004)
Peronist	**−0.823**
	(0.153)
Radical	−0.139
	(0.173)
Log population	0.086
	(0.043)
Municipal expenditures per capita	**−0.002**
	(0.001)
Buenos Aires	0.909
	(0.214)
Córdoba	**0.996**
	(0.203)
Misiones	**0.732**
	(0.300)
Constant	−0.578
	(0.741)

Source: Authors' compilations.
Notes: Standard errors in parentheses. Boldface indicates coefficient is
statistically significant at p < .05. N = 1,920.
Favor: dummy for response, "people support the most important party
in this neighborhood because it does favors for people."

Mexico Our findings in Mexico generally match our Argentine findings. We find a clear link between economic development and democracy, but our survey results lend less than overwhelming support to
hypotheses linking development and democratization to the forging of
a democratic political culture. As explained earlier, in Mexico there
were strong regional gradients in the pace and level of democratization.
Hence in Mexico we are able to test the development hypothesis with
electoral and socioeconomic data collected at the municipal level (see

Cleary 2004). We treat the PRI's vote share, and the opposition's ability to attain office, as measures of democratization and study the impact of development on democratization. As previous scholarship has shown (Hernández Valdez 2000), developmental theories of democratization generate roughly the same implications for comparisons across regions within a country as they do across countries, and generally explain democratization as a function of literacy, wealth, and urbanization. We test these propositions by estimating models of municipal political competition (see table 5.9).

Our dependent variables are two measures of electoral competition: the average vote share for the PRI in municipal elections in the 1990s, and a dummy variable indicating whether, before 2000, an opposition party ever defeated the PRI and was installed in the mayor's office. Our independent variables include each municipality's literacy rate, poverty rate, and total population (logged), as well as controls for turnout, population growth, the proportion of indigenous residents, and spending by the Programa Nacional de Solidaridad (PRONASOL), a broad infrastructure and development program run out of the president's office during the presidency of Carlos Salinas.[12] In models 2 and 4, we also include dummy variables for each of the states. The dataset includes virtually all municipalities that held elections in the 1990s.[13]

Indeed, development encouraged democratization. Models 1 and 2 in table 5.9 show that the PRI took a larger share of the vote in municipalities that were poor, illiterate, and sparsely populated.[14] Figure 5.3 is a simulation based on model 2. Holding all else equal, we expect the PRI to win an additional 10 percentage points in a municipality with high poverty and low literacy, versus one that is relatively wealthy and literate. We expect the PRI to win an additional 18 points in a small municipality (population thirty-two hundred) compared to a large one (population sixty-six thousand two hundred).[15] Models 3 and 4, which estimate the probability of party alternation in the mayor's office, show similar results. Poverty, literacy, and population size are not the only factors that matter. Higher voter turnout also predicts lower vote shares for the PRI and higher probabilities of party alternation. More lavish PRONASOL spending predicts higher support for the PRI—not surprisingly, given the political motivations of the program. Hence our findings in Mexico lend strong support to the hypothesis that development causes democratization: democratization was more likely in places that were more urban, more literate, and less poor.[16]

Along with electoral democratization in Mexico, did economic development also encourage the democratization of political culture? As with our Argentine surveys, we test a series of four propositions: that personal wealth is predictive of institutional trust, that poverty breeds clientelism, that personal wealth is related to postures toward the rule

Table 5.9   Causes of Municipal-Level Democratization in Mexico

Dependent Variable	(1) PRI Vote Share	(2) PRI Vote Share	(3) Alternation	(4) Alternation
Model	Log-Odds OLS	Log-Odds OLS	Logit	Logit
Turnout	**−1.662**	**−1.520**	**3.709**	**5.029**
(average 1990s)	(0.218)	(0.243)	(0.481)	(0.597)
Poverty rate	**0.984**	0.503	**−2.949**	**−2.549**
(1990)	(0.297)	(0.325)	(0.642)	(0.777)
Literacy rate	−0.241	**−1.014**	−0.234	**2.343**
(1990)	(0.276)	(0.334)	(0.588)	(0.781)
Log population	**−0.300**	**−0.283**	**0.346**	**0.482**
(1990)	(0.024)	(0.027)	(0.053)	(0.067)
Population growth	−0.171	**−0.455**	0.106	**1.011**
(percentage, 1990	(0.116)	(0.123)	(0.245)	(0.305)
to 2000)				
Indigenous	0.167	0.040	−0.454	−0.007
population	(0.112)	(0.129)	(0.241)	(0.300)
(1990)				
PRONASOL	**0.111**	**0.082**	**−0.313**	**−0.211**
(total per capita,	(0.024)	(0.025)	(0.076)	(0.083)
in thousands)				
State dummy	(excluded)	(included)	(excluded)	(included)
variables[a]				
Constant	**4.216**	**4.990**	**−4.046**	**−9.012**
	(0.378)	(0.571)	(0.830)	(1.273)
N	1953	1953	1953	1953
R-squared	0.172	0.250		
Percentage correctly			65.8	68.6
predicted				

Sources: Authors' analysis based on Banamex (2001); INEGI (2000).
Notes: Bold coefficients significant at $p < .05$; standard errors in parentheses.
[a]Model 2 includes a dummy variable for each state, save one. Model 4 includes the same dummy variables, except that three were dropped because of perfect collinearity with the dependent variable. Coefficients were not reported simply for presentational reasons.
PRI vote share: The vote share for the PRI in municipal elections, averaged for every election held in the 1990s.
Alternation: Dummy indicating whether the municipality had ever had party alternation in the mayor's office prior to the year 2000.
Turnout: average participation rate in municipal election held between 1990 and 1999.
Poverty rate: percentage of economically active population earning less than the official minimum wage, 1990.
Literacy rate: percentage of adult population literate, 1990.
Population: Natural log of the total municipal population, 1990.
Population growth: percentage increase in total municipal population, 1990 to 2000.
Indigenous: percentage of municipal population that speaks an indigenous language, 1990.
PRONASOL: Total PRONASOL spending per capita in the municipality, 1989 to 1994.

Figure 5.3   Mexico: Simulated Expected Vote Share for PRI

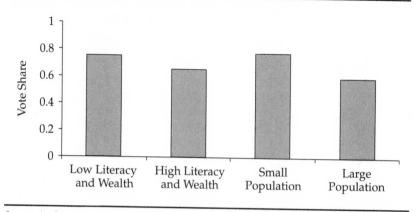

Source: Authors' compilations.
Notes: Low and high literacy and wealth, and small and large populations, refer to the 10th and 90th percentile scores in the sample for those two variables. *Clarify* simulations draw on Table 5.9 Model 2, and hold all other explanatory variables at their sample means.

of law, and that community economic development encourages democratization of the political culture.

We indeed find an impact of social class on people's responses to questions such as whether having good, committed people staffing government, or having mechanisms of accountability, is a better explanation for responsive government[17] (see table 4A.2). The direction of the effect, however, is not what modernization theory predicts. As in Argentina, the higher the respondent's social class, the less attuned she was to institutional mechanisms of accountability, and the more attuned she was to the role of individual character traits in inducing governments to act in constituents' interests.

Socioeconomic development might also encourage democratization by reducing clientelism and personalistic citizen-party linkages. We saw in chapter 4 that respondents from Baja California (our most democratic state) were far less likely than respondents from the other three states to have personal ties to political parties. Because Baja California is also the wealthiest state of the four, we might surmise that economic development in that state has produced a relatively large middle class and reduced the effectiveness of clientelism.

Yet differences in wealth among individuals do not drive these regional differences. Nor does education. Indeed, a respondent's income and level of education were not significant predictors of his propensity to go to a party for help in solving a problem, to consider going to one in search of a job, or even to have received a gift during the recent electoral campaign. People with higher incomes were slightly less likely to believe that campaign-season handouts make people feel obligated to vote for the donor party, but the estimated effect is counterbalanced by the effect of class, which runs in the opposite direction. In fact, by all of our measures, upper-class respondents were more likely, not less likely, to give answers indicating personalistic party linkages (see table 4A.6). Of course, upper-class respondents are probably not enmeshed in clientelist linkages that leave them dependent on their party patrons for small personal favors and handouts. Rather, the positive relationship between class and personalism probably indicates increased social contact or familiarity between party officials and upper-class individuals. This finding is at odds with our findings for Argentina, where we uncovered more evidence of a relationship between poverty and personalism. But the findings in the two countries are consistent on one important point. Even controlling for wealth and education, we find cross-regional differences in levels of personalism, and these differences map onto variation in the quality of democracy.

Another way to evaluate the relationship between socioeconomic development and the culture of democracy is to analyze responses to several questions about the rule of law. In chapter 4 we introduced several survey questions that probed whether the respondent thought that one was occasionally justified to break a law (see table 4.7). Recall that we asked whether one might be justified in not paying a bus fare, evading taxes, or buying stolen property. If socioeconomic modernization encourages the democratization of political culture, we might expect wealth and education to encourage a proceduralist mindset. And we have seen that upper-income Argentines were somewhat more proceduralist, or more prone to contingent consent, than their lower-income compatriots.

In Mexico as in Argentina, wealth encouraged proceduralism. But in Mexico there were nuances. The effect only held in our most democratic region. In our other three regions, the effect was the reverse: wealth was associated with the view that rules are to be broken.

If we focus on the effect of income, we find that Mexicans with higher incomes were likely to say that breaking the law was never justified. The effect was substantial: as income goes from lowest category to highest, the probability of a "never justified" response jumps by 15 to 20 points, depending on the question (see table 4A.7). Yet self-proclaimed upper-class respondents were far less likely to offer a "never justified" response, and the size of the effect is about the same as that of income. The probability that someone from the highest class will say that avoiding military service was "never justified" is about 20 points lower than the probability that a lower-class person would an-

Table 5.10   Mexico: Opposition to Law-Breaking

	Baja California	Chihuahua	Michoacán	Puebla	Total
Class					
Lower	66.5%	73.7%	58.0%	51.0%	62.0%
Middle	70.5	73.8	56.0	48.2	63.0
Upper	76.7	30.2	26.2	32.2	39.0
Total	69.7%	66.7%	53.7%	47.3%	

Source: Authors' compilations.
Note: Each cell reports the percentage of valid responses stating that breaking a rule or law was "never justified," averaged across the six primary questions presented in table 4.7.

swer this way. Also, the higher a person's self-declared social class, the more he or she was willing to evade taxes and claim undeserved public services.

Differences in political culture across Mexico's regions persist even when we control for wealth and education. Indeed, region was the most powerful predictor of proceduralism. Hence, for example, holding all other variables at their median values, a respondent from Baja California has an 89 percent probability of saying that taking a bribe is "never justified." If we move this median respondent to Puebla, the probability of the proceduralist response falls to 61 percent, a 28-point drop.

A closer look at the survey results gives us a better sense of how to interpret the findings for social class. In table 5.10, the number in each cell is the percentage of respondents, broken down by social class and state, who said that breaking the law (avoiding military service, evading taxes) was "never justified," averaged across the six questions introduced in chapter 4. This table shows that respondents from Baja California were much more likely to disapprove of rule-breaking than respondents from Puebla. But the class pattern in Baja California was strikingly different than in the other three states. In Chihuahua, Michoacán, and Puebla, people who identified themselves as upper class were far more likely to approve of rule-breaking. But in Baja California, the pattern was reversed. This supports the proposition that economic development alters the mindset of the upper class, making it more supportive of democracy (see Lipset 1959). Generalizing from these questions about the rule of law to a democratic culture more broadly, this evidence supports the hypothesis that development encourages a prodemocratic political culture.

Yet note that the lower and middle classes in Baja California and Chihuahua are more legalistic than their counterparts in Michoacán and Puebla. In fact, the lower class in Baja California is more legalistic than any social class in Michoacán and Puebla. Thus proceduralism differs across states, no matter what social class the respondent belongs to.

Turning to the impact of community development, rather than individuals' incomes or class, on democratic political culture, we find no significant relationship between the level of development of the municipality the respondent lives in and expectations of accountability. We estimated multivariate regression models of Favor (a dummy for someone who attributes local party support to the distribution of favors, rather than the party's concern for people), and of Attention (a dummy for someone who agrees that politicians "pay attention to people like me" because they want to be reelected; see table 5A.7). We included either the total revenues per capita of the respondent's municipality or the municipality's poverty rate as indicators of the overall level of development in his or her community.[18] If development encourages democratization, we would expect revenue to be positively correlated with our two dependent variables and poverty rates to be negatively correlated. We find, however, no significant relationship between municipal wealth and individual beliefs: community development does not predict institutional trust.

Regarding proceduralism, community development seems to impede rather than encourage democratic outlooks. Wealthier communities contain people who were less likely to categorically disapprove of rule breakers (see table 5A.8). Simulations show that the impact of municipal wealth (revenues) was considerable. A shift in local revenues from the 10th to the 90th percentile predicts a 15- to 20-percent drop (depending on the question) in the probability that the respondent would say that the violation of the law was "never justified." The higher the poverty rate, furthermore, the more likely respondents were to evince respect for the rule of law. Rather than economic development predicting a stronger attachment to the rule of law, we find that wealthier communities exhibited a weaker attachment. Again, regional differences remain, even when we control for potentially confounding factors.

When we studied the factors influencing democratization and the decline of one-party dominance in Mexico, we found that municipal factors such as poverty and literacy rates strongly predicted local democratization. The underlying explanation for that relationship, however, remains in question. Whereas economic development clearly encouraged democratization in Mexico, the impact of development on Mexico's political culture was much less straightforward. In the most democratic region we studied, people who saw themselves as middle or upper class evinced a greater commitment to the rule of law. Outside of this region, wealth had the opposite effect: it discouraged proceduralism. Nor did wealth undermine personalism in Mexico: the tendency to trust individual politicians and to turn to them for help was more pronounced among the wealthy. We return to this fact, and its implications, shortly.

The Mexican evidence has repeatedly failed to indicate that development fosters democratization by occasioning a shift in people's mindsets. We have indeed found significant cross-state differences in political attitudes, which on the whole sustain the idea of a link between more consolidated regions and democratized political culture. Baja Californians, for instance, were more legalistic, less enmeshed in personal relationships with parties, and more attuned to institutional accountability. Yet we have been unable to tie these regional differences to economic development. In Argentina, economic development did have the expected effect of undercutting clientelism. In turn, the decline of clientelism, rather than development per se, encouraged the emergence of a democratic political culture of skepticism.

Socioeconomic Inequality Enhances Democracy

Several theories link socioeconomic equality to the emergence, stability, and quality of democracy. According to Lipset (1959), economic development enhances and stabilizes democracy by bringing greater equality to the class structure. Greater equality makes people at the top regard those at the bottom as more like them and hence more deserving of participation in collective decisions. According to Carles Boix (2003), and to Daron Acemoglu and James Robinson (2003), equality encourages democracy by making people at the top less afraid of allowing the median voter to decide the level of taxation. This is because in a society in which the distribution of income is relatively equal, the median voter favors less redistribution of wealth than would the median voter in an unequal society. We also have good theoretical reasons to predict that rising equality undermines political clientelism. Clientelism—parties' distribution of private benefits as quid pro quos for electoral support— flourishes in settings where these private benefits are worth a lot to the targeted voters but little, per vote bought, to the party that purchases them. Both will be the case if voters' marginal utility diminishes with income, and if the resources that parties have to buy votes are a function of per capita income (Stokes 2005). We now test the proposition that equality promotes a democratic political culture and, in Mexico, democratization.

Mexico   In Mexico, we find some evidence that equality is related to democratic consolidation. We do not, though, have a direct indicator of economic inequality in Mexican municipalities. Our best available measure is the poverty rate, which we introduced earlier as a measure of community wealth, but which we might also reasonably interpret as a proxy for inequality. For example, that Baja California (our most democratic and wealthiest state) had an unusually large middle class (see table 5A.9).

If we were to find a significant effect of municipal poverty rates on respondents' absorption of a democratic culture, it would be difficult for us to determine whether the effect was due to poverty, or to the inequality that almost certainly accompanies it. We are spared this difficulty by the fact that the poverty rate is not a significant predictor of a democratic political culture in Mexico. In the single instance in which the poverty rate is (weakly) significantly related to beliefs, the relationship runs opposite to the predicted direction: the higher the poverty rate in his or her municipality, the more likely a person was to say that it was never justified to claim an undeserved public service (see table 5A.8, model 3). Also, in contrast to Argentina (as we shall see), we find no evidence that municipal poverty rates (as opposed to low incomes of individual respondents) predicted clientelism. We find no relationship between municipal poverty (or local revenue) and the respondent's propensity to claim that voters in their communities are swayed by pre-election handouts. Thus our evidence indicates that, in Mexico, growing equality does not modify beliefs in ways favorable for democracy.

Argentina   Turning to our Argentine samples, we use two measures of inequality. Neither is ideal; both rely on the claim that the larger the proportion of poor people in a municipality, the greater the inequality there. Clearly this is not a logical necessity: a municipality in which all assets are divided into tiny allotments of equal size is both very poor and perfectly equal. But it appears to be an empirical fact in Argentina that widespread poverty goes with a relatively small middle class. For some supporting evidence, consider again table 5.7, which lists the self-reported incomes of respondents in the four locations we surveyed. The province with the largest percentage of low-income respondents (Misiones, 57 percent) was also the province with the smallest proportion of middle-income respondents (39 percent), and the region with the largest proportion of middle-income respondents (Mar del Plata, 59 percent) also had the smallest proportion of low-income respondents (27 percent).

One of our measures of inequality is the proportion of people in a municipality who lived in substandard housing, designated in the Argentine census as "B housing" or "casa b"—hence our variable name, Casa B. The other is the proportion of people in a municipality designated as having "unsatisfied basic needs" (necesidades básicas insatisfechas, NBI).[19] Casa B is a good measure of rural poverty, NBI of poverty in urban and rural areas. The two measures are correlated at the 0.90 level; therefore, to avoid multicollinearity, we do not include them simultaneously in specifications. Levels of municipal inequality vary sharply across our regions. Municipalities in Misiones have the highest levels of poverty by both measures, and therefore (we infer) the greatest inequality (see table 5A.10). Multivariate regression analysis confirms that, in the presence of controls, being located in Misiones powerfully predicts that a municipality will have high levels of poverty.

Because the regions vary strongly on our measures of poverty and inequality, we might find that differences in the structure of their residents' beliefs actually reflect differences in levels of inequality. That is, we might find that (apparent) regional differences disappear in the presence of controls for inequality. But this is not the case: in the presence of controls for inequality, regional differences persist. More to the point, municipal inequality either had no effect or it had the "wrong" effect on beliefs. For example, municipal poverty rates (whether measured by the percentage of poor-quality housing or of people living under the poverty line) had no significant impact on people's likelihood of saying that governments provide good services because they are under the watch of third parties.

We find no effect of municipal inequality on people's trust in politicians. For instance, people living in areas of high inequality (Casa B) were no more or less likely to offer an institutional trust answer to the question about good municipal services (see table 5A.11).

Whereas equality does not, as we have just seen, greatly influence institutional trust, it does influence perceptions of clientelism, and in the expected way. The belief that "people in my neighborhood support the locally most prominent party because it gives things out in the campaign" (rather than "because it has a better program") was sensitive to levels of poverty (see models 2 and 3 in table 5.11).

Our interpretation is that people perceive clientelism as more widespread in poor than in wealthy communities because it *is* more widespread. Hence, in Argentina, income equality improves the quality of democracy by eroding clientelism.

But what lies behind higher poverty—and greater inequality—is, in part, economic stagnation.[20] Or, stated the other way around, economic development increases equality and equality in turn erodes clientelism. Our prediction, then, is that if we include measures of both municipal economic development and inequality in the same model, the development variable should drive inequality, the intervening variable, to statistical insignificance. Consider model 4 in table 5.11, a specification that includes only municipal expenditures per capita (in 1998) and not our measures of inequality. The coefficient relating expenditures to Handout is negative and significant, indicating that municipal eco-

Table 5.11   Argentina: Models of Beliefs that Neighbors Supported Party Because of Campaign Handouts

Dependent Variable	(1) Handout	(2) Handout	(3) Handout	(4) Handout	(5) Handout
Model	Logit	Logit	Logit	Logit	Logit
Income	−0.056	−0.050	−0.042	−0.051	−0.049
	(0.038)	(0.038)	(0.038)	(0.044)	(0.037)
Education	0.039	0.034	0.036	0.035	0.034
	(0.041)	(0.041)	(0.041)	(0.041)	(0.041)
Housing	−0.009	−0.007	−0.001	0.013	0.011
	(0.102)	(0.103)	(0.004)	(0.104)	(0.104)
Gender	0.013	0.021	0.029	−0.001	0.004
	(0.107)	(0.107)	(0.107)	(0.106)	(0.105)
Age	−0.001	−0.001	−0.001	−0.001	−0.001
	(0.004)	(0.004)	(0.004)	(0.004)	(0.004)
Peronist	**−0.557**	**−0.563**	**−0.583**	**−0.597**	**−0.594**
	(0.156)	(0.156)	(0.156)	(0.155)	(0.155)
Radical	**−0.671**	**−0.705**	**−0.690**	**−0.695**	**−0.705**
	(0.186)	(0.185)	(0.186)	(0.185)	(0.185)
Log population	−0.030	0.008	−0.007	−0.065	−0.047
	(0.041)	(0.043)	(0.040)	(0.045)	(0.053)
Buenos Aires	**1.387**	**1.319**	**1.233**	**1.067**	**1.080**
	(0.216)	(0.220)	(0.227)	(0.268)	(0.271)
Córdoba	**1.100**	**1.127**	**1.115**	**0.972**	**0.997**
	(0.257)	(0.255)	(0.256)	(0.270)	(0.271)
Misiones	**1.746**	**1.428**	**1.305**	**1.163**	**1.117**
	(0.258)	(0.318)	(0.315)	(0.380)	(0.381)
Casa B		0.014			0.005
		(0.008)			(0.009)
NBI			0.045		
			(0.017)		
Municipal expenditures per capita				−0.002	−0.002
				(0.001)	(0.001)
Constant	−0.975	−1.582	−1.858	0.296	−0.080
	(0.595)	(0.645)	(0.645)	(0.798)	(1.041)

Source: Authors' compilations.
Notes: Standard errors in parentheses. Boldface indicates coefficient is statistically significant at $p < .05$. N = 1,920. For variable definitions see tables 4A.1 and 5A.10.

nomic development undermines clientelism. Model 5 is a specification that simultaneously controls for municipal development and poverty (inequality). Comparing models 2 and 5, we see that controlling for municipal wealth reduces the magnitude of the inequality effect by two-thirds.[21] This result is consistent with our interpretation that development in Argentina undermines clientelism by reducing inequality.

Recall that without controls for municipal poverty, region strongly affects perceptions of clientelism: these perceptions are least wide-spread in the most-democratic region, most widespread in the least-democratic one. (These regional effects show up, for instance, in the large positive and significant coefficient on the provincial dummies in model 1, table 5.11.) But equality also varies with the quality of democracy across regions. Perhaps these regional differences in perceptions of clientelism were in fact stand-ins for differences in equality. To some degree this is true. Controlling for poverty (in model 2), the apparent difference between Buenos Aires and Misiones largely disappears, as indicated by the fact that the three regional coefficients are roughly equal in model 2. Thus, the apparently more widespread perception of clientelism in Misiones than in Buenos Aires turns out to be explained by higher poverty rates in Misiones. That is, we would expect percep-tions of clientelism to be equally widespread in municipalities with the same level of inequality, whether they are located in the province of Buenos Aires, Córdoba, or Misiones. But the large and positive coeffi-cients for all three regional dummies in model 2 indicate that the per-ceptions of clientelism are rare in Mar del Plata. A person in a Misiones city with the same proportion of substandard dwellings as Mar del Plata's (6 percent) would still be more likely to perceive his or her neighbors as succumbing to clientelist inducements. Holding other variables, such as income and education, at their sample means, the Misiones resident's probability of attributing clientelist decision rules to his neighbors is 48 percent, whereas the Mar del Plata resident's is 18 percent.[22]

Introducing our second measure of poverty, NBI, as a proxy for in-equality has the same effect (see column 3, table 5.11). Regional differ-ences between Misiones, on the one hand, and Córdoba and the prov-ince of Buenos Aires, on the other, become insignificant: not region per se, but higher rates of poverty in Misiones explain the more widespread perceptions of clientelism there. But even with controls for poverty, perceptions of clientelism remain less widespread in Mar del Plata than elsewhere.

Figure 5.4 illustrates the joint effects of region and poverty on expec-tations of clientelism. When we assume a resident of a Misiones munici-pality with that province's highest rate of poverty (WBI = 35 percent), the expected percentage of clientelist responses is 71 percent. When we assume a resident of a Misiones municipality with that province's low-est poverty (17 percent), the probability of a clientelist response drops to 52 percent. When we assume a Misiones municipality with Mar del Plata's poverty rate (11 percent), the probability of a clientelist response drops to 45 percent. And when we assume a resident of Mar del Plata (and a poverty rate of 11 percent), the probability of a clientelist response drops to 18 percent.[23] The explanation for these powerful regional effects, which go well beyond the greater poverty of a region like Misiones and

Figure 5.4   Argentina: Simulated Expected Probability of Believing Neighbors Support Parties Because of Clientelist Inducements, by Region and Poverty Rate (NBI)

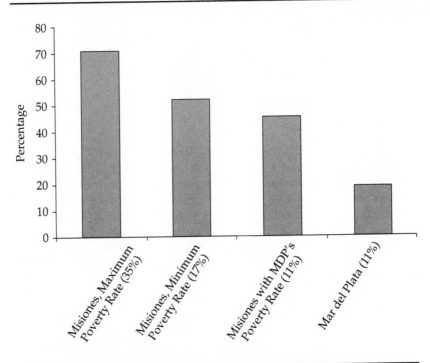

Source: Authors' compilations.
Notes: Clarify simulations. We hold household income, education level, quality of housing, and size of respondent's municipality at the sample median.

the greater affluence of a district like Mar del Plata, is that regional political leaderships also adopt policy stances that then become a part of the regional political culture. Our case study of Mar del Plata in chapter 3 offered evidence for just such regional strategic choices and the way they led constituents to think differently about politics.

To summarize, we find no effect of municipal economic development on political culture or perceptions of clientelism in Mexico. In Argentina as well, individual and community economic development did not influence political culture. But we found one crucial exception: income equality reduced perceptions of clientelism, and when clientelism eroded, so did a personalistic political culture more generally. Hence, in Argentina, economic development and the greater income equality that it generated helped instill a political culture of skepticism and accountability via the mechanism of reduced clientelism. To some degree the poverty effect erased apparent cross-regional differences. But not entirely. Clientelism was less prevalent in our most democratic region, even considering relatively low poverty rates there. Economic development increases equality, and equality erodes clientelism. Regional political parties' strategic choices also played an independent part in explaining different levels of clientelism, at least at the extremes of the most and least democratic regions.

Conclusions

In chapter 4 we showed that regions of Argentina and Mexico where democracy functioned well sustained cultures of political trust that were different than the cultures found in regions where democracy worked badly. In high-quality regional democracies, we found a culture of institutional trust. In low-quality regional democracies, we found a culture of personal trust in politicians. In Argentine regions where democracy worked well, we also found widespread contingent consent: citizens were willing to comply with the demands of government, particularly fiscal demands, only when the demands were fair and furthered constituents' interests. In the Mexican states where democratization had gone furthest, we found a commitment to proceduralism. These regional differences have proved mightily robust; they were almost never reducible to other kinds of differences among the regions' populations. Try as we may through statistical manipulations, we have not been able to eliminate the effect of geographic region on democratic political culture. Our qualitative accounts in Part II (chapters 2 and 3) indicate that the strategic choices of regional political elites drive some of these persistent regional differences in political culture and the deepening of democracy.

The strategic intervention of politicians, then, is part of the explanation for differences in political cultures of trust across Argentina and Mexico, and for cross-regional differences in the quality of democracy. Still, we have tried here to push further and look for other factors that explain why democracy deepens in some regions but not in others. Social capital did not get us very far in explaining these differences. Our evidence confounded most predictions of social capital theory. More democratic regions were not richer in social capital; indeed, in less democratic regions people were more active in civic associations, met more frequently, collaborated more to solve common problems, and went to church more regularly. In Argentina, the only group activity that people in consolidated democratic regions engaged in more was playing soccer. Those active in civic associations did trust other people more in the abstract, and to cooperate in personal endeavors. But they did not trust their fellow citizens to monitor politicians. Nor were the active more prone to support compliance with onerous burdens, such as paying taxes or serving in the military. Nor, finally, did those well endowed with social capital believe that third-party constraints on governments caused governments to perform well.

In turn, economic development matters in explaining cross-regional variation in the quality of democracy and the structure of beliefs, but not for the reasons commonly offered. Wealthier individuals did not believe in institutional constraints, and in fact evinced greater personal trust in politicians. Community economic development had little effect on institutional or personal trust. It did have the effect of reducing clientelism sharply, especially in Argentina. The reason, we contend, is that underdeveloped regions are also those with significant income inequality, and income inequality tempts political parties to use resources that emanate, ultimately, from the elite to buy votes of people at the bottom. Hence underdevelopment leads to inequality, and inequality shapes the strategies of political parties, leading them to pursue less democratic means of mobilization than are viable in wealthier and more equal regions.

One of the most startling findings in this chapter has to do with a contrast between Argentina and Mexico. In Argentina, economic development had noticeable effects on the political culture of democracy. To some degree, wealth encouraged proceduralism and contingent consent. Most notably, wealth—whether of individuals or communities—undercut clientelism. In Mexico, by contrast, wealth clearly encouraged electoral democratization but had little visible effect on political culture. Economic development only shaped the political culture of the state that, in electoral terms, had democratized earliest and most fully.

Our evidence leads us to conclude that economic development and income equality only modify the political culture once democracy has become well established. Skepticism and institutional trust, proceduralism and contingent consent, the demise of clientelism—in short, the political culture of democracy—do not cause democratization. What does is, among other factors, economic development and the equalization of incomes and social status. What's more, under nondemocratic conditions, people who enjoy greater wealth do not become democrats because they adopt democratic beliefs. They become democrats, as has been repeatedly emphasized in recent studies, because they are less threatened by the prospect of redistribution that democracy is likely to bring about (Boix 2003; Acemoglu and Robinson 2003). Once democratization has taken place, however, wealth does encourage a more democratic culture in a broader sense.

Whatever the effects of development and equality on political culture, our statistical results in the end draw us back to the notion of regional political cultures. Even when we bring in other factors that covary with region—factors such as clientelism, poverty, and inequality—we have not been able to completely efface the independent effects of region. Especially when we compare our extremes with Mar del Plata and Baja California at one end, and Misiones and Puebla at the other, differences of many sorts remain irreducible to structural factors or to the underlying characteristics of regional citizenries. These differences show up in how skeptical people are about politicians, how sensitive they are to the constraining effects of institutions, including elections, whether they trust their fellow citizens to hold political leaders accountable and not be swayed by minor blandishments, and in their commitment to legal rules and norms. We now turn to some more general reflections, emerging from the Mexican and Argentine experiences, about trust and the nature of democratic culture.

Appendix

Table 5A.1   Argentina: Model of Church Attendance

Dependent Variable	(1) Religion
Model	Ordered logit
Income	−0.014
	(0.034)
Education	−0.038
	(0.029)
Housing	0.037
	(0.072)
Gender	**0.646**
	(0.092)
Age	**0.020**
	(0.003)
Peronist	0.005
	(0.120)
Radical	0.056
	(0.135)
Log population	0.026
	(0.037)
Buenos Aires	−0.144
	(0.152)
Córdoba	**0.393**
	(0.160)
Misiones	**1.271**
	(0.174)
Cut 1	**1.558**
	(0.538)

(*Table continues on p. 166.*)

Table 5A.1 *Continued*

Dependent Variable	(1) Religion
Cut 2	**3.161**
	(0.545)
Cut 3	**4.059**
	(0.556)

Source: Authors' compilations.
Notes: Standard errors in parentheses. Boldface indicates coefficient is statistically significant at p < .05. N = 1,920.

Table 5A.2   Mexico: Models of Civic Participation

Dependent Variable	(1) Meet	(2) Comprob	(3) Belong
Model	Logit	Logit	Ordered logit
Income	0.097	−0.027	0.116
	(0.064)	(0.062)	(0.074)
Education	0.066	0.085	**0.241**
	(0.069)	(0.072)	(0.074)
Class	**0.501**	**0.434**	0.222
	(0.116)	(0.127)	(0.122)
Gender	0.164	−0.072	**−0.295**
	(0.133)	(0.120)	(0.135)
Age	**0.100**	0.077	0.043
	(0.049)	(0.053)	(0.058)
PRI supporter	**0.896**	**0.384**	0.210
	(0.239)	(0.187)	(0.230)
PAN supporter	**0.809**	0.277	0.222
	(0.238)	(0.193)	(0.225)
PRD supporter	**0.798**	−0.146	0.032
	(0.325)	(0.289)	(0.385)
Rural	0.025	−0.024	0.102
	(0.148)	(0.147)	(0.123)
Chihuahua	**0.946**	0.276	0.369
	(0.246)	(0.231)	(0.265)
Michoacán	**0.943**	0.201	**0.777**
	(0.286)	(0.245)	(0.250)
Puebla	**0.542**	−0.091	0.236
	(0.266)	(0.229)	(0.285)
Constant	**−4.180**	**−2.394**	
	(0.563)	(0.502)	
Cut 1			**3.339**
			(0.535)
Cut 2			**5.481**
			(0.557)
Cut 3			**6.809**
			(0.596)

Source: Authors' compilations.
Notes: See table 5.2 for a description of the dependent variables. Standard errors in parentheses. Boldface indicates coefficient is statistically significant at p < .05. N = 1,598.

Table 5A.3   Argentina: Models of Interpersonal Trust

Dependent Variable	(1) Neighbor	(2) Advantage	(3) Trust
Model	Logit	Logit	Ordered logit
Income	**0.115**	**0.085**	**0.071**
	(0.041)	(0.036)	(0.034)
Education	−0.044	**0.054**	**0.088**
	(0.039)	(0.029)	(0.030)
Housing	**0.172**	0.100	**−0.193**
	(0.081)	(0.082)	(0.080)
Gender	**−0.262**	0.106	**−0.217**
	(0.118)	(0.101)	(0.092)
Age	−0.001	**0.012**	**0.007**
	(0.004)	(0.003)	(0.003)
Peronist	0.038	0.041	**0.337**
	(0.138)	(0.121)	(0.119)
Radical	0.094	0.212	0.194
	(0.162)	(0.161)	(0.144)
Log population	**−0.084**	−0.038	−0.000
	(0.035)	(0.035)	(0.042)
Buenos Aires	0.211	0.139	0.296
	(0.209)	(0.142)	(0.159)
Córdoba	−0.188	0.084	−0.090
	(0.206)	(0.177)	(0.218)
Misiones	**−0.442**	−0.007	−0.365
	(0.225)	(0.202)	(0.232)
Belong	0.188	0.105	**0.301**
	(0.113)	(0.086)	(0.073)
Comprob	**0.545**	0.048	**0.434**
	(0.116)	(0.104)	(0.126)
Constant	**1.381**	**−1.380**	
	(0.556)	(0.538)	
Cut 1			−0.825
			(0.613)
Cut 2			**2.086**
			(0.595)

Source: Authors' compilations.
Notes: Standard errors in parentheses. Boldface indicates coefficient is statistically significant at p < .05. N = 1,920.
Neighbor: Dummy for response, "I would leave my home in the care of a neighbor."
Advantage: Dummy for response, "The majority of people would not take advantage of you if they could."

Table 5A.4   Mexico: Models of Interpersonal Trust

Dependent Variable	(1) Neighbor	(2) Advantage	(3) Trust
Model	Logit	Logit	Ordered logit
Income	−0.037	**−0.200**	**−0.133**
	(0.052)	(0.064)	(0.045)
Education	**0.210**	0.080	0.086
	(0.059)	(0.056)	(0.050)
Class	**0.205**	−0.074	0.165
	(0.101)	(0.113)	(0.094)
Gender	**−0.253**	−0.018	−0.128
	(0.113)	(0.128)	(0.102)
Age	0.026	0.000	0.042
	(0.042)	(0.044)	(0.042)
PRI supporter	0.343	0.081	0.133
	(0.179)	(0.173)	(0.186)
PAN supporter	**0.394**	−0.006	**0.419**
	(0.183)	(0.167)	(0.147)
PRD supporter	−0.136	0.393	0.329
	(0.224)	(0.272)	(0.213)
Rural	0.100	0.177	−0.050
	(0.098)	(0.094)	(0.099)
Chihuahua	0.052	−0.243	**0.403**
	(0.186)	(0.185)	(0.155)
Michoacán	−0.210	−0.138	0.014
	(0.200)	(0.207)	(0.227)
Puebla	−0.260	0.179	0.238
	(0.180)	(0.214)	(0.185)
Belong	0.154	−0.144	0.187
	(0.127)	(0.119)	(0.106)
Comprob	**0.288**	0.014	**0.348**
	(0.132)	(0.130)	(0.156)
Constant	**−1.090**	−0.065	
	(0.350)	(0.384)	
Cut 1			−0.612
			(0.403)
Cut 2			**1.575**
			(0.400)

Source: Authors' compilations.
Notes: Standard errors in parentheses. Boldface indicates coefficient is statistically significant at p < .05. N = 1,598.

Table 5A.5 Argentina: (Non-) Impact of Social Capital on Compliance

Dependent variable	(1) Handout	(2) Favor	(3) Taxes	(4) Claim	(5) Military	(6) Stolen	(7) Corrupt	(8) Admission
Model	Logit	Logit	Ordered logit	Ordered logit	Ordered logit	Ordered logit	Ordered logit	Ordered logit
Income	−0.057	−0.052	**0.090**	**0.110**	−0.031	0.084	0.041	0.049
	(0.038)	(0.040)	(0.036)	(0.040)	(0.030)	(0.054)	(0.091)	(0.047)
Education	0.036	0.019	0.023	0.046	0.039	0.007	0.112	0.019
	(0.041)	(0.035)	(0.031)	(0.036)	(0.032)	(0.046)	(0.080)	(0.041)
Housing	−0.008	0.058	−0.036	0.019	**0.198**	0.004	**0.382**	0.033
	(0.102)	(0.086)	(0.086)	(0.086)	(0.076)	(0.099)	(0.181)	(0.104)
Gender	0.016	0.030	−0.047	0.000	0.148	**0.523**	0.110	0.079
	(0.107)	(0.101)	(0.093)	(0.109)	(0.090)	(0.134)	(0.247)	(0.109)
Age	−0.001	**−0.014**	**0.015**	**0.018**	−0.012	**0.042**	**0.034**	**0.028**
	(0.004)	(0.004)	(0.003)	(0.003)	(0.003)	(0.006)	(0.009)	(0.005)
Peronist supporter	**−0.562**	**−0.778**	−0.164	**−0.376**	−0.130	−0.315	−0.513	−0.217
	(0.156)	(0.148)	(0.121)	(0.132)	(0.120)	(0.175)	(0.330)	(0.131)
Radical supporter	**−0.672**	−0.121	0.132	−0.285	−0.143	−0.081	−0.128	0.338
	(0.187)	(0.177)	(0.168)	(0.159)	(0.162)	(0.223)	(0.440)	(0.227)
Log Pop	−0.028	**0.120**	**−0.075**	**−0.115**	0.022	−0.063	0.000	−0.023
	(0.041)	(0.042)	(0.036)	(0.041)	(0.046)	(0.050)	(0.072)	(0.049)
Buenos Aires	**1.385**	**1.241**	0.059	−0.037	−0.239	0.044	0.428	**0.928**
	(0.216)	(0.195)	(0.173)	(0.187)	(0.150)	(0.246)	(0.469)	(0.216)
Córdoba	**1.101**	**1.124**	0.204	−0.295	−0.002	0.153	−0.385	0.163
	(0.258)	(0.196)	(0.204)	(0.191)	(0.174)	(0.284)	(0.427)	(0.222)
Misiones	**1.741**	**1.347**	0.365	−0.278	0.171	−0.211	−0.003	0.445
	(0.257)	(0.237)	(0.230)	(0.204)	(0.240)	(0.268)	(0.474)	(0.252)
eet	0.097	−0.084	−0.173	0.140	−0.016	**0.489**	0.006	−0.221
	(0.131)	(0.138)	(0.108)	(0.127)	(0.116)	(0.181)	(0.282)	(0.146)
Constant	−1.005	**−1.880**						
	(0.593)	(0.625)						
Cut 1			**−2.171**	**−2.811**	0.400	**−2.200**	−1.783	**−2.176**
			(0.531)	(0.641)	(0.677)	(0.752)	(1.151)	(0.746)
Cut 2			0.421	−1.033	**2.014**	−0.289	−0.411	0.215
			(0.529)	(0.644)	(0.682)	(0.753)	(1.172)	(0.694)

Source: Authors' compilations.
Notes: Standard errors in parentheses. Boldface indicates coefficient is statistically significant at < .05. N = 1,920.

Table 5A.6   Mexico: (Non-) Impact of Social Capital on Compliance

Dependent Variable	(1) Handout	(2) Favor	(3) Taxes	(4) Claim	(5) Military	(6) Stolen	(7) Corrupt	(8) Fare
Model	Logit	Logit	Ordered logit	Ordered logit	Ordered logit	Ordered logit	Ordered logit	Ordered logit
Income	−0.069	0.087	0.062	0.080	0.090	**0.214**	**0.213**	**0.192**
	(0.064)	(0.057)	(0.058)	(0.064)	(0.069)	(0.061)	(0.068)	(0.073)
Education	−0.018	**0.146**	0.029	−0.017	−0.011	−0.065	−0.060	−0.097
	(0.062)	(0.060)	(0.054)	(0.051)	(0.057)	(0.062)	(0.064)	(0.060)
Class	0.179	−0.184	**−0.273**	**−0.204**	**−0.349**	**−0.559**	**−0.821**	**−0.513**
	(0.106)	(0.116)	(0.098)	(0.103)	(0.115)	(0.118)	(0.118)	(0.125)
Gender	0.125	−0.089	−0.026	0.126	−0.045	−0.050	0.066	0.069
	(0.108)	(0.114)	(0.109)	(0.106)	(0.115)	(0.100)	(0.115)	(0.103)
Age	−0.028	0.079	0.076	0.011	0.025	−0.033	0.024	0.090
	(0.045)	(0.047)	(0.041)	(0.039)	(0.046)	(0.052)	(0.052)	(0.050)
PRI supporter	−0.153	**−0.745**	−0.290	−0.284	−0.208	−0.033	−0.388	−0.072
	(0.205)	(0.199)	(0.162)	(0.145)	(0.167)	(0.171)	(0.213)	(0.179)
PAN supporter	−0.343	**−0.738**	−0.186	−0.238	−0.164	−0.177	−0.290	−0.131
	(0.180)	(0.212)	(0.156)	(0.135)	(0.154)	(0.177)	(0.222)	(0.186)
PRD supporter	0.297	−0.591	−0.087	−0.155	−0.136	0.152	−0.220	0.010
	(0.229)	(0.316)	(0.222)	(0.214)	(0.248)	(0.233)	(0.281)	(0.235)
Rural	**−0.261**	−0.157	0.019	0.104	−0.001	−0.025	0.053	−0.018
	(0.101)	(0.123)	(0.107)	(0.092)	(0.099)	(0.143)	(0.170)	(0.145)
Chihuahua	0.421	0.326	−0.394	0.216	−0.137	−0.016	**−0.896**	−0.066
	(0.226)	(0.199)	(0.220)	(0.221)	(0.195)	(0.259)	(0.279)	(0.254)
Michoacán	**0.600**	0.180	**−1.021**	−0.398	**−0.718**	**−0.601**	**−1.457**	−0.370
	(0.221)	(0.221)	(0.205)	(0.208)	(0.183)	(0.279)	(0.284)	(0.261)
Puebla	0.245	**0.604**	**−1.101**	**−0.537**	**−0.883**	**−0.832**	**−1.718**	**−0.886**
	(0.192)	(0.208)	(0.198)	(0.210)	(0.191)	(0.263)	(0.272)	(0.232)
Meet	0.237	−0.180	−0.238	**−0.461**	−0.215	−0.266	**−0.369**	**−0.357**
	(0.154)	(0.151)	(0.142)	(0.146)	(0.162)	(0.159)	(0.158)	(0.169)
Constant	−0.499	−0.438						
	(0.423)	(0.384)						
Cut 1			**−2.860**	**−2.261**	**−2.910**	**−4.142**	**−5.117**	**−3.457**
			(0.448)	(0.416)	(0.378)	(0.536)	(0.576)	(0.518)
Cut 2			**−0.829**	**−0.329**	**−1.058**	**−1.904**	**−3.304**	**−1.345**
			(0.430)	(0.421)	(0.370)	(0.567)	(0.579)	(0.515)

Source: Authors' compilations.
Notes: Standard errors in parentheses. Boldface indicates coefficient is statistically significant $p < .05$. N = 1,598.

Table 5A.7   Mexico: Effect of Municipal Economic Development on Institutional Trust

Dependent Variable	(1) Attention	(2) Attention	(3) Favor	(4) Favor
Model	Logit	Logit	Logit	Logit
Income	0.125	0.114	0.086	0.078
	(0.071)	(0.071)	(0.058)	(0.057)
Education	−0.062	−0.066	**0.137**	**0.136**
	(0.059)	(0.059)	(0.060)	(0.061)
Class	**−0.563**	**−0.554**	−0.206	−0.192
	(0.122)	(0.125)	(0.114)	(0.112)
Gender	−0.185	−0.189	−0.098	−0.100
	(0.127)	(0.127)	(0.115)	(0.115)
Age	−0.050	−0.046	0.075	0.073
	(0.052)	(0.052)	(0.047)	(0.047)
PRI supporter	**−0.939**	**−0.946**	**−0.773**	**−0.766**
	(0.223)	(0.222)	(0.200)	(0.200)
PAN supporter	**−0.660**	**−0.677**	**−0.764**	**−0.759**
	(0.205)	(0.206)	(0.216)	(0.215)
PRD supporter	−0.172	−0.176	−0.611	−0.617
	(0.298)	(0.297)	(0.319)	(0.318)
Rural	0.043	0.128	−0.112	−0.089
	(0.132)	(0.137)	(0.134)	(0.132)
Chihuahua	−0.120	−0.057	0.298	0.337
	(0.242)	(0.234)	(0.200)	(0.199)
Michoacán	**−1.125**	**−0.916**	0.240	0.301
	(0.406)	(0.284)	(0.300)	(0.250)
Puebla	−0.128	0.144	**0.684**	**0.775**
	(0.386)	(0.309)	(0.285)	(0.260)
Municipal own revenue	−0.000		0.001	
	(0.002)		(0.001)	
Municipal poverty rate		−1.780		−1.463
		(1.273)		(1.143)
Constant	**2.936**	**2.858**	−0.565	−0.407
	(0.666)	(0.463)	(0.501)	(0.386)
N	1588	1598	1588	1598

Source: Authors' compilations.
Notes: Standard errors in parentheses. Boldface indicates coefficient is statistically significant at p < .05.
Favor: dummy for response, "people support the most important party in this neighborhood because it is concerned for everyone" (rather than because it does favors for people).
Attention: dummy for response, "when politicians pay attention to people like me, it is because they want to be reelected."

Table 5A.8   Mexico: Effect of Municipal Economic Development on Proceduralism

Dependent Variable	(1) Taxes	(2) Taxes	(3) Claim	(4) Claim	(5) Fare	(6) Fare
Model	Ordered logit	Ordered logit	Ordered logit	Ordered logit	Ordered logit	Ordered logit
Income	0.062	0.076	0.082	0.085	**0.188**	**0.206**
	(0.058)	(0.057)	(0.067)	(0.065)	(0.074)	(0.072)
Education	0.032	0.028	−0.009	−0.012	−0.097	−0.094
	(0.054)	(0.054)	(0.050)	(0.051)	(0.059)	(0.058)
Class	**−0.300**	**−0.271**	**−0.256**	**−0.221**	**−0.547**	**−0.526**
	(0.100)	(0.099)	(0.104)	(0.103)	(0.127)	(0.120)
Gender	0.027	−0.039	0.118	0.125	0.064	0.052
	(0.108)	(0.109)	(0.105)	(0.106)	(0.103)	(0.104)
Age	0.074	0.077	0.009	0.008	0.085	0.087
	(0.041)	(0.042)	(0.039)	(0.039)	(0.051)	(0.051)
PRI supporter	**−0.334**	**−0.352**	**−0.351**	**−0.376**	−0.127	−0.156
	(0.161)	(0.162)	(0.147)	(0.149)	(0.180)	(0.179)
PAN supporter	−0.217	−0.217	**−0.285**	**−0.301**	−0.173	−0.182
	(0.158)	(0.159)	(0.137)	(0.135)	(0.191)	(0.188)
PRD supporter	−0.119	−0.129	−0.200	−0.218	−0.033	0.031
	(0.220)	(0.219)	(0.218)	(0.219)	(0.232)	(0.230)
Rural	−0.043	−0.107	0.000	−0.021	−0.050	−0.182
	(0.130)	(0.118)	(0.108)	(0.104)	(0.162)	(0.150)
Chihuahua	**−0.473**	**−0.510**	0.064	0.053	−0.147	−0.217
	(0.226)	(0.227)	(0.221)	(0.226)	(0.260)	(0.255)
Michoacán	**−1.196**	**−1.560**	**−0.721**	**−0.990**	−0.495	**−1.093**
	(0.255)	(0.306)	(0.237)	(0.356)	(0.338)	(0.347)
Puebla	**−1.294**	**−1.640**	**−0.882**	**−1.101**	**−1.007**	**−1.607**
	(0.261)	(0.307)	(0.275)	(0.336)	(0.306)	(0.318)
Municipal poverty rate	1.319		2.428		0.712	
	(1.216)		(1.298)		(1.652)	
Municipal own revenue		−0.004		−0.004		−0.005
		(0.002)		(0.002)		(0.002)
Cut 1	**−2.943**	**−3.737**	**−2.376**	**−3.179**	**−3.544**	**−4.653**
	(0.455)	(0.585)	(0.421)	(0.572)	(0.522)	(0.632)
Cut 2	**−0.915**	**−1.693**	**−0.451**	**−1.251**	**−1.437**	**−2.524**
	(0.437)	(0.567)	(0.427)	(0.574)	(0.522)	(0.626)
N	1598	1588	1598	1588	1598	1588

Source: Authors' compilations.
Note: Standard errors in parentheses. Boldface indicates coefficient is statistically significant at p < .05.

Table 5A.9   Mexico: Self-Reported Social Class and Family Income, by State

	Baja California	Chihuahua	Michoacán	Puebla	Total
Social class					
Lower	28%	36%	41%	37%	35%
	(111)	(142)	(163)	(147)	(563)
Middle	64%	45%	42%	50%	50%
	(254)	(180)	(166)	(200)	(800)
Upper	6%	12%	9%	7%	9%
	(25)	(49)	(37)	(29)	(140)
No answer	3%	7%	9%	6%	6%
	(10)	(27)	(34)	(24)	(95)
Family monthly income					
Low	33%	36%	36%	33%	34%
	(131)	(145)	(144)	(130)	(550)
Middle	41%	38%	23%	40%	36%
	(164)	(153)	(93)	(158)	(568)
High	18%	5%	5%	5%	8%
	(69)	(21)	(20)	(21)	(131)
No answer	9%	20%	36%	23%	22%
	(36)	(79)	(143)	(91)	(349)

Source: Authors' compilations.
Notes: Total number of responses in parentheses.
Low income: 0 to 2,400 pesos per month.
Middle income: 2,401 to 8,000 pesos per month.
High income: 8,001 or more pesos per month.

Table 5A.10   Argentina: Average Municipal Poverty Rates, by Region (in Percentage)

Province	Casa B	NBI
Mar del Plata	6.4	10.9
Buenos Aires	13.4	14.8
Córdoba	8.8	11.4
Misiones	36.5	22.7

Source: Authors' compilations.
Notes: Casa B: Percentage of households in the respondent's municipality with one of the following indicators of inadequate housing: No running water; no toilet facilities with sewage connection; dirt floors.
NBI: Percentage of households in the respondent's municipality with one of the following indicators of poverty: three or more inhabitants per room; precarious house not owned by residents; no indoor toilet facilities or toilets not connected to sewage system; one school-age child who does not attend school; households with four or more persons per employed member and in which the head of household has two years or less of schooling. See INDEC, Situación y Evolución Social (Sintesis N°4).

Table 5A.11 Argentina: (Non-) Impact of Poverty on Institutional Trust

Dependent Variable	(1) Service
Model	Logit
Income	−0.052
	(0.043)
Education	0.037
	(0.036)
Housing	−0.006
	(0.077)
Gender	**−0.313**
	(0.103)
Age	**−0.013**
	(0.004)
Peronist	**−0.234**
	(0.117)
Radical	−0.082
	(0.142)
Log population	0.041
	(0.038)
Buenos Aires	**−0.470**
	(0.189)
Córdoba	**−0.595**
	(0.186)
Misiones	**−1.387**
	(0.303)
Casa B	0.013
	(0.007)
Constant	1.054
	(0.570)

Source: Authors' compilations.
Notes: Standard errors in parentheses. Boldface indicates coefficient is statistically significant at p < .05. N = 1,920.

PART IV

THE POLITICAL CULTURE OF
DEMOCRACY RECONSIDERED

Chapter 6

Region, Democratization, and Political Culture

A S DEMOCRACY in a country or a region deepens, the nature of political trust is likely to change. Citizens will turn from the belief that what matters for producing responsive government is that politicians be personally trustworthy, to the belief that what matters is that institutions constrain politicians to be trustworthy. Our findings generally—although not universally—support this basic claim. Here we consider the lessons these findings contain for our understanding of why democracy deepens and why it causes a shift in political trust.

We then step back and make broader claims. One is that the questions perpetually asked about the transition of countries from authoritarianism to democracy should also be asked about the transition of regions within countries from a more superficial to a deeper democracy. Our second claim is that the distinctiveness of regions and regional cultures calls for some deeper thinking about the processes that produce a geographic or jurisdictional boundedness of political culture. Our third claim is that the fabric of beliefs and practices we have studied are best considered political cultures. Hence, although our study has challenged the idea that democratic culture is a culture of personal trust, still we have sought to resuscitate the concept of political culture. Our final claim is that, notwithstanding the displacement of personal trust by institutional trust in mature democratic regions, democracy remains inevitably personalized, to some degree, even in strongly institutionalized regions.

Political Trust and Democracy: A Review of the Findings

Our basic findings are the following:

- The quality of democracy—as reflected in the fiscal behavior of provincial and state governments, levels of political violence, the competitiveness of elections, electoral participation of voters, ticket-splitting, voters' willingness to discuss politics, and in a series of other practices—varied sharply from region to region in the two countries we studied, making possible a ranking of regions according to this quality.

- Political beliefs also diverged widely across regions in both countries.

- People in the more democratized regions
  —identified institutional constraints, and not the character of officeholders, as the chief determinant of government responsiveness, and hence had a finer appreciation of mechanisms of accountability;[1]
  —were less prone to clientelism and saw their neighbors as less prone to it; and
  —were more likely to voice respect for the rule of law, either absolutely (in Mexico) or contingently (in Argentina).

- People in the less democratized regions
  —identified the character of politicians, and not institutional constraints, as the chief determinant of government responsiveness;
  —were more prone to clientelism and saw their neighbors as more prone to it; and
  —were less inclined to voice unconditional support for the rule of law.

- In both countries, economic development caused regional democratization. In Argentina, development and income equality created a more democratic regional political culture. In Mexico, economic development did not change political culture, but it did increase political competition.

- In both countries, development fails to explain the full extent of cross-regional differences in trust, perceptions of accountability, and proceduralism; some differences are purely regional, probably reflecting the strategic choices of regional political leaders.

Processes of Regional Democratization

A central task of this book was to explain why democracy works well in some regions and not in others. Here we lay out two conjectures about processes of change that have led some regions to democratize and others to remain less democratic.[2]

The Civic Culture Scenario

In a democracy in which government generally performs badly, one region develops a rich associational life, spawning many organizations and clubs that involve much of the citizenry. People who work together in civic associations come to trust one another, and to believe that others are doing their part to make sure that local and regional governments run well. This interpersonal trust in turn makes citizens more willing to do their part to monitor the government. Their involvement in civic associations also gives them optimistic expectations about the compliance of others with burdensome government requirements. Both monitoring and compliance allow regional democracy to function well. Hence a rich associational life, and the personal trust it encourages, improves the quality of democracy in this region.

We raised theoretical doubts about this scenario, and our empirical findings led us to dismiss it as an account of the varying quality of democracy in the two new democracies we studied. Instead, we found theoretical and empirical support for a second stylized process.

The Development Scenario

In a country that is formally democratic but in which government functions badly, poverty is widespread and inequality is high. Political parties use public and party resources to give out minor private benefits to poor voters, hoping that such private favors will engender political support. They portray these favors as the personal benevolence of political leaders, engendering a culture of personalized political trust. For exogenous reasons, one region grows economically and income distribution there becomes more equal. Parties in that region find that favors of ever-increasing value are needed to mobilize political support among their increasingly middle-class constituents. Clientelism declines and political competition increases. The political leadership, discouraged from clientelism, sees institutionalization as a way of getting voters to give it a broader authority and strengthens institutional mechanisms of accountability. Hence economic development and income equality spark a series of changes that culminate in greater institutional trust (displacing personal trust), and explain the unusually high quality of democracy in this region.

The development scenario has a particularly tight fit with our evidence from Argentina. Regarding Mexico, our evidence was ambiguous on the origins of the democratic culture of skepticism. But we have nevertheless shown that the more democratic regions in both countries were distinguished by higher levels of development and a distinctive political culture. The theoretical reasoning and evidence in this book support the development scenario, but undercut the civic culture scenario.

From the Democratization of Countries to the Democratization of Regions

Most studies of democratic consolidation have focused on countries. Our study is one of a few—Robert Putnam's *Making Democracy Work* being the leading example—to focus on the democratic consolidation of regions within countries. Democratization means something different when the unit of analysis is countries and not regions. The dominant perspective in comparative politics, and one with which we have considerable sympathy, is to treat countries as having achieved democratization when certain conditions are met: presidents and parliaments are elected and step down when they lose elections, a threshold percentage of the adult population is enfranchised, civilians control the military, civilian leaders are subject to the rule of law, etc. (see, for example, Dahl 1971; Przeworski and colleagues 2000; Boix 2003; Karl 1990; Collier 1999). This conditional approach implies that democracy is a dichotomous state, and countries are either in that state or they are not. Yet scholarly treatments, supported by lay common sense, have difficulty giving up entirely on a continuous understanding of democracy—that democratic countries may nonetheless be more or less democratic. This persistent idea of democracy as a continuous variable explains the continued use by empirical researchers of, for instance, the Polity and Freedom House measures. We cannot seem to rid ourselves of the intuition that some democracies are more, and some less, democratic.

Democracy as a quality that places have to greater or lesser degrees makes all the more sense when we consider politics in regions of a single democracy—that is, in a single country where elections are competitive, civilians control the military, and so on. The conditions that make a country a democracy generally make all regions of that country democratic, at least in the dichotomous sense. If elections are free and fair at the national level, and if a large proportion of the adult population enjoys the right to vote, then these conditions tend to hold across all regions of the country. Were the contrary true—were it the case, for instance, that national elections were free and fair but regional politics was controlled by nonelected military officers, or that large swaths of the electorate were barred, locally, from participation—one would question the label democracy as applied to the country as a whole.

Yet there is no question that democracy works better in some regions than in others, that some are more democratic than others. What's more, we suspect that this regional unevenness is present in nearly every democracy, though it will be more marked in some countries than in others. (Our guess is that this variation is greater in newer and poorer democracies than in older and wealthier ones.)

These conceptual points suggest an advantage to studying democratization across regions within countries. Certain factors that are known to matter in the democratization of nations are held constant when one considers subnational regions. Studying regions, then, may help us identify factors that are difficult to measure at the country level, and may help us to make sense of the mechanisms linking causal factors to the outcome of democratization.

A good example from this study is income equality. The mechanisms theorists have identified linking income equality to democratization include a greater tendency of those at the top to acknowledge the basic humanity of those at the bottom when the gulf between them is not too wide (Lipset 1959, 1960), and a greater willingness of those at the top to open decisions about income distribution to those in the middle when the gap is not too wide (Boix 2003; Acemoglu and Robinson 2003). Our study focuses attention yet again on the (regional) democratization effects of growing income equality. Yet it seems unlikely that the Boix and Acemoglu-Robinson mechanism is at work here: in Mexico and Argentina, taxation and redistribution schemes were largely established at the national level. Therefore we must search for a different mechanism linking income equality with democratization. We identified two: the demand for political rights on the part of the middle class; and the decline of clientelism, which becomes prohibitively expensive when votes must be purchased not with a bag of food but with a public sector job or an automatic washing machine. These two mechanisms may be at work as well in the democratization of countries. Here, then, is an example of propositions generated by research into regional democratization that should be considered in studies of the democratization of countries.

Why Are Regions So Different?

Having laid out two conjectures about regional differentiation in the quality of democracy—the second one supported by our study, the first one not—we admit that the degree of distinctiveness of regional political cultures surprised us. This distinctiveness rests to some degree on the kinds of processes and factors we just laid out. But not entirely. We did find that we could make some apparent regional differences "go away" with the appropriate statistical controls: for instance, the high levels of poverty in Misiones, rather than its geographic location, explain its high rate of clientelism. Generally speaking, however, this was not the case, and where a person lived remained an unexpectedly persistent factor shaping his or her political beliefs.

Our general position in this book has been that region stands for something else: the quality of democratic governance and practices. Indeed, we were at length in Part II to rank the four regions in each country on a scale, from most to least democratic. The quality of democracy, then, was generally the explanatory factor for features of political culture; each region was a stand-in for democracy of a given quality. Yet we came to believe in the course of our research that these regional differences amounted to even more than proxies for democracies of differing qualities.

We posit two other dynamics that help explain the robustness of geographic place as a cause of distinct patterns of beliefs. The first has to do with strategic choices made by regional political leaders. These leaders, individuals whose jurisdictions or range of influence correspond to discrete districts, states, or provinces, make choices about what kinds of strategies to follow and what kinds of institutions to build (or to neglect). Their choices then reverberate into the political culture and beliefs of the citizenry.

To translate this idea into the language of game theory, the strategy of clientelism relies on repeated interactions between parties and voters, a repeated game for which clientelism is one possible equilibrium among others. The same can be said of the strategic interaction between voters and elites leading to a strengthening of accountability, in which voters gain the ability to monitor and to contingently renew or fire officeholders, and officeholders gain authority over a broader range of policy areas. But the game has other equilibria and the leaders could have chosen another path. The jurisdiction or, more loosely, field of action of these political elites is geographically defined: they are governors of states, mayors of cities, and secretaries-general of regional branches of political parties. Hence, for example, the strategic choice to follow through on a promise to give a job in the public sector to a political supporter, rather than reneging, reinforces the public belief that favors, and not programmatic appeals, explain a party's public support. The political leaders in a similar, neighboring region might chose to renege, which in turn might lead to the unraveling of clientelism and to leaders' finding alternative, perhaps more programmatic, strategies of mobilization.

A second cause of regional distinctiveness is a dynamic of mutual persuasion. Here, admittedly firmly in the realm of conjecture, we encounter more tension with a rationalist account. We posit that regional differences in political culture are to some degree the result of people exposing others who live nearby to certain beliefs. Mere exposure to these beliefs makes their adoption, among coworkers, neighbors, schoolmates, and fellow churchgoers, more likely. Of course not all communications are geographically bounded, and one may be exposed to, and persuaded by, arguments about the nature of politics and government carried in messages from distant figures on television, radio, or in print. Yet geographic proximity brings with it greater occasion to send informal and daily messages that influence how we think about politics. For instance, parents might bring children up to be deferential to political leaders and to attribute good performance of the government to the beneficence of these leaders, independent of any evidence in favor of such an interpretation. To the extent that the beneficiaries infer that likeable, trustworthy governors personally see to it that their constituents' needs are met, and persuasively communicate this belief to those with whom they have direct contact, the regional political culture will be personalistic.

Why Political Culture?

How does the construct of a political culture help us understand the dynamics of democratic consolidation? By political culture we mean patterns of political action and a related web of political beliefs and preferences, beliefs and preferences that tend to show some logical coherence as well as empirical covariation. People who lived in more democratic regions in Argentina and Mexico participated in political cultures featuring the beliefs that institutions constrain politicians and that their neighbors respond to programmatic appeals by parties and not to personal inducements. They preferred respect for the rule of law or contingent consent to the law. Regarding actions and practices, they tended to vote rather than to abstain, to get their news from written rather than from broadcast sources, and to speak freely about their political choices. The beliefs, preferences, and actions of people living in less democratic regions were starkly different. (In some theoretically important ways the political cultures of more and less democratic regions were not different: people in them displayed the same levels of interpersonal trust, and participated equally in civic associations.)

One might object that invoking the concept of political culture obscures more than it clarifies. Differences in perceptions across our regions to some extent reflected real differences in how well democracy worked. If we were merely dealing with a set of accurate perceptions of better functioning (or worse functioning) political institutions, then we could discard the construct of political culture, and instead conclude that cross-regional differences in political beliefs and preferences were simply an artifact of cross-regional variation in the quality of democracy. In some ways this objection is fair. It is probably the case that more people in Baja California than in Puebla believed that elections were clean because they *were* cleaner in Baja California. People in Mar del Plata saw clientelism as less widespread than those in Misiones did because it *was* less widespread in Mar del Plata.

Yet not all of the systematic differences we detected between the skeptical, democratic cultures and the trusting, less democratic ones were simple reflections of distinct realities. Respect for the rule of law is a preference that one comes to hold, rather than a reflection of the quality of democracy. It may be that these preferences become more widespread as the flouting of law becomes less common. Even if this is so, the preference is distinct from the behavioral pattern. More central to our defense of the construct of political cultures is the fact that people who participated in more and less democratic cultures hold systematically different beliefs about matters that they cannot observe. Consider the belief, more widespread in the more democratic regions in both countries, that other voters take into account political programs and universalistic concerns, rather than particularistic favors, when deciding how to vote. When people respond to questions by speculating about the motives of other voters, they are doing just that—speculating. The number of other voters about whom any person knows the precise voting decision rules is limited. Hence we find, as a component of political culture, beliefs that run well beyond one's experiences or observations.

The motivations of politicians are particularly difficult for citizens to discern through direct observation. We have seen that a central element in the democratic culture of skepticism is the belief that politicians are only responsive when they are under institutional constraints. A prominent element in the culture of personal trust in our less consolidated regions was the belief that politicians who act responsively must be inherently good people. Few citizens of any country have the opportunity to look deeply into the character and motivations of elected officials. We can only speculate that people acquire institutional trust by inferring motives from the actions of politicians. For some voters in new democracies, belief in the trustworthiness of politicians arises from the voter's status as client: from their face-to-face contact and receipt of pseudo-gifts of food, clothing, or cash. For all these reasons, we hold, perceptions can diverge from reality.

We now further develop our claim that the cross-regional divergences in political outlooks and actions are best described as a skeptical culture in more democratic regions, and a personally trusting culture in less democratic ones.

What Kind of Political Culture of Democracy?

Our objections to the civic culture tradition, as we have explained, are in part theoretical. It fails to provide persuasive arguments about why a lively community associational life is critical to improving the quality of democracy, just as it fails to provide persuasive arguments about why interpersonal trust among citizens enhances democratic governance. Among several theoretical objections outlined in chapter 1, we doubt that private citizens who trust each other also trust one another to keep tabs on elected officials. The belief that your neighbors are trustworthy, in the sense that you might leave your home under their care, does not imply that they will look out for your interests in city hall or in the national bureaucracy. To the extent that you believe that third parties are promoting your interests in these spheres, the third parties are institutions—the press, lobbies, nongovernmental organizations, and the like—and not our neighbors. Finally, the mutual familiarity and bonds of reciprocity that social capital theorists celebrate often, in democracies in the developing world, undermine the anonymity and freedom from reprisals that meaningful citizenship requires.

Our objections to the civic culture tradition are empirical as well as theoretical. The evidence presented in earlier chapters has contradicted civic cultural arguments at nearly every turn. Democratization certainly brings with it a reshaping of political culture, but the culture of democracy is not the one envisioned in the civic culture tradition. Democratic political culture may be a culture of citizenship, awareness, and participation. But it is also a culture of skepticism, of contingent consent, and of conditional, weak trust in government.

As a system of preferences and beliefs, the democratic culture of skepticism departs sharply from the political culture of trust. As a system of patterned actions and practices, the departure is equally sharp. Theorists from de Tocqueville to Putnam have described the civic culture of democracy as one in which democratic citizens participate heavily in civic associations. There are some ways in which the citizens of our consolidated regions resembled the figure of the civic participant. Compared to their compatriots in less democratic regions, they split their tickets more frequently, and hence presumably were more thoughtful voters. They read newspapers more frequently. And they felt freer to report their vote choices to survey interviewers. Yet in other ways these same citizens looked very different from the image of the civic participant. They joined fewer civic associations. They went to church less frequently. They had looser links to political parties. They were no more trusting of their neighbors and were less personally trusting of politicians. They were less likely to have turned to local political figures or party operatives or to the municipal government to solve a problem. In both Argentina and Mexico, people from the most democratic regions were the least likely to report that they had turned to their municipal administration to solve some problem in recent years. This held true even in the presence of controls for income, education level, housing quality, and other possible confounding variables. Far from civic activists or participants, they looked like people who, though politically informed and aware, spent more time on private matters than on civic affairs.

This lesser participation in civic life and greater absorption in private concerns may be a function of community development and democratic consolidation itself. We argued in the first chapter that civic activism may, indeed, be self-limiting, with people turning away from civic involvement when their demands are met and community development advances. Reflecting on this decline in civic activism, a city councilman from the Argentine city of Mar del Plata we interviewed reflected on the quiescence of his neighbors, a quiescence about which he was not entirely pleased:

> I'm a member of community development organizations, I go to their meetings. There are never more than eight, ten, twelve of us. There is no atmosphere of community or neighborhood participation. The development associations have turned into places where the only thing they do is cut the grass, they give free classes in Tai Kwan Do, and there's a dentist. . . . But there's no complex participation, on neighborhood themes, about the improvement of services. The thing is that the infrastructure of services is almost covered. . . . So those social entities that call themselves Societies for Development . . . in time have changed into places where old people go to play cards. (Norberto Pérez, February 25, 2004)

Certainly the social effects of "old people" playing cards in a neighborhood club as against playing solitaire at home may be significant. Still, the picture that emerges from his words and from our analysis is one of a democratic subculture that is skeptical and, in its relations to civic associations, if not to voting and to political attentiveness, inactive.

As an empirical matter, our findings were not in all respects at odds with those of the civic culture tradition. We have already mentioned some practices that made the inhabitants of our more democratic regions look like civic activists: they split tickets more, were more willing to talk about politics, paid more attention to it, and got their news from more sophisticated sources. And the civic culture tradition is not univocal in linking interpersonal trust to participation—a link that our research failed to uncover. Almond and Verba found this link in the advanced democracies they studied but not in their less stable democracies:

> In the United States and Britain the belief that people are generally cooperative, trustworthy, and helpful is frequent. . . . Belief in the benignity of one's fellow citizen is directly related to one's propensity to join with others in political activity. General social trust is translated into politically relevant trust. In [Germany, Italy, and Mexico] the absence of a cooperative, group-forming political style appears to be related . . . to the fact that even that trust expressed does not increase the probability that an individual will think of working with others in trying to influence the government. (1963, 285)

Our study, like theirs, found that a person who believed in the "benignity of one's fellow citizens" was also more likely to "join with others in political activity," or at least join civic organizations. And we found this in two less developed, new democracies, one of which (Mexico) Almond and Verba also studied and the other of which (Argentina) was, like Italy and Germany in the early 1960s, a recently re-democratized country at a moderate level of economic development.

Yet we also found, in our cross-regional studies, that civic participation was higher in the less democratic regions than in the more democratic ones. Also at odds with the civic culture tradition is the propensity of people who took part in civic associations in Mexico and Argentina to evince less institutional trust and more personal trust in politicians. If civic action is supposed to breed political sophistication and beliefs supportive of democratic consolidation, the supposition is contradicted by the experiences of our new Latin American democracies.

In fact, our evidence shows that interpersonal trust, which is central to the civic culture theory of democracy, did not predict any of the political-cultural features that distinguished the more democratic regions of Argentina and Mexico. As tables 6.1 and 6.2 show, respondents who expressed high levels of interpersonal trust were significantly less likely to express institutional trust, and more likely to personally know a local party operative. The interpersonally trustworthy were also no less likely to be enmeshed in clientelist relationships; nor were they more likely to express respect for the rule of law.

Personal Trust and Institutional Trust

Another of our central aims was to examine the role of trust in politics, and, in particular, in the dynamics of regional democratization. Our theoretical predispositions left us more sympathetic to institutional than to personal trust as a foundation for democracy. In general, citizens cannot know enough about politicians' inherent qualities to be able to confidently use elections to select the ones who are trustworthy and reject the ones who are not. A more solid foundation for democracy, our initial instincts told us, were institutions that constrained politicians to act in constituents' interests. The institutionally shaped self-interest of politicians is a surer foundation for responsiveness than were the strengths of their characters. When it comes to trusting politicians, weak trust is better than strong trust.

Our research confirmed these instincts in many ways. People in more democratic regions understood that their ability to trust politicians depended on institutions that monitor the actions of these politicians, rather than on their inherent honesty or competence. A broad range of evidence generated from our sample surveys supported this view.

Table 6.1   **Argentina: Interpersonal Trust and the Democratic Culture of Skepticism**

	Level of Interpersonal Trust	
	Low	High
Institutional trust		
Percentage who say government provides good services when it is monitored (Services)	58	53
Percentage who say governments are efficient because they want to be reelected (Efficient)	77	70
Percentage who say "no" politicians can be trusted if they are not monitored (Trustpol)	51	29
Clientelism		
Percentage who know local party representative (Know Party)	24	36
Percentage who would go to a party rep. for employment help (Job)	35	37
Percentage who received handouts during the campaign (Gift)	9	8
Proceduralism		
Percentage saying it is "never justified" to avoid paying taxes one owes (Taxes)	44	47
Percentage saying it is "never justified" to claim undeserved services (Claim)	68	71
Percentage saying it is "never justified" to not pay admission to a public event (Admission)	80	81

Source: Authors' compilations.

Yet our research has reminded us that politics is always personalized to some degree. Although people in our more democratic regions had a finer appreciation of institutional trust and were more skeptical about the trustworthiness of politicians, still, like people everywhere, they made inferences about what their elected leaders were like as people and about how, for good or ill, leaders' personal traits influenced their capacity to govern and to govern well. In theory, there are some conditions under which it is not unreasonable for constituents to trust their representatives in a strong, personal sense (Fearon 1999). But beyond whether it is rational or reasonable to do so, it is probably inevitable that voters think about politicians as people who have inherent personality traits, traits that matter for public affairs. Voters may be especially prone to consider the personalities of politicians when they are electing politicians to executive offices.

Given our predilections, we were surprised to find a personalizing

Table 6.2   Mexico: Interpersonal Trust and the Democratic Culture of Skepticism

	Level of Interpersonal Trust	
	Low	High
Institutional trust		
Percentage who say government provides good services when it is monitored (Services)	63	51
Percentage who say governments are efficient because they want to be reelected (Efficient)	74	52
Percentage who say "no" politicians can be trusted if they are not monitored (Trustpol)	33	11
Clientelism		
Percentage who know local party representative (Know Party)	21	26
Percentage who would go to a party rep. for employment help (Job)	27	33
Percentage who received handouts during the campaign (Gift)	17	15
Proceduralism		
Percentage saying it is "never justified" to avoid paying taxes one owes (Taxes)	46	49
Percentage saying it is "never justified" to claim undeserved services (Claim)	47	49
Percentage saying it is "never justified" to avoid paying a public transportation fare (Fare)	64	61

Source: Authors' compilations.

of politics in our more democratic regions, even if that personalizing was less pronounced than in our less democratic ones. We were surprised by the evident importance of the force of personality of Ernesto Ruffo, Baja California's first PAN governor, and of Patricio Martínez, the PRI leader who won Chihuahua back for the PRI after a period of opposition control. We also learned a valuable lesson about personality, trust, and democracy from leaders such as Elio Aprile, the Argentine mayor. More people in his region (than in the others we studied) believed that, when politicians are trustworthy, it is simply because they want to win more votes or because they fear reprisals. But Mayor Aprile still knew that, at key moments, his constituents would be swayed not by appeals to institutions or interests but by his personal reputation. When he first ran for office, and had no political record to appeal to, he courted voters by projecting an image of honesty. When he sought a popular mandate for a major development project, he found that technical appeals alone did not move people; he had to back them up with his own "affable" personal presence.

Aprile's constituents were not crazy to withhold support from a risky project until he made a personal appeal. We speculate that their reasoning might have gone like this. They believed that their mayor was honest and capable, but knew that many politicians and officials were neither. They therefore considered the ambitious and costly proposals to be a risky proposition: they might be the scheme of dishonest or incompetent politicians, or they might be taken over by such politicians in the future. Skeptical, these constituents therefore required the personal backing of their honest and capable mayor before they would give their approval.

Yet if this case reminds us that personalities inevitably, and sometimes sensibly, come into play in democratic politics and that trust always involves an assessment of personalities, not just of institutions, it also illustrates the pitfalls of personal trust. The mayor's constituents were probably right when they initially inferred that he was honest. But in bad times it was easy for his opponents to persuade citizens that they had misjudged, and that in fact Aprile was dishonest. As we saw in chapter 3, when their leader took missteps, his constituents made incorrect suppositions about the personality flaws that led him astray.

The lesson goes far beyond events in one city in one developing democracy. And the lesson is sobering. Whether or not it is rational to do so, we as citizens will never stop trying to understand the personalities, qualities of mind, and character of politicians when we assess whether they deserve our support. Especially when politicians seek executive office, citizens will show interest in where they were born and grew up, in their religious beliefs, their spouses and their families. We will always want to know how honest they are, how shrewd, how passionate, and how steadfast. Yet we are likely to attain only a blurred vision of our leaders as people and fail to anticipate which qualities matter for a leader in an uncertain future. Citizens are likely to trust their leaders, and distrust them, for the wrong reasons.

Still, despite this inevitable personalization and search for leaders whom we can trust, to consolidate new democracies and to deepen old ones what we need is not civic-minded citizens who are ready to trust their neighbors or their elected officials. What we need instead are institutions that generate trustworthiness by making governments more transparent and leaders more responsive to the interests of their constituents.

Appendix

Methodology

Imputation of Missing Data

All of our survey questions elicited non-responses, with people either declining to answer or responding, "don't know." We report the non-response rates in all of the cross-tabular tables, and we include them in our calculations of cross-regional variation in the responses of interest (see for example table 4.1). The cross-regional patterns shown in these tables generally hold, whether or not we include the non-responses in our percentage calculations.

In all multivariate analyses, we treat non-responses as missing data. We use the multiple imputation techniques described in King et al. (2001) and implemented in the *Amelia* program to generate imputed values for missing data (see also Honaker et al. 2003). We generated five datasets each from the original Argentine and Mexican datasets, and substituted the imputed values for the missing values. We estimated multivariate models using *Clarify*'s *estsimp* command in combination with the *mi* option, specifying the use of all five datasets (we discuss our use of *Clarify* in the section on Simulations).

Thus, except where noted, all multivariate models for Argentina are based on 1,920 observations (480 in each of 4 regions), and those for Mexico are based on 1,598 observations (400 for each of four states, less two cases in the state of Chihuahua that are completely missing). In virtually no instances did the models that drew on imputed datasets generate substantively different results than those that employed listwise deletion.

Model Specification and Multi-Level Data

In the multivariate analyses of survey responses, all of the dependent variables are categorical; thus all of our models are logit, ordered logit, or multinominal logit estimations, as appropriate. As explained, we used clustered sample designs, which means that our observations within clusters are potentially non-independent. To correct for this potential non-independence, in all models using survey data we estimate and report robust standard errors, using Stata 8.0's *cluster* option in all of our estimations (see Kish and Frankel 1974 and White 1980).

Many of our specifications include a mix of variables that were observed at individual and municipal levels, such as the population size of a respondent's municipality, its poverty rate, and the revenues raised locally. Because individual respondents were drawn in ten-person clusters from within municipalities, and because large municipalities produced multiple clusters, in some models there may be additional non-independence that robust standard errors do not account for. It is possible to compensate for the potential inefficiency of estimates produced by this non-independence by estimating hierarchical linear models (HLM; see Raudenbush and Bryk 2002). However, given that we are already correcting for non-independence within clusters, an HLM approach would have added much complexity to analyses and interpretations without significantly improving the precision of our estimates.

Simulations

Throughout the book we use simulations to help illustrate the substantive significance of statistical effects that we identify in multivariate analyses. All of these simulations are generated in Stata 8.0 using the *Clarify* program (Tomz, Wittenberg, and King 2001; King, Tomz, and Wittenberg 2000). *Clarify* draws simulations of parameters of statistical models from their sampling distribution and then converts these simulated parameters into expected values, such as expected probabilities of an answer to a survey question, given hypothetical values of explanatory variables. Thus the program offers a convenient way to interpret and illustrate how a given change in the value of an explanatory variable affects an outcome of interest. *Clarify* software and documentation are available from Gary King's website at http://gking.harvard.edu.

Survey Questions and Translations

This appendix lists the exact wording of the survey questions discussed in this book, particularly in chapters 4 and 5. Many questions were worded differently in Argentina and Mexico. We list both versions, with English translations, and we note which questions were asked in each country.

Services

Some governments provide good services to the people, others don't. In your opinion, those that provide good services, why do they do so?

1) Because they are watched by the courts, congress, or the press,

2) (Mexico) Because they are honorable people?

2) (Argentina) Because they are good, committed people?

Algunos gobiernos proveen buenos servicios a la gente, otros no. En su opinión, los que proveen buenos servicios, ¿por qué lo hacen?

1) Porque están bajo la vigilancia de la justicia, el congreso, o la prensa,

2) (Mexico) Porque son personas honradas

2) (Argentina) Por que son personas de bien y comprometidas?

Efficient

Mexico

Some municipalities provide public services like street repairs in an efficient way, others don't. When municipal governments function efficiently, is it because . . .

1) The mayor, the comptroller and the city councillors are committed people,

2) They know that if they don't work well, the voters won't reelect them?

Algunos municipios proveen servicios públicos como reparación de calles de una forma eficiente, otros no. Cuando los gobiernos funcionan eficientemente, ¿Es porque . . .

1) El Presidente municipal, los síndicos y los regidores son personas comprometidas

2) Saben que si no trabajan bien los votantes no los volverán a elegir?

Argentina

When municipal governments function efficiently, is it because . . .

1) The mayor, the city council and members of the accounts tribunal are committed people,

2) They know that if they don't work well, the voters won't reelect them?

Cuando los gobiernos funcionan eficientemente, ¿Es porque . . .

1) El Intendente, los concejales y miembros del tribunal de cuentas son personas comprometidas

2) Saben que si no trabajan bien los votantes no los volverán a elegir?

Attention

(Previous question: Do you think that politicians pay attention to the opinions of people like you?

¿Piensa que los políticos prestan atención a las opiniones de personas como Usted?)

Thinking about politicians who do pay attention, do you think they do it because it really matters to them or because they want to be reelected?

Pensando en los políticos que sí prestan atención, ¿Usted cree que lo hacen porque realmente les importa o porque quieren ser reelegidos?

Bribe

Mexico

When a politician abusing his position is trying to act illegally or is accepting bribes, how likely is it that he will be discovered, for example by the press or the authorities?

1) Very likely
2) Not very likely
3) Not likely at all

Cuando algún político abusando de su posición está tratando de actuar ilegalmente o está aceptando sobornos, ¿qué tan probable es que lo descubra por ejemplo la prensa o las autoridades?

1) Muy probable
2) Poco probable
3) Nada probable

Argentina

When a politician accepts bribes, how likely is it that he will be discovered, for example by the press or the authorities?

1) Very likely
2) Not very likely
3) Not likely at all

Cuando algún político acepta coimas ¿qué tan probable es que lo descubra por ejemplo la prensa o las autoridades?

1) Muy probable

2) Poco probable

3) Nada probable

Trustpol

Thinking in general about people who hold public office, how many do you think are trustworthy and will behave correctly without being monitored?

1) All

2) A majority

3) A minority

4) None

Pensando en las personas con cargos públicos en general, cuántos piensa Ud. que son confiables y que se portarán de una forma correcta (Argentina: bien) sin ser vigilados.

1) Todos

2) La mayoría

3) La minoría

4) Ninguno

Personal Trust

Tell me please which of the following expression is closest to your way of thinking:

1) I believe that you can trust a majority of people

2) I believe you can only trust a minority of people

3) I don't trust anyone (spontaneous)

Dígame por favor cuál de las siguientes expresiones se acerca más a su manera de pensar:

1) Creo que se puede confiar en la mayoría de la gente

2) Creo que sólo se puede confiar en una minoría de la gente

3) No confío en nadie (espontánea)

Patron

Mexico

(Previous question: Who do you believe is the most important person in politics in this area?

¿Quién cree usted que es el personaje más importante en la política en esta localidad?)

In recent years, have you turned to this person to resolve some problems?

En los últimos años, ¿Usted ha recurrido a esa persona para resolver algún problema?

Argentina

(Previous question: Apart from whether you like this person or not or voted for this person or not, who do you believe is the most important person in politics in this part of the city?

Más allá que le guste o no, lo vote o no ¿Quién cree usted que es el personaje más importante en la política en esta área de la ciudad?)

In recent years, have you turned to this person to resolve some problems?

En los últimos años, ¿Usted ha recurrido a esa persona para resolver algún problema?

Know Party

Do you know some representative of a political party in your neighborhood or locality?

¿Conoce usted a algún representante de un partido político en su colonia o localidad?

Party Help

In recent years, have you turned to a representative of some political party to resolve a problem?

En los últimos años, ¿Ud. ha recurrido a un representante (Argentina: puntero or referente) de algún partido político para resolver un problema?

Job

If the head of your family lost his or her job and the family needed help, would you turn to a party representative of a political party?

Si el jefe de su familia perdiera su trabajo y la familia necesitara ayuda, ¿Ud. recurriría al representante (Argentina: puntero o referente) de un partido político?

Party Give, Gift

Mexico

The following statement preceded the questions listed below as Party Give and Gift:

This past [date of election], there were elections for governor,[1] state legislators, and mayors. Which of the following activities occurred in this city or community before the elections?

El pasado [date of election], hubo elecciones para Gobernador, Diputados Locales y Presidente Municipal. ¿Cuáles de las siguientes actividades ocurrieron en esta ciudad o comunidad antes de las elecciones?

Party give

During the campaign, did a candidate or party distribute things to people?

¿Durante la campaña, un candidato o un partido repartió cosas a la gente?

Gift

Did you receive something from a party or candidate?

¿Usted recibió algo de algún partido o un candidato?

Argentina

Party give

Here in this neighborhood, did any candidate or party distribute things to people in the campaign?

¿Acá en este barrio, algún candidato o un partido repartió cosas a la gente en campaña?

Gift

Did you receive something from a candidate, party, or public organism during the campaign?

¿Usted recibió algo de algún candidato, partido u organismo público en campaña?

Does Obligate

Mexico

Sometimes candidates or representatives of political parties distribute things during electoral campaigns, for example bags of food. Do you think that the people who receive these things feel obligated to vote for that party or candidate?

A veces los candidatos o representantes de los partidos políticos reparten cosas durante las campañas electorales, como por ejemplo despensas. ¿Usted cree que las personas que reciben esas cosas se sienten obligadas a votar por ese partido o candidato?

Argentina

When candidates or party representatives distribute things during election campaigns, such as bags of food or mattresses, do you believe that the people who receive these things feel obliged to vote for that party or candidate?

Cuando los candidatos o punteros de los partidos políticos reparten cosas durante las campañas electorales, como por ejemplo bolsones, colchones. ¿Usted cree que las personas que reciben esas cosas se sienten obligadas a votar por ese partido o candidato?

Should Obligate

And do you believe they should feel obliged?

¿Y cree que deberían sentirse obligadas?

Claim

Mexico

In general, do you believe that claiming public goods and services or public benefits that one does not deserve is . . .

1) Always justified
2) Sometimes justified
3) Never justified?

En general, ¿Usted cree que reclamar bienes y servicios públicos o beneficios públicos que no le corresponden a uno . . .

1) Siempre se justifica
2) A veces se justifica
3) Nunca se justifica?

Argentina

Do you believe that claiming something from the government that one does not deserve is

1) Always justified
2) Sometimes justified
3) Never justified?

¿Usted cree que reclamar algo del gobierno que no corresponde reclamar . . .

1)   Siempre se justifica

2)   A veces se justifica

3)   Nunca se justifica?

Claim Many

Mexico

If many people claimed public goods and services or public benefits knowing that they didn't deserve them, is it justified for someone to do so as well?

Ahora bien, si dado que mucha gente reclama bienes y servicios públicos o beneficios públicos sabiendo que no les corresponden, ¿es justificable que uno también lo haga?

Argentina

If many people claimed goods, services, or benefits from the government knowing that they didn't deserve them, is it justified for one to do so as well?

Si mucha gente reclama bienes, servicios o beneficios del gobierno sabiendo que no les corresponden, ¿es justificable que uno también lo haga?

Taxes

Mexico

Thinking again in general terms, do you believe that not paying taxes that one owes is . . .

1)   Always justified

2)   Sometimes justified

3)   Never justified?

Pensando nuevamente en términos generales, ¿usted cree que no pagar impuestos que le corresponden a uno . . .

1)   Siempre se justifica

2)   A veces se justifica

3)   Nunca se justifica?

Argentina

Thinking again in general terms, do you believe that not paying taxes is

1) Always justified
2) Sometimes justified
3) Never justified?

Pensando nuevamente en términos generales, ¿usted cree que no pagar impuestos . . .

1) Siempre se justifica
2) A veces se justifica
3) Nunca se justifica?

Taxes Many

Mexico

If many people didn't pay taxes, knowing that this means that there will be fewer public services in this locality, is it justified that one also doesn't pay?

Ahora bien, si dado que mucha gente no paga impuestos sabiendo que esto significa que habrá menos servicios públicos en su localidad ¿es justificable que uno también no los pague?

Argentina

If many people didn't pay taxes, knowing that this means that there will be fewer public services in this locality, is it justified that one also doesn't pay?

Si es que mucha gente no paga impuestos sabiendo que esto significa que habrá menos servicios públicos en su localidad ¿es justificable que tampoco los pague?

Military

Mexico

Now please tell me, do you think that avoiding military service that one is supposed to do is . . .

1) Always justified
2) Sometimes justified
3) Never justified?

Ahora dígame por favor ¿usted cree que evitar cumplir con el servicio militar que debe hacer uno . . .

1) Siempre se justificaba
2) A veces se justificaba
3) Nunca se justificaba?

Argentina

Until recently obligatory military service existed. Do you believe that not complying with military service in that era was

1) Always justified
2) Sometimes justified
3) Never justified?

Hasta hace poco existía el Servico Militar Obligatorio ¿usted cree que el no cumplir con el servicio militar en aquella época . . .

1) Siempre se justificaba
2) A veces se justificaba
3) Nunca se justificaba?

Military Many

Mexico

If many people do not comply with military service, is one also justified in not complying?
     Ahora bien, si dado que mucha gente no cumple con el servicio militar ¿es justificable que uno también no lo cumpla?

Argentina

If many people didn't comply with military service, was one also justified in not complying?
     Si mucha gente no cumplía con el servicio militar ¿era justificable que uno tampoco lo cumpliera?

Stolen

Mexico

Buying an article that might be stolen is

1) Always justified
2) Sometimes justified
3) Never justified

Comprar algún artículo aunque sea robado

1) Siempre se justifica
2) A veces se justifica
3) Nunca se justifica

Argentina

Buying an article that one suspects is stolen is

1) Always justified
2) Sometimes justified
3) Never justified

Comprar algún artículo que se sospecha es robado

1) Siempre se justifica
2) A veces se justifica
3) Nunca se justifica

Corrupt

That an authority or functionary accepts a bribe is

1) Always justified
2) Sometimes justified
3) Never justified

Que una autoridad o funcionario acepte un soborno o "mordida" (Argentina: soborno o coima)

1) Siempre se justifica
2) A veces se justifica
3) Nunca se justifica

Fare

Mexico Only

To not pay the fare for public transportation is

1) Always justified
2) Sometimes justified
3) Never justified

No pagar el boleto o "el pasaje" en el transporte público

1) Siempre se justifica
2) A veces se justifica
3) Nunca se justifica

Admission

Argentina Only

To not pay for admission to a public event is

1) Always justified
2) Sometimes justified
3) Never justified

No pagar una entrada de un espectáculo público

1) Siempre se justifica
2) A veces se justifica
3) Nunca se justifica

Handout, Favor, Past

Thinking now about the most important political party in this area (Argentina: the political party you mentioned as the most important [in your neighborhood]), would you say that the people support it because . . .
   Favor
   . . . it is concerned for everyone or because it has done them some favor?
   Handout
   . . . Because the party has given out things during the campaign or because it has a better program?
   Pensando ahora en el partido político más importante de esta localidad usted diría que la gente lo apoya porque:
   ¿Se preocupa por todos o Porque les ha hecho algún favor?
   ¿Porque el partido ha repartido cosas en la campaña o porque tiene una mejor propuesta?

Meet

During the last 12 months, have you attended an assembly or meeting about some problem in your community or in the school?

Durante los últimos 12 meses, ¿Usted asistió a una asamblea o una reunión sobre algún problema en su comunidad o en la escuela?

Sport

This variable is a dummy for people who answered "athletic" when read the following list:

I am going to read you a list of organizations that some people belong to. If you belong to one please tell me what type it is. There are associations that are:

1) Athletic

2) Artistic and cultural

3) Parents in the schools

4) Community or of neighbors

5) Of peasants

6) Professional

7) Youth

8) Unions

9) Trade groups

10) Political groups or political parties

11) Non-governmental or civic organizations

12) Other

Voy a leerle una lista de organizaciones a las cuales algunas personas pertenecen. Si usted pertenece a alguna dígame por favor de que tipo es. Existen asociaciones:

1) Deportivas

2) Artísticas y culturales

3) De padres de familia en las escuelas

4) Comunales o de vecinos

5) De campesinos

6) Profesionales

7) Juveniles

8) Sindicatos

9) Gremios

10) Grupos políticos o partidos políticos

11)   Organizaciones no gubernamentales o civiles

12)   Otra

Belong

At the moment, to how many organizations do you belong?

¿En este momento, a cuántas organizaciones calcula Ud. que pertenece?

1)   0

2)   1

3)   2–3

4)   Más que 3

Time

During the last 12 months, about how much time have you dedicated to the activities of these organizations?

1)   Just 1 day

2)   1 week

3)   Between 2 and 3 weeks

4)   Between 1 or 2 months

5)   More than 3 months

Durante los últimos 12 meses, ¿aproximadamente cuánto tiempo ha dedicado Ud. a actividades de esa(s) organización(es)?

1)   Sólo 1 día

2)   1 semana

3)   Entre 2 y 3 semanas

4)   Entre 1 o 2 meses

5)   Más de 3 meses

Comprob

During the last 12 months, have you collaborated with other people who are not your relatives to try to resolve some problem that confronted your community?

Durante los últimos 12 meses, ¿ha usted colaborado con otras personas que no sean familiares suyos para tratar de resolver algún problema que enfrente su comunidad?

Workprob

Other than your work duties, during the last 12 months have you collaborated with other people you work with to try to resolve some problem in common?

Más allá de sus deberes en el trabajo, ¿Durante los últimos 12 meses ha colaborado con otras personas que trabajen con usted para tratar de resolver algún problema en común?

Religion

Thinking now about religion, about how many times per month do you go to mass or to another religious service?

Pensando ahora en la religión, ¿aproximadamente cuántas veces por mes va Ud. a misa o a otro servicio religioso?

1) 0

2) 1–2

3) 3–4

4) Más de 4

Neighbor

Thinking about the locality or neighborhood where you live, if you were to leave on a trip, do you have some neighbors whom you could trust to watch your house while you were away?

Pensando ahora en la localidad o colonia donde usted vive, ¿si usted se fuera de viaje, tiene algunos vecinos en quienes podría confiar para que le cuiden la casa mientras está afuera?

Advantage

Do you think that most people would try to take advantage of you if they were given the chance, or do you think that they would not try to take advantage?

¿Cree que la mayoría de la gente trataría de aprovecharse de usted si se le presentara la oportunidad, o cree que no trataría de aprovecharse?

Income

Adding the income of all the people in your house who work, how much do all those who work in your family earn per month?

Sumando los ingresos de todas las personas que trabajan en su casa, ¿Cuánto ganan todos los que trabajan en su familia al mes?

Mexico

1) Hasta $800
2) $801–$2,400
3) $2,401–$4,000
4) $4,001–$8,000
5) $8,001–$16,000
6) Más de $16,000

Argentina

1) Hasta 100 pesos
2) Entre 101 a 300 pesos
3) Entre 301 a 500 pesos
4) Entre 501 a 700 pesos
5) Entre 701 a 1000 pesos
6) Entre 1001 a 1500 pesos
7) Entre 1501 a 2000 pesos
8) Más de 2001 pesos

Education

Up to what year did you study?
¿Hasta qué año escolar estudió usted (grado máximo)?

Mexico

1) Ninguno (None)
2) Primaria (Primary)
3) Secundaria (Secondary)
4) Preparatoria (Preparatory)
5) Universidad (University)
6) Universidad y más (Beyond university)
7) Otros estudios (Other studies)

Argentina

1) Sin estudio (No studies)
2) Primario incompleto (Primary incomplete)
3) Primario completo (Primary completed)

4)   Secundario incompleto (Secondary incomplete)

5)   Secundario completo (Secondary completed)

6)   Terciario incompleto (Tertiary incomplete)

7)   Terciario completo (Tertiary completed)

8)   Universitario incompleto (University incomplete)

9)   Universitario completo (University completed)

Class

To what social class do you think you belong?

The upper class

The middle class

The lower class

¿A cuál clase social considera Ud. que pertenece?

La clase alta

La clase media

La clase baja

Housing

Argentina Only

This variable is a 5-point ordinal scale based on the interviewer's assessment, according to the following guidelines:

1)   General shantytown dwellings

2)   Typical workers' housing

3)   Medium-sized or small houses of simple design

4)   Traditional or modern house construction, made with high-quality materials

5)   Single-family homes (modern, or well-preserved older home), located in a residential neighborhood, with a garage and garden.

1)   Generalmente villa miseria

2)   Casas de Barrios típicos obreros

3)   Casas o chalets de dimensiones medianas o pequeñas y de diseño simple

4) Construcción tipo chalet tradicional o moderno, Hechos con materials de calidad

5) Casa aislada (moderna o antigua bien conservada), situada en barrio residencial, con garaje y jardín

Age

How old are you?
¿Cuántos años cumplidos tiene usted?

1) 18 to 25 years old
2) 26 to 35 years old
3) 36 to 45 years old
4) 46 to 55 years old
5) More than 55 years old

PRI, PAN, and PRD Supporter

Mexico Only

Independently of whom you have voted for in the past, with which
party do you most identify? How much?

1) PAN strongly
2) PAN somewhat
3) PRI strongly
4) PRI somewhat
5) PRD strongly
6) PRD somewhat
7) Other
8) None

Independientemente de por quién ha votado en el pasado, ¿Con cuál
partido se identifica usted más? ¿Cuánto?

1) PAN mucho
2) PAN algo
3) PRI mucho
4) PRI algo
5) PRD mucho

6) PRD algo

7) Otro

8) Ninguno

Peronist and Radical

Argentina Only

Regardless of who you have voted for in the past, which party do you like more?

1) Peronists

2) Radicals

3) Other (which?)

Independientemente de por quién ha votado en el pasado, ¿Cuál partido le gusta más?

1. PJ

2. UCR

3. Otro (¿cuál?)

Notes

Preface

1. Robert Putnam (2000, 47) bemoans a sharp decline, between the mid-1960s and the 1990s, in the number of survey respondents in the United States who agreed that you could "trust the government in Washington to do what is right all or most of the time." Other prominent studies linking trust to democracy include Almond and Verba (1963, 490), Dahl (1971, 150–2), Hetherington (2005), and Inglehart (1988).
2. For similar arguments see Hibbing and Theiss-Morse (2002) and Uslaner (2002).

Chapter 1

1. Societies that achieve these ends, Warren writes, are ones in which the associational life is "multifaceted and cuts across identities, communities, geographies, and other potential cleavages" (3).
2. In his study of Italy, Putnam considers the problems of cooperation in a clientelistic political culture. He focuses on the ways in which clientelism can thwart cooperation. Our point here is that cooperation itself is undemocratic when it means enforcing the implicit clientelist rule of exchange (a vote in exchange for a handout or a job).
3. The interview was conducted by Valeria Brusco, Lucas Lázaro, and Susan Stokes in July 2003.
4. Assume that the total dollar amount that a party has at its disposal for vote buying is a function of the country's per capita income. Gifts will be effective in winning over people's votes only if they increase a person's income by some minimum amount. The party will be able to buy a larger number of votes when incomes are highly unequal and there are many poor voters than when incomes are equal and the amount it must spend per vote grows.
5. Although our conceptualization of trust is not exactly the same, we adopt the A-B-X framework from Russell Hardin (2002).
6. In what sense are the former versions weak and the latter strong? In two

211

senses. First, whether trust is sustained by a spontaneous convergence of interests, by direct sanction, or by third-party sanction, X is unambiguously in B's interest. B simply shares with A an interest in X, or, once the costs of punishment for not doing X enter B's calculations, B prefers X to not-X. But when trust is personal—when it is sustained by A's belief that B's inherent qualities induce him to do X—B has some discernable interests in not doing X. B's personal qualities override his interests. The mayor would be better off stealing from the public till and would do so if it were not for his inherent honesty.

The second reason why personal trust, in comparison to the other forms we have identified, is a strong version is that it is portable across many settings in which A and B interact. If a citizen knows that the mayor is honest and frugal, he will trust her not only as mayor but also as a business partner and treasurer of a sports club and in any other setting in which honesty and frugality are called for. Portability, in this example, is not complete: he ought not entrust her, say, with writing a play or winning the tournament in which the sports club competes in. If he needs someone for these purposes, then rather than the honest and frugal mayor he would do better trusting the local bohemian or the swaggering athlete. Perhaps the strongest form of trust is personal trust with perfect portability, as when A regards B as so wise an actor and so in sympathy with A's interests that he will remain trustworthy in any conceivable setting.

7.   Yet it is also true that the nature and effects of clientelism will turn out to be different in Mexico, where a ruling party had vast fiscal resources available to it for decades, and Argentina, where politics was competitive and parties had much smaller clientelism budgets when they found themselves in opposition.

8.   The typical question about political trust simply asks the respondent whether he or she trusts a given institution or actor (the courts, the parliament, the president). Because the question does not stipulate what the respondent might or might not trust the institution or politician to do, these questions probably elicit the respondents' general feelings about the institution or politician. The question becomes indistinguishable from one that simply asks, "Do you like or approve of" the president, the parliament, and so forth.

9.   The Federal District of Mexico City and the federal capital in Argentina are additional subnational units, and very large ones. We do not use data from either, though our Buenos Aires province sample did include large municipalities in Greater Buenos Aires, such as La Matanza.

Chapter 2

1.   The Federal District (Mexico City) is neither a state nor a municipality.
2.   Just over 10 percent of the population self-identifies as indigenous. The 2000 census reports that 7 percent of the population speaks an indigenous language, and that over 1 million Mexicans (about 1.2 percent of the population) speak only an indigenous language (see Serrano Carreto, Embriz Osorio, and Fernández Ham 2002).

3. This view is overwhelmingly accepted in the literature on Mexico, with good reason. Many authors view the period from 1983 to 2000 as a single, protracted democratic transition, in which opposition groups chipped away at the PRI's electoral hegemony from below, starting with a few municipal contests, expanding to state-wide races, and culminating in Vicente Fox's presidential victory in 2000 (see Lujambio 2000; Chand 2001; Eisenstadt 2004). Others argue that competitive elections contribute to democracy by improving political outcomes or by causing institutional changes, such as creating stronger state legislatures (Rodríguez 1998; Beer 2003). Both lines of reasoning imply that subnational units are more democratic when they have real electoral competition.

4. For example, between 1989 and 1998 the PRI's electoral advantage was strongest in Puebla, Tamaulipas, and Veracruz, each of which the party won by 20- to 30-point margins. But most contests were much closer, and even these overwhelming victories look competitive compared to the 60- to 80-point margins that were common in gubernatorial elections just ten years earlier.

5. The two cases in which the PRI has won back the governors office (Chihuahua in 1998 and Nuevo León in 2003) bear out this conjecture. In neither case did the opposition attempt (or even discuss attempting) to subvert the electoral outcome or the transfer of power.

6. Resolutions varied across these three states. In Guanajuato the PRI and PAN eventually came to a compromise agreement, by which the fraudulently elected PRI governor resigned and was replaced by an interim (PAN) governor until 1995. In Michoacán, the PRI and PRD failed to reach any post-election agreement, and the PRI governor remained in office. In Tabasco, as noted, the PRI governor successfully held his ground in spite of an agreement between Zedillo and the PRD to force his resignation (see Eisenstadt 2004).

7. See, for example, *Keesing's Record of World Events* (April 1990), and various articles in *El Universal* (August 2004).

8. As of March 2005, the fourteen states in which the PRI has never lost the governorship are: Campeche, Coahuila, Colima, Durango, Hidalgo, México, Oaxaca, Puebla, Quintana Roo, Sinaloa, Sonora, Tabasco, Tamaulipas, and Veracruz. The PRI lost the gubernatorial election in Guerrero in February 2005.

9. Mike Alvarez and colleagues (1996) argue, with regard to countries, that cases like these can fairly be coded as democratic if the ruling party concedes a loss at a later point in time. That is, if a party that has stayed in power by winning several consecutive elections later loses and steps down, its willingness to cede power at that later point can be used to infer that it would also have ceded power earlier. But this coding rule seems unwise in our context, given the PRI's contradictory responses to the gubernatorial elections in Chihuahua in 1986 and 1992. In 1986, the PRI was unwilling to recognize a PAN victory even though many observers argued that the PAN candidate was the true winner of the election. In 1992, the PRI did abide by the outcome, according to which the PAN's Francisco Barrio took the governorship. It would be problematic to infer that the

state PRI was willing to abide by democratic norms in 1986, because it eventually conceded an election in 1992.

10. The Acteal massacre was just one of many in recent years. In 1995, seventeen peasants were murdered in Coyuca de Benítez, Guerrero. All of the victims were members of an opposition peasant organization. Several police officers were later implicated in the massacre. In May 2002, mestizo gunmen ambushed and killed twenty-six Zapotec Indian peasants in the village of Santiago Texitlán, Oaxaca. The violence was related to a land dispute between the Zapotecs and mestizo peasants.

11. The CNDH issues a "recommendation" when an investigation determines that a public official has committed a human rights violation. The CNDH does not have enforcement authority, but its formal report includes a stipulation of the facts of the case and recommendations for how the public official should change policy, behavior, or both.

12. Beer asked legislators to estimate the percentage of bills that were generated in the legislature. She received responses from 146 legislators in seventeen states. Table 2.2 lists the median response within each state.

13. The other four countries were the United States, the United Kingdom, Germany, and Italy. In Mexico, 42 percent expected equal treatment from the bureaucracy, and 50 percent expected unequal treatment. In Italy, 53 percent expected equal treatment and only 13 percent expected unequal treatment. In the United States, the UK, and Germany, strong majorities expected equal treatment (83 percent, 83 percent, and 65 percent, respectively), and fewer than 10 percent expected unequal treatment (Almond and Verba 1963, 108).

14. Our case selection method required us to choose from among the twelve states that held elections in 2001, so that we could have postelection surveys. From among these, we chose for variation in the level of democracy and geographic location, but were also guided toward states with which we were more familiar, and on which strong political science literatures already existed.

15. Baja California Norte is typically referred to simply as Baja California, whereas Baja California Sur, which became a state in 1974, requires the "Sur."

16. As is true in many closely contested elections, Rodríguez and Ward report that "many observers felt" that the PAN won this election, but that the PRI committed fraud and reversed the outcome. Although such claims are often plausible, the fact that opposition parties occasionally cry wolf makes it exceedingly difficult to know whether the charge is true in particular cases. But whether or not this election was fraudulent, it is clear that the PAN "made a very strong showing" and that the PRI "carried out violent attacks against the PANistas" after the election (Rodríguez and Ward 1994, 27). Eisenstadt concurs, characterizing fraud in the 1959 election as "particularly unconscionable" (2004, 169).

17. The only previous victory of an opposition candidate in Baja California had been in Ensenada in 1983, when a disgruntled PRI leader defected from the party and won the municipality under the banner of the Partido Socialista de los Trabajadores (PST) (see Espinoza Valle 1998, 33–34).

18. This is partly a consequence of a proportional representation scheme that moderates the effect of lopsided election returns.

19. This does not mean that they do so happily, and it is important to keep in mind that the local leadership of the PRI often dissented from the federal government's willingness to negotiate with the PAN. But the main actors all abide by electoral outcomes in a way consistent with Przeworski's (1991) characterization of democratic consolidation.

20. The PAN's eight victories in 1983 also included the large cities of Hidalgo del Parral and Delicias, meaning that the PAN won in four of Chihuahua's five largest municipalities that year.

21. See Vikram Chand (2001, 37–38). Alberto Aziz Nassif (1987) offers a detailed analysis of the official voting returns from the 1986 election, providing a wealth of circumstantial evidence of fraud.

22. At the time, Chihuahua's state legislature was comprised of eighteen single-member plurality districts and ten proportional representation (PR) seats. The PRI won five of the ten PR seats as well, yielding a PRI bloc of twenty-two seats in a twenty-eight-seat legislature (Lujambio 2000).

23. Another reason not to overemphasize this election, hinted at by several analysts we interviewed, is that there may have been a large sympathy vote that made the outcome an anomaly. Barrio's teenaged daughter was killed in an automobile accident two weeks before the election.

24. For example, according to the survey responses we collected in four states in 2001, Michoacán had the highest rate of self-reported church attendance (see table 5.2).

25. It might be more accurate to ascribe the clientelist label to the two main parties in the state (the PRI and the PRD), rather than to the state of Michoacán per se. For example, Enrique Semo describes the PRD as a "federation of *caudillos*," and describes this personalist structure as the party's "Achilles heel" (Semo 2003, 125–32; see also Sánchez 1999). Nevertheless, the behavior of the two parties makes it fair to describe the general political climate of the state as traditional and clientelistic.

26. Michoacán has an odd election calendar, with nonconcurrent elections. It held state legislative elections on July 2, 1989, and municipal elections on December 3, 1989 (de Remes 2000).

27. See, for example, *Keesing's Record of World Events* (April 1990).

28. Many leaders of the PRD opposed the protest movements undertaken by their supporters, but they were not always able to effectively control the protesters. Nor did politicians like Cárdenas hesitate to publicly blame the PRI for the violence that occurred (Eisenstadt 2004).

29. We are aware of no evidence to indicate that the fraud in Puebla decided the outcome. According to official returns, the PRI won handily, with 66 percent of the vote (to the PAN's 30 percent). But the reports of fraud and intimidation allow us to infer that, in contrast to Chihuahua, the PRI would not have conceded defeat in Puebla even had it lost in the voting.

30. Microcredits are small-scale loans given directly to individuals or small community groups, typically directly from the federal government, and typically with the aim of providing "seed money" for a small entrepreneurial venture or business.

31. The story was reported in a series of articles in *El Sol de Puebla* (see October 17, 2001, p. 4; October 25, 2001, p. 4; November 15, 2001, p. 4; November 22, 2001, p. 4).

Chapter 3

1. Democratization in Mexico took the form of a gradual erosion of single-party rule of the PRI. Therefore the magnitude of opposition-party electoral support, and whether opposition parties had ever held office, were appropriate measures of democratization in Mexico. The Argentine experience of democratization was different, and hence we need different measures—in this case not of "democratization," but of the quality of democracy. That is, autocratic rule in Argentina in the period before 1983 was not organized by a political party but by the armed forces, and the electoral dominance of a single party in an Argentine municipality does not necessarily signal a lack of democracy.

2. The fact that our samples are drawn from different kinds of political units—in one case, a district, roughly equivalent to a U.S. county, dominated by a single city; in the other, provinces composed of a number of municipalities—raises some methodological issues. One is that population size varies widely. All regressions include a control for (logged) population size, allowing us to directly inspect the impact of population size on our dependent variables. Another concern is heteroskedasticity. We account for this complication by reporting robust (cluster-corrected) standard errors in all of our regressions (this technique is required by our clustered survey design).

3. The UNDP defines economic competitiveness as "the ability or capacity of the economy of a country, region or territory, to achieve sustainable economic development" (UNDP 2002, 7–8). The UNDP measures human development as a function of longevity, educational attainment, and standard of living (GDP per capita in purchasing power parity dollars).

4. According to the UNDP, Catamarca and San Luis are special cases that fall outside of this framework, Catamarca because of new mining activities, San Luis because "a process of reinvestment of residences based originally on fiscal incentives" has left it with low unemployment rates and a solvent fiscal situation (UNDP 2002, 13, our translation).

5. When coding provinces for data analysis, Gibson and Calvo count as "metropolitan" provinces Buenos Aires, Córdoba, Mendoza, and Santa Fe, as well as the Federal District; they count all other provinces as "peripheral."

6. We included all provinces for which data were available.

7. We include two measures of poverty, NBI—the proportion of residents in the municipality who fall below the poverty line—and Casa B—the proportion of residents who live in sub-standard housing. Both measures come from the 2001 census.

8. In the vast majority of municipalities, the percentage of the budget spent on personnel fell between 30 to 70% percent; therefore it was unnecessary to transform the dependent variable into a log-odds ratio.

9. Data for Catamarca are only available for 1995. Not all mayors were Peronists and Radicals. The most frequent third party to win local elections were local or "neighborhood parties" (partidos vecinales), parties that are usually particular to a given province. The municipal database for these analyses was assembled by Stokes, Valeria Brusco, and Marcelo Nazareno.

10. Others have argued—see in particular Mainwaring (1999)—that electoral volatility in third-wave democracies is high compared to volatility in advanced industrialized democracies, and that this high volatility reflects badly on the quality of democracy in the former. The greater the volatility, in this view, the less congealed are party identities and the less meaningful the vote. But note that "supply-side" factors influence differences in volatility among countries. That is, if, say, Peru's volatility is much higher than Britain's, to a large degree the difference is due to variation over time in the set of parties that Peruvian voters can choose among. This in contrast to Britain, where the party system has been fairly stable for a century. Analyzing differences in volatility across regions in a single country allows us to hold constant the party-system or supply side of volatility. The remaining variation in volatility, we argue, reflects the greater or lesser hold of clientelist ties on voters.

11. Fernando de la Rúa resigned the presidency in December 2001, escaping in a helicopter from the rooftop of the Casa Rosada from angry mobs in the streets below. For an analysis of the political crisis leading up to these events, see Novaro (2002).

12. Mar del Plata is the major city in a department or "partido" called General Pueyrredón. There are several other towns in General Pueyrredón, but only one full-fledged municipal government (the one housed in Mar del Plata).

13. The discussion of the popular consultation that follows draws heavily on studies by, and discussions with, a team of researchers that comprise the Grupo de Análisis Político at the Universidad Nacional Mar del Plata: Fabio Albo, Rosa Duarte, Daniela Filieri, Fernando Folcher, Gabriel Rodríguez, and Gustavo Vela. Our discussion here also draws on a series of interviews with local political elites carried out by Stokes and Fernando Folcher in February 2004.

14. Aprile was elected in May 1995 but only took office in December of that year. In an interview he said that he came up with the idea for the public works drive, and for the financing scheme and referendum, only during this long transition period. All other officials whom we interviewed concurred that the idea was Aprile's.

15. For the purpose of local taxation, the city is divided into zones, some of which pay at a higher rate and some at a lower rate. The zone that a household was located in would determine whether the special tax would be three or four pesos. The special tax would be a part of people's contributions for lighting and conservation of public routes (Alumbrado y Conservación de la Vía Pública), which in Mar del Plata, as in other municipalities in the province of Buenos Aires, accounts for most locally raised municipal revenues.

16. Interview with Walter Malagutti, city council member, February 25, 2004.
17. Throughout the translations are ours.
18. Albo and colleagues (2000) use official sources and a day-by-day review of the local newspapers, such as *Diario el Atlántico* and *Diario la Capital* in April and May 1996, to reconstruct this debate. One of the co-authors, Gustavo Vela, was a staff member of the city council during this period.
19. The mayor put the number at between five thousand and seven thousand. Some critics put it at five hundred. See Albo and colleagues (2000), and Folcher and colleagues (2002). In interviews in 2004, supporters of the plan admitted that it had failed to produce as many new jobs as they had anticipated.
20. In our interview, former Mayor Aprile spoke candidly about the period of more than a year after his resignation, describing what appears to have been a severe bout of depression and anxiety. He said that he resigned because he was "morally broken."

Chapter 4

1. To select the Argentine sample, we used multistage cluster sampling procedures, as follows. From the full set of census tracts in each province (and in Mar del Plata) we selected forty-eight, in each of which we interviewed ten people. To select the forty-eight tracts, we divided the entire population of the province by forty-eight, using the result as a cut-off point. We then drew tracts at random, using a skip number, from the full list of tracts, summing the population of each tract drawn as we proceeded. When the addition of a tract's population put the total over the cut-off point, this tract entered our sample. We repeated the procedure until we had selected forty-eight tracts. We used maps to develop a sample frame of streets in each of the selected tracts, and then used random numbers to select square blocks in which to conduct the interviews. Interviewers chose the houses on the blocks by skip numbers. Within each household, interviewers requested interviews with the adult family member who had had the most recent birthday.
2. To select the Mexican sample, our polling firm randomly chose forty electoral sections (secciones electorales) in each state. Electoral sections are similar to census tracts but are created by the Federal Electoral Institute (IFE) for the purpose of administering elections. Within each selected section, we interviewed ten respondents in face-to-face interviews, using a protocol to ensure that the gender and age range of the respondent pool was evenly distributed. The distribution of municipal size, neighborhood type (urban/rural), age, and gender of our respondents roughly matches the distribution of the population as reported in the 2000 census.
3. See appendix for precise question wording in Spanish and English.
4. According to Pearson's chi-squared tests, the differences between Mar del Plata and Misiones (the most and least democratic regions, respectively) for the first three questions in table 4.1 are statistically significant at $p < .001$, $p < .10$, and $p < .01$, respectively.
5. Here and in chapter 5, when indicated, we present multivariate models in

an appendix, to facilitate presentation. All multivariate models of survey responses reported in this book report robust standard errors that are designed to account for correlated errors, due to the clustered sample design of the survey.

6. Here and throughout the book we generated the simulations using the *Clarify* program (Tomz, Wittenberg, and King 2001, and King, Tomz, and Wittenberg 2000). *Clarify* draws simulations of parameters of statistical models (in this case, logit regressions) from their sampling distribution and then converts these simulated parameters into expected values, such as expected probabilities of an answer to a survey question, given hypothetical values of explanatory variables. *Clarify* software and documentation are available from Gary King's website at http://gking.harvard.edu. For this simulation we held household income, education level, quality of housing, age, and population size of the respondents' community at their sample medians, and assumed a female Peronist supporter.

7. Multivariate analysis reveals some striking effects on respondents' personal trust of politicians. Higher-income respondents were more trusting than lower-income ones. Respondents who supported either the Peronist party or the Radical party (in contrast, mainly, to those who supported no party) were more personally trusting of politicians, as were people from smaller towns and cities. We reasoned that people who were more personally trusting of others in general would also be more trusting of politicians, and therefore included a control for Personal Trust—whether they said, in response to another survey question, that one can trust no one, a minority, or a majority of people. And indeed, the more trusting respondents were of people in general, the more trusting they were of politicians. John Brehm and Wendy Rahn (1997) and Eric Uslaner (2002) find a similar relationship between interpersonal trust and trust in government in the United States, and Timothy Power and Mary Clark (2001) find that respondents who express interpersonal trust in Costa Rica, Mexico, and Chile are more likely to express support for democracy. Uslaner points out that the two types of trust are not always related: in countries with communist legacies, for example, the relationship is the reverse—individuals expressing interpersonal trust are less likely to express trust in the government (2002, 220). Nevertheless, the relationship that we find in Argentina (and in Mexico) suggests a link between interpersonal trust and personal trust in politicians. However, in chapter 5 we show that cross-regional differences in interpersonal trust do not map onto differences in the actual level of democracy.

8. In this case, people who were more institutionally trusting—believed bribe-takers would be caught—were also more personally trusting, believing that politicians could be trusted even without monitoring.

9. This simulation draws on the parameter estimates in the model in table 4A.1. In it we assumed a female Peronist supporter of median income, education, and housing quality for the sample, who lives in an average-sized city. Only the difference between Misiones and the other three regions is statistically significant.

10. Since 1994, Argentine presidents are permitted to run for reelection only

once. Neither members of the national legislature nor members of provincial legislatures face term limits. Some provinces impose term limits on governors, but most do not, and few municipalities do.

11. The dummy variable for Chihuahua also has a positive coefficient, though it is not statistically significant at conventional levels.

12. The question was "How clean do you think this year's elections will be—totally clean, more or less clean, not very clean, or not at all clean?" (Lawson and colleagues 2002, 28). (¿Qué tan limpias cree Ud. que serían las elecciones de este año—totalmente limpias, más o menos limpias, poco limpias o nada limpias?)

13. With a national sample of about twenty-four hundred respondents, the total number of respondents per state is low, especially for some of the smaller states. Thus, we suspect that the state-level percentages we are reporting here have large and unequal variances, limiting the confidence we can have in this comparison. Still, the results are in line with the other findings we report in this section, and thus comprise suggestive evidence in favor of our hypothesis.

14. For this simulation we assumed a female nonpartisan citizen whose income, education, and age match the median for our sample.

15. According to a Pearson's chi-squared statistic, the differences in response frequencies between Baja California and the other three states, displayed in table 4.4, are all statistically significant at $p < 0.05$.

16. It is intriguing to note, referring back to table 4.3, that the same pattern holds for Argentina. Mar del Plata, which tends to have lower non-response rates, has the highest non-response rate for Favor.

17. Model 4 in table 4A.3 also shows a substantial effect of partisanship on the likelihood that someone would believe that parties have support because they are "concerned for people." Partisans of all three major parties are significantly more likely to believe this.

18. We return to the potential causal relationship between economic development and clientelism in the next chapter.

19. These are expected simulated probabilities, generated by *Clarify* (see note 6), drawing on model 1 in table 4A.5. In the simulations we hold income, education, housing quality, and community size at their sample medians, and assume a female Peronist sympathizer from Misiones.

20. Some scholars argue that parties can play on norms of reciprocity by offering material incentives before an election and asking for a vote in return. Even if the ballot is secret, some voters may repay the favor and vote for the clientelist party out of a sense of obligation (see Auyero 2000). Yet respondents in our least democratized region were less likely than those in our most consolidated one to assert that these handouts did, or should, create a sense of obligation in their recipients to vote for the donor party. The explanation may be that these handouts actually were ineffective in mobilizing support for the parties, and people in the region where these handouts were common knew they were ineffective. But we just saw in the previous section that the influence of gifts was greater in less-democratic regions. Instead, handouts probably are often effective and the claim

that they are not may be a self-justification on the part of people who felt defensive about receiving them. In Argentina, receiving a handout had no effect on whether a respondent believed that the recipient should return the favor, but people who received them were significantly less likely to believe that they did cause such a sense of obligation. This is what we learn from the negative and significant coefficient relating Received Goods to Does Obligate (see model 5 in table 4A.4). The effect is not negligible. In simulations, a hypothetical Misiones resident who did not receive a handout had a 48 percent probability of saying that such handouts create a sense of obligation; if she did receive one, the probability dropped to 35 percent.

21. The fact that fewer Mexicans than Argentines acknowledge clientelist distribution of goods in their neighborhoods might also be explained by differences in the manner of distribution, with more public disbursement—for example, at campaign events and rallies—in Argentina, and more private disbursement—for example, in private homes—in Mexico. Given the historically symbiotic relationship between the state and the PRI, it may also be difficult for Mexican respondents to distinguish whether the source of such goods is the political party or the government.

22. We coded those who responded to this question by saying that they did not know a party representative as not having gone to one for help. We reasoned that anyone who did go to a party representative for help would have answered that he or she knew such a person. But the absolute numbers, listed in parentheses in the table, show that even among those who knew a party representative, Baja Californians were (slightly) less likely than residents of the other three states to turn to the representative for help.

23. Political parties and candidates distribute minor goods—food, clothing, building materials, for example—to voters to instill in voters a sense of obligation to vote for the party. As in Argentina, we can use survey evidence to see how influential norms of reciprocity were. We asked respondents whether they thought that people felt obliged to support a party that had distributed goods or favors, and whether recipients of such gifts ought to feel obliged. Overall, a majority (56 percent) believed that recipients of clientelist inducements do not feel obliged to support the donor party. But a non-negligible proportion—37 percent—believed that they do feel obliged. This is a sizeable number, suggesting that clientelist mobilization can influence the outcome of elections. We do not find strong cross-state differences in recipients' belief that clientelist gifts do induce in the recipients a sense of obligation. But when we asked respondents whether recipients of these favors ought to feel obligated (deberían sentirse obligadas), the differences across states were greater. An overwhelming majority of respondents in each state rejected the notion that minor gifts should engender loyalty (see table 4.6, Should Obligate). Thus a large majority of citizens in each state rejected the moral claims of clientelism. Baja Californians, however, stand out as particularly dismissive of this notion, agreeing with it only half as frequently as respondents in the other three states. Note that the effect of democratization on moral claims of clientelism is

exactly the reverse of Argentina's, where people in the least democratized region were the most dismissive of these claims.

24. Partisans of either the PRI or the PAN are more likely than non-partisans to know a party representative (Know Party), to have gone to one for help (Party Help), and to consider going to one hypothetically (Job). In table 4A.6 model 1, the difference between the coefficients for PRI and PAN partisanship is statistically significant (at p = 0.012), meaning that PRI partisans are more likely to know a local party operative than PAN partisans. But in the second and third models, the coefficients for these two variables are roughly similar, meaning that partisanship in either party predicts more personalism than when the respondent is not a partisan of either party.

25. This was the reverse of the Argentine pattern, where people from the least consolidated region were *less* likely to believe that clientelist handouts do—and ought to—create obligations.

26. Power and Clark analyze similar questions collected in the 1998 Hewlett Foundation survey in Chile, Costa Rica, and Mexico (2001). They use responses to these questions as a measure of "civismo," which they believe measures the respondent's "propensity to intervene against free-riding or norm-transgressing individuals" (59). They find a cross-country link between civismo and democracy, analogous to the findings we report here.

27. The question also added "knowing that there will be fewer public services in your neighborhood."

28. In fact, respondents in all four states were significantly more likely to say that the action was not justified after being prompted that "many other people" were doing it. We expected our hypothetical suggestion that "others were doing it" to have the opposite effect, softening the respondents' views about the rule of law. Instead, our suggestion seems to have provoked a legalistic reaction, causing respondents to condemn such actions in even greater numbers.

29. Income is a 6-point ordinal variable coded according to the respondent's self-reported household income. Social class is a 3-point ordinal variable reflecting whether the respondent described himself as lower, middle, or upper class. The two variables are significantly, but only weakly, correlated (rho = 0.15, p < 0.001).

30. To see this, note that each of the state dummies has a negative coefficient (predicting lower values on the dependent variable than for Baja California, the excluded dummy), and that the relative size of the three state dummy coefficients always ranks them in the same order: Chihuahua's coefficients are the smallest, Puebla's are in the middle, and Michoacán's are the largest (in absolute value).

31. By their appraisal, compliance with municipal taxes is, under normal circumstances, around 65 percent. We have been unable to find comparative data from other regions, but Mar del Plata's leaders assert that this compliance rate is high by Argentine standards.

32. Authors' translation.

33. The simulation assumes a female Peronist supporter who is otherwise average for the sample.

Chapter 5

1. In Mexico, we asked the respondent to estimate the average number of hours per week, over the previous twelve months.

2. In Mexico, sports clubs were the second most frequently mentioned, behind parent-teacher associations.

3. The third option, "I don't trust anyone," was not read to the interviewees, but was recorded if the response was volunteered spontaneously.

4. Both simulations assume a female Peronist supporter who resides in Mar del Plata and whose housing quality and municipality size are at the sample median.

5. No other measures of social capital had significant effects on institutional trust, but their coefficients generally carried negative signs; in no case was there a positive and significant effect of social capital on institutional trust. Model 3 in table 5.5 shows that people more involved in civic associations were somewhat more personally trusting of politicians than those who did not participate.

6. Simulations generated with *Clarify*. The 95 percent confidence intervals were 46 to 63 percent for an institutional response to Service when Comprob = 0 and Belong = 0, and 21 to 44 percent when Comprob = 1 and Belong = 3.

7. These conclusions are based on models 1 and 2 in table 5A.3, and on other models not shown.

8. The only exception is that Argentines who met to solve problems also said they would not knowingly buy stolen goods (see model 6 in table 5A.5).

9. To see this effect, the reader can refer to table 4A.1, model 4.

10. Higher incomes often failed to produce pro-democratic beliefs and preferences. Wealthier Argentines were not more likely to say that people supported political parties for universalistic rather than for particularistic reasons, nor that they considered past performance rather than future-oriented promises in deciding how to vote. Surprisingly, they were not less likely to say that parties gave things out in their neighborhoods (though they were less likely to have taken handouts themselves). In other respects the evidence in favor of individual wealth predicting democratic attitudes in Argentina was mixed.

11. Of course, only a fraction of municipal expenditures are financed by locally raised taxes. But transfers from the provincial and national governments tend to be based on population formulas. So differences among municipalities in the level of outside financing they receive tend to wash out in revenue per capita measures.

12. Population size is conceptually distinct from urbanization: in principle a municipality could have a large but geographically dispersed population. In practice, large municipalities in Mexico are almost always urban. In the absence of measures of population density, total municipal population is an appropriately close proxy measure for urbanization.

13. We exclude from the analysis 418 indigenous municipalities that use customary forms of rule (rather than multiparty elections), as well as a handful more where data are missing.

14. Most of the coefficients of interest are statistically significant, and their substantive impact is considerable. The dependent variable is a log-odds transformation of the PRI's vote proportion. Using the transformed variable avoids problems that could arise when using OLS on a proportional dependent variable (see Greene 1997, 895). The substantive size of the coefficients is difficult to interpret directly, so we use *Clarify* simulations to translate the predicted effects back into percentage terms.

15. These population sizes represent the 10th and 90th percentile scores in the sample.

16. Hernández Valdez (2000) finds similar support for socioeconomic factors in his analysis of state-level democratization in Mexico.

17. In the Mexican surveys, we tend to prefer our measure of class over our measure of income. Table 5A.9 shows our respondents' reported income and self-perceived social class, by state. The high nonresponse rate to our questions about household earnings (especially in the poorer states) gives us pause in using this measure. It may be that many respondents did not feel comfortable answering this question; it may also be that many did not know, as the question asked them for their family's total monthly income. We should also note that income may not be a perfect indicator of wealth, since current monthly income does not reflect savings and the ownership of assets. But our income and class variables are the best indicators we have of the characteristics that Lipset (1959) and others had in mind when they attributed democratization to changes in attitudes brought about by economic development.

18. The revenue measure is the amount of municipal revenue raised locally, per capita per annum, averaged across the 1990s after adjusting for inflation. We use local revenue generation because it is more closely tied to local wealth (as opposed to federal and state transfers, which are apportioned by spending formula, often inversely to local wealth). Models using this variable have 1,588 observations instead of 1,598, because ten cases are from a municipality that was created in 1995 and lacks revenue data. The poverty rate is the percentage of economically active adults in the municipality in the year 2000 who earn less than the official minimum wage.

19. See note to table 5A.10 for more detailed explanations of Casa B and NBI. A drawback of both measures is that the most recent year for which they are available is 1991. As of November 2004, neither measure has been reported at the municipal level out of the 2001 census.

20. Our measure of municipal wealth—expenditures per capita—is negatively correlated with poor-quality housing (−0.64) and with the percentage of residents below the poverty line (−0.67). These correlations indicate that community wealth and poverty rates are negatively related, but not so strongly as to be collinear and hence preclude simultaneous inclusion in model specifications.

21. Note also that the coefficient for Casa B in model 2 is weakly significant ($p = 0.07$), whereas the coefficient in model 5 is clearly not significant.

22. These are simulated expected probabilities, produced by *Clarify*, and assume in both cases a male Peronist supporter who lives in a municipality

in which 6.4 percent of the population lives in substandard housing (the level of Casa B for Mar del Plata). In all other respects the hypothetical individual is typical for the sample. Ninety-five percent confidence intervals are between 7 and 16 percent for the Mar del Plata case, and between 24 and 7 percent for the Misiones case.

23. Simulated expected probabilities produced by *Clarify*. We assume a male Peronist sympathizer who in all other respects is average for the sample. In estimations not shown, the coefficient relating Casa B to the probability that a person would respond that people in her neighborhood support the locally prominent party because it has given out favors (rather than because it is concerned with everyone; variable name Favor) is positive but falls short of statistical significance. As in model 2, table 5.11, even in the presence of this control for poverty, Mar del Plata residents were significantly less likely to offer the clientelist answer than were Misiones residents. Exactly the same can be said for models of Favor that control for NBI.

Chapter 6

1. Of course we are using a shorthand here. People in these regions were more likely to hold these beliefs, but both kinds of beliefs could obviously be found in both kinds of regions.
2. Because our research design is mainly cross-sectional, we offer these dynamic scenarios as conjectures.

Appendix

1. The elections in Chihuahua and Michoacán included a gubernatorial contest; Baja California and Puebla held midterm elections for state congress and mayors only.

References

Abers, Rebecca. 1998. "From Clientelism to Cooperation: Local Government, Participatory Policy, and Civic Organizing in Porto Alegre, Brazil." *Politics and Society* 26(4): 511–37.

Acemoglu, Daron, and James Robinson. 2003. "Political Origins of Dictatorship and Democracy." Unpublished manuscript. Political Science Department, University of California, Berkeley.

Ackerman, Bruce, and Ian Ayres. 2002. *Voting with Dollars: A New Paradigm for Campaign Finance.* New Haven. Conn.: Yale University Press.

Albo, Fabio, Daniela Filieri, and Gustavo Vela. 2000. *Votos, Obras y Economía: Mar del Plata y la Consulta Popular de 1996.* Unpublished manuscript. Universidad Nacional Mar del Plata.

Almond, Gabriel A., and Sidney Verba. 1963. *The Civic Culture: Political Attitudes and Democracy in Five Nations.* Princeton, N.J.: Princeton University Press.

Alvarez, Mike, and colleagues. 1996. "Classifying Political Regimes." *Studies in Comparative International Development* 31(summer): 3–36.

Arnold, Douglas. 1993. "Can Inattentive Citizens Control their Elected Representatives?" In *Congress Reconsidered*, 5th ed., edited by Lawrence C. Dodd and Bruce I. Oppenheimer. Washington, D.C.: CQ Press.

Auyero, Javier. 2000. *Poor People's Politics: Peronist Survival Networks and the Legacy of Evita.* Durham, N.C.: Duke University Press.

———. 2003. *Contentious Lives: Two Argentine Women, Two Protests, and the Quest for Recognition.* Durham, N.C.: Duke University Press.

Axelrod, Robert. 1984. *The Evolution of Cooperation.* New York: Basic Books.

Aziz Nassif, Alberto. 1987. *Prácticas electorales y democracia en Chihuahua.* Mexico City: CIESAS.

———. 2000. *Los ciclos de la democracia: Gobierno y elecciones en Chihuahua.* Mexico City: CIESAS and Porrua.

Banamex. 2001. *México Electoral: Estadísticas Federales y Locales, 1970–2000.* CD-ROM. Mexico City: Banamex.

Beer, Caroline C. 2003. *Electoral Competition and Institutional Change in Mexico.* Notre Dame, Ind.: University of Notre Dame Press.

Boix, Carles. 2003. *Democracy and Redistribution.* New York: Cambridge University Press.

Boix, Carles, and Daniel Posner. 1998. "Social Capital: Explaining its Origins and Effects on Government Performance." *British Journal of Political Science* 28(4): 686–93.

Brehm, John, and Wendy Rahn. 1997. "Individual-Level Evidence for the Causes and Consequences of Social Capital." *American Journal of Political Science* 43(3, July): 999–1023.

Bruhn, Kathleen. 1996. *Taking on Goliath: The Emergence of a New Left Party and the Struggle for Democracy in Mexico*. University Park: The Pennsylvania State University Press.

Bruhn, Kathleen, and Keith Yanner. 1995. "Governing Under the Enemy: The PRD in Michoacán," in *Opposition Government in Mexico*, edited by Victoria E. Rodríguez and Peter M. Ward. Albuquerque: University of New Mexico Press.

Brusco, Valeria, Marcelo Nazareno, and Susan C. Stokes. 2004. "Vote Buying in Argentina." *Latin American Research Review* 39(2): 66–88.

Cady, Frederic. 2005. "Filling the Power Void: Candidate Selection Changes in the Partido Revolucionario Institucional (PRI) in Mexico." Paper presented at the annual meeting of the Midwest Political Science Association, Chicago (April).

Calvo, Ernesto, and Victoria Murillo. 2004. "Who Delivers? Partisan Clients in the Argentine Electoral Market." *American Journal of Political Science* 48(4): 742–57.

Chand, Vikram K. 2001. *Mexico's Political Awakening*. Notre Dame, Ind.: University of Notre Dame Press.

Cleary, Matthew R. 2004. "Electoral Competition and Democracy in Mexico." Ph.D. diss., University of Chicago.

Cohen, Joshua, and Joel Rogers. 1995. "Secondary Associations and Democratic Governance." In *Associations and Democracy*, edited by Joshua Cohen and Joel Rogers. London: Verso.

Collier, Ruth Berins. 1999. *Paths Toward Democracy: The Working Class and Elites in Western Europe and South America*. Cambridge: Cambridge University Press.

Cornelius, Wayne A. 1986. "Political Liberalization and the 1985 Elections in Mexico." In *Elections and Democratization in Latin America, 1980–1985*, edited by Paul W. Drake and Eduardo Silva. San Diego: University of California, San Diego.

———. 1999. "Subnational Politics and Democratization: Tensions between Center and Periphery in the Mexican Political System." In *Subnational Politics and Democratization in Mexico*, edited by Wayne A. Cornelius, Todd A. Eisenstadt, and Jane Hindley. San Diego: University of California, San Diego, Center for U.S.-Mexican Studies.

Courchene, Thomas, and Alberto Díaz Cayeros. 2000. "Transfers and the Nature of the Mexican Federation." In *Achievements and Challenges of Fiscal Decentralization: Lessons from Mexico*, edited by Marcelo Giugale and Steven B. Webb. Washington, D.C.: The World Bank.

Dahl, Robert A. 1971. *Polyarchy: Participation and Opposition*. New Haven, Conn.: Yale University Press.

De Remes, Alain. 2000. "Municipal Electoral Processes in Latin America and

Mexico." Working Paper No. 125. Mexico City: División de Estudios Políticos, CIDE.

Diaz-Cayeros, Alberto, Beatriz Magaloni, and Barry R. Weingast. 2003. "Tragic Brilliance: Equilibrium Hegemony and Democratization in Mexico." Unpublished manuscript, Department of Political Science, Stanford University.

Dixit, Avinash, and John Londregan. 1996. "The Determinants of Success of Special Interests in Redistributive Politics." *Journal of Politics* 58(4):1132–55.

Domínguez, Jorge I., and James A. McCann. 1996. *Democratizing Mexico: Public Opinion and Electoral Choices*. Baltimore, Md.: Johns Hopkins University Press.

Eisenstadt, Todd A. 2004. *Courting Democracy in Mexico: Party Strategies and Electoral Institutions*. New York: Cambridge University Press.

Espinoza Valle, Victor Alejandro. 1998. *Alternancia Política y Gestión Pública: El Partido Acción Nacional en el gobierno de Baja California*. Tijuana: El Colegio de la Frontera Norte.

Fagen, Richard R., and William S. Touhy. 1972. *Politics and Privilege in a Mexican City*. Stanford, Calif.: Stanford University Press.

Fearon, James. 1999. "Electoral Accountability and the Control of Politicians: Selecting Good Types Versus Sanctioning Poor Performance." In *Democracy, Accountability, and Representation*, edited by Adam Przeworski, Susan C. Stokes, and Bernard Manin. New York: Cambridge University Press.

Ferejohn, John. 1999. "Accountability and Authority: Toward a Theory of Political Accountability." In *Democracy, Accountability, and Representation*, edited by Adam Przeworski, Susan C. Stokes, and Bernard Manin. New York: Cambridge University Press.

Folcher, Fernando, Daniela Filieri, Gabriel Rodríguez, Gustavo Vela, Fabio Albo, and Rosa Duarte. 2002. "Votos, obra pública, y economía: Mar del Plata y la Consulta Popular de 1996." Paper presented to the Conference on Local Democracy: Poverty, Social Capital, and Clientelism in Argentina. University of Chicago (March 8–9, 2002).

Fox, Jonathan. 1994. "The Difficult Transition from Clientelism to Citizenship: Lessons from Mexico." *World Politics* 46(2): 151–84.

García García, Raymundo. 1998. *Puebla: Elecciones, Legalidad y Conflictos Municipales, 1977–1995*. Puebla, Mexico: Benemérita Universidad Autónoma de Puebla.

Garrido, Luis Javier. 1993. *La Ruptura: La Corriente Democrática del PRI*. Mexico City: Grijalbo.

Gibson, Edward. 2004. "Subnational Authoritarianism: Dilemmas of Territorial Governance in Contemporary Democracies." Paper presented to the Latin America Regional Workshop, Kellogg Institute for International Studies. University of Notre Dame (May 12, 2004).

Gibson, Edward, and Ernesto Calvo. 2000. "Federalism and Low-Maintenance Constituencies: Territorial Dimensions of Economic Reform in Argentina." *Studies in Comparative International Development* 35(3): 32–55.

Greene, William H. 1997. *Econometric Analysis*. Third Edition. Upper Saddle River, N.J.: Prentice Hall.

Guillén López, Tonatiuh. 1993. *Baja California 1989–1992: Alternancia Política y Transición Democrática*. Tijuana: El Colegio de la Frontera Norte.

———. 1995. "The 1992 Elections and the Democratic Transition in Baja California." In *Opposition Government in Mexico*, edited by Victoria E. Rodríguez and Peter M. Ward. Albuquerque: University of New Mexico Press.

Hardin, Russell. 1998. "Trust in Government." In *Trust and Governance*, edited by Valerie Braithwaite and Margaret Levi. New York: Russell Sage Foundation.

———. 2002. *Trust and Trustworthiness*. New York: Russell Sage Foundation.

Hart, Vivien. 1978. *Distrust and Democracy*. New York: Cambridge University Press.

Hernández Valdez, Alfonso. 2000. "Las causas estructurales de la democracia local en México, 1989–1998", *Política y Gobierno* 7(1): 101–44.

Hetherington, Marc J. 2005. *Why Trust Matters: Declining Political Trust and the Demise of American Liberalism*. Princeton, N.J.: Princeton University Press.

Hibbing, John R., and Elizabeth Theiss-Morse. 2002. *Stealth Democracy: Americans' Beliefs about How Government Should Work*. Cambridge: Cambridge University Press.

Hiskey, Jonathan T. 1999. *Does Democracy Matter? Electoral Competition and Local Development in Mexico*. Ph.D. diss., University of Pittsburgh.

Honaker, James, Anne Joseph, Gary King, Kenneth Scheve, and Naunihal Singh. 2003. "Amelia: A Program for Missing Data." Unpublished manuscript, Department of Government, Harvard University.

Huntington, Samuel P. 1991. *The Third Wave: Democratization in the Late Twentieth Century*. Norman: Univeristy of Oklahoma Press.

Inglehart, Ronald. 1988. "The Renaissance of Political Culture." *American Political Science Review* 82(4): 1203–30.

Instituto Nacional de Estadística y Censos (INDEC). 2001. *Censo Nacional de Población, Hogares, y Viviendas del Año 2001*. Buenos Aires: Ministerio de Economica de la República Argentina.

Instituto Nacional de Estadísticas, Geografía e Informática (INEGI). 2000. *XII Censo General de Población y Vivienda*. Aguascalientes and Mexico City: INEGI.

Karl, Terry Lynn. 1990. "Dilemmas of Democracy in Latin America." *Comparative Politics* 23(1): 1–21.

Keesing's Record of World Events. 1990. "Ending of Town Hall Occupations." Vol. 36, Number 4 (April). Washington, D.C.: Keesing's Worldwide.

King, Gary, James Honaker, Anne Joseph, and Kenneth Scheve. 2001. "Analyzing Incomplete Political Science Data: An Alternative Algorithm for Multiple Imputation." *American Political Science Review* 95(1, March): 49–69.

King, Gary, Michael Tomz, and Jason Wittenberg. 2000. "Making the Most of Statistical Analyses; Improving Interpretation and Presentation." *American Journal of Political Science* 44(2): 347–61.

Kish, Leslie, and Richard Frankel. 1974. "Inference from Complex Samples." *Journal of the Royal Statistical Society*. Series B. 36(1): 1–37.

Langston, Joy. 2003. "Rising from the Ashes? Reorganizing and Unifying the PRI's State Party Organizations after Electoral Defeat." *Comparative Political Studies* 36(3): 293–318.

Lawson, Chappell. 2000. "Mexico's Unfinished Transition: Democratization and Authoritarian Enclaves in Mexico." *Mexican Studies/Estudios Mexicanos* 16(2): 267–87.

Lawson, Chappell (principal investigator), with Miguel Basañez, Roderic Camp, Wayne Cornelius, Jorge Domínguez, Federico Estévez, Joseph Klesner, Beatriz Magaloni, James McCann, Alejandro Moreno, Pablo Parás, and Alejandro Poiré. 2002. "Mexico 2000 Panel Study." Funding for study was provided by the National Science Foundation (SES-9905703) and *Reforma* newspaper.

Levi, Margaret. 1988. *Of Rule and Revenue.* Berkeley: University of California Press.

———. 1997. *Consent, Dissent, and Patriotism.* New York: Cambridge University Press.

Levitsky, Steven. 2003. *Transforming Labor-Based Parties in Latin America: Argentine Peronism in Comparative Perspective.* New York: Cambridge University Press.

Linz, Juan J., and Alfred Stepan. 1996. *Problems of Democratic Transition and Consolidation: Southern Europe, South America, and Post-communist Europe.* Baltimore, Md.: Johns Hopkins University Press.

Lipset, Seymour Martin. 1959. "Some Social Requisites of Democracy: Economic Development and Political Legitimacy." *American Political Science Review* 53(1): 69–105.

———. 1960. *Political Man: The Social Bases of Politics.* Garden City, N.Y.: Doubleday.

Lujambio, Alonso, with the collaboration of Horacio Vives Segl. 2000. *El Poder Compartido: un ensayo sobre la democratización mexicana.* Mexico City: Oceano.

Macías Palma, Carlos. 1998. *De Moreno Valle a Bartlett: 30 años de historia política de Puebla.* Puebla, Mexico.

Madison, James. 1787/1982. *The Federalist Papers,* edited by Gary Wills. New York: Bantam Books.

Mainwaring, Scott P. 1999. *Rethinking Party Systems in the Third Wave of Democratization: The Case of Brazil.* Stanford: Stanford University Press.

Mizrahi, Yemile. 1994. "Rebels without a Cause? The Politics of Entrepreneurs in Chihuahua." *Journal of Latin American Studies* 26(1): 137–58.

———. 1995. "Entrepreneurs in the Opposition: Modes of Political Participation in Chihuahua," in *Opposition Government in Mexico,* edited by Victoria E. Rodríguez and Peter M. Ward. Albuquerque: University of New Mexico Press.

Novaro, Marcos, ed. 2002. *El Derrumbe Político en el Ocaso de la Convertibilidad.* Buenos Aires: Grupo Editorial Norma.

O'Donnell, Guillermo, and Philippe Schmitter. 1986. *Transitions from Authoritarian Rule: Tentative Conclusions about Uncertain Democracies.* Baltimore: Johns Hopkins University Press.

Paxton, Pamela. 2002. "Social Capital and Democracy: An Interdependent Relationship." *American Sociological Review* 67(2): 254–77.

Power, Timothy J., and Mary A. Clark. 2001. "Does Trust Matter? Interpersonal Trust and Democratic Values in Chile, Costa Rica, and Mexico." In *Citizen Views of Democracy in Latin America,* edited by Roderic Ai Camp. Pittsburgh, Pa.: University of Pittsburgh Press.

Przeworski, Adam. 1991. *Democracy and the Market*. New York: Cambridge University Press.

Przeworski, Adam, Michael E. Alvarez, José Antonio Cheibub, Fernando Limongi. 2000. *Democracy and Development: Political Institutions and Well-Being in the World, 1950–1990*. Cambridge: Cambridge University Press.

Putnam, Robert. 1993. *Making Democracy Work: Civic Traditions in Modern Italy*. Princeton, N.J.: Princeton University Press.

———. 2000. *Bowling Alone: The Collapse and Revival of American Community*. New York: Simon & Schuster.

Raudenbush, Stephen W., and Anthony S. Bryk. 2002. *Hierarchical Linear Models: Applications and Data Analysis Methods*. 2nd ed. Thousand Oaks, Calif.: Sage.

Remmer, Karen, and Eric Wibbels. 2000. "The Subnational Politics of Economic Adjustment: Provincial Politics and Fiscal Performance in Argentina." *Comparative Political Studies* 33(4): 419–51.

Rodríguez, Victoria E. 1998. "Opening the Electoral Space in Mexico: the Rise of the Opposition at the State and Local Levels." In *Urban Elections in Democratic Latin America*, edited by Henry A. Dietz and Gil Shidlo. Wilmington, Del.: SR Books.

Rodríguez, Victoria E., and Peter M. Ward. 1994. *Political Change in Baja California: Democracy in the Making?* San Diego: Center for U.S.-Mexican Studies, University of California, San Diego.

Sánchez, Marco Aurelio. 1999. *PRD: la elite en crisis*. Mexico City: Plaza y Valdez.

Sandel, Michael. 1996. *Democracy and its Discontents: America in Search of a Public Philosophy*. Cambridge, Mass.: Harvard University Press.

Santos, Boaventura de Souza. 1998. "Participatory Budgeting in Porto Alegre: Toward a Redistributive Democracy." *Politics and Society* 26(4): 461–510.

Semo, Enrique. 2003. *La Búsqueda: la izquierda mexicana en los albores del siglo XXI*. Mexico City: Oceano.

Serrano Carreto, Enrique, Arnulfo Embriz Osorio, and Patrician Fernández Ham, eds. 2002. *Indicadores socioeconómicos de los pueblos indígenas de México, 2002*. Mexico City: INI-Programa de las Naciones Unidas para el Desarrollo.

Stokes, Susan C. 2005. "Perverse Accountability: A Formal Model of Machine Politics with Evidence from Argentina." *American Political Science Review* 99(3, August): 315–25.

Szwarcberg, Mariela L. 2001. "Feeding Loyalties: An Analysis of Clientelism, the Case of the Manzaneras." Unpublished manuscript. Buenos Aires: Universidad Torcuato di Tella.

Tomz, Michael, Jason Wittenberg, and Gary King. 2001. "*Clarify*: Software for Interpreting and Presenting Statistical Results," Unpublished paper. Harvard University.

Trocello, María Gloria. 2003. "Clientelismo y populismo: Prácticas y discursos legitimadores del régimen político puntano." Unpublished paper. Universidad Nacional de San Luis, Argentina.

United Nations Development Program (UNDP). 2002. *Hacia una integracion cooperativa y solidaria del territorio nacional*. Buenos Aires: PNUD.

Urquiza, Yolanda. 2002. *Las eternas internas: política y faccionalismo en un muni-*

cipio radical, 1983–1999. Unpublished paper. Universidad Nacional de Misiones, Argentina.

Urquiza, E. Yolanda. 2004. "Las eternas internas: Políitica y faccionalismo en un municipio radical, 1983–1999." In *La democracia local en Argentina: Clientelismo, capital social, e innovación en Argentina*, edited by Samuel Amaral and Susan Stokes. Buenos Aires: Universidad Tres de Febrero.

Uslaner, Eric M. 2002. *The Moral Foundations of Trust*. New York: Cambridge University Press.

Valdiviezo Sandoval, René. 1998. *Elecciones y Desarrollo en Puebla, 1959–1989*. Puebla, Mexico: Benmérita Universidad Autónoma de Puebla.

Vela, Gustavo, and Gabriel Rodríguez. 2001. "Relación entre el poder local y las Asociaciones Vecinales de Fomento en la ciudad de Mar del Plata: Una responsabilidad de dos vías." Paper presented to the V Congress of Political Science, Sociedad Argentina de Análisis Político. Río Cuarto, Argentina (November 14–17, 2001).

Ward, Peter M. and Victoria E. Rodríguez, with Enrique Cabrero Mendoza. 1999. *New Federalism and State Government in Mexico*. Austin: Lyndon B. Johnson School of Public Affairs, University of Texas, Austin.

Warren, Mark E. 2001. *Democracy and Association*. Princeton, N.J.: Princeton University Press.

White, Halbert. 1980. "A Heteroskedasticity-Consistent Covariance Matrix Estimator and a Direct Test for Heteroskedasticity." *Econometrica* 48(4): 817–38.

Index

Boldface numbers refer to figures and tables.